SOCIAL CHANGES IN A GLOBAL WORLD

Sara Miller McCune founded SAGE Publishing in 1965 to support the dissemination of usable knowledge and educate a global community. SAGE publishes more than 1000 journals and over 800 new books each year, spanning a wide range of subject areas. Our growing selection of library products includes archives, data, case studies and video. SAGE remains majority owned by our founder and after her lifetime will become owned by a charitable trust that secures the company's continued independence.

Los Angeles | London | New Delhi | Singapore | Washington DC | Melbourne

ULRIKE SCHUERKENS

SOCIAL CHANGES IN A GLOBAL WORLD

Los Angeles | London | New Delhi
Singapore | Washington DC | Melbourne

Los Angeles | London | New Delhi
Singapore | Washington DC | Melbourne

SAGE Publications Ltd
1 Oliver's Yard
55 City Road
London EC1Y 1SP

SAGE Publications Inc.
2455 Teller Road
Thousand Oaks, California 91320

SAGE Publications India Pvt Ltd
B 1/I 1 Mohan Cooperative Industrial Area
Mathura Road
New Delhi 110 044

SAGE Publications Asia-Pacific Pte Ltd
3 Church Street
#10-04 Samsung Hub
Singapore 049483

Typeset by: C&M Digitals (P) Ltd, Chennai, India
Printed and bound by CPI Group (UK) Ltd,
Croydon, CR0 4YY

Library of Congress Control Number: 2017930217

British Library Cataloguing in Publication data

A catalogue record for this book is available from
the British Library

ISBN 978-1-4739-3021-6
ISBN 978-1-4739-3022-3 (pbk)

At SAGE we take sustainability seriously. Most of our products are printed in the UK using FSC papers and boards.
When we print overseas we ensure sustainable papers are used as measured by the PREPS grading system.
We undertake an annual audit to monitor our sustainability.

CONTENTS

ABOUT THE AUTHOR

Ulrike Schuerkens studied at the Universities of Cologne (Germany) and Rennes (France). She has doctorates in both sociology, and social anthropology and ethnology, from the École des Hautes Études en Sciences Sociales in Paris. She received the diploma *Habilitation à diriger des recherches* from the University Paris V – René Descartes. Currently, she is a professor of sociology at the University Rennes 2, France. She also teaches in the master and PhD program of the *École des Hautes Études en Sciences Sociales*, Paris, France. She also taught as a lecturer at the University Lille 3 (France) and at Humboldt University, Berlin (Germany). She was a visiting professor at the Universities Paris 1 and Paris V, University of Cologne (Germany), Rouen Business School and others. Ulrike Schuerkens has served for many years in different functions as a member of the board of the Research Committee on Social Transformations and Sociology of Development, RC 09 of the International Sociological Association. She is presently the co-president of RC 09 and is on the editorial board of several international journals. She has published extensively on globalization, glocalization, socio-economic development, social change, transnational migrations, multiculturalism, and colonialism. Her latest monographs are *Soziale Transformationen und Entwicklung(en) in einer globalisierten Welt* (Juventa, 2014), *Global Management, Local Resistances* (ed., Routledge, 2014), *The Socio-economic Outcomes of the Global Financial Crisis* (ed., Routledge, 2012), *Globalization and Transformations of Social Inequality* (ed., Routledge, 2010), *Globalization and Transformations of Local Socio-Economic Practices* (ed., Routledge, 2008), Transnational Migrations and Social Transformations (ed., *Current Sociology*, 2005, 53 (4)), *Global Forces and Local Life-Worlds: Social Transformations* (ed., Sage, 2004), *Changement social sous régime colonial: Du Togo allemand aux Togo et Ghana indépendants* (L'Harmattan, 2001), *Transformationsprozesse in der Elfenbeinküste und in Ghana* (Lit, 2001).

PREFACE

I want to thank my colleagues Professor Nina Bandelj, Professor Habibul H. Khondker, and Professor Dieter Neubert for the valuable information and helpful comments on an earlier version of this book. My thanks also go to the Publisher for Politics, Criminology, & Sociology at SAGE Publishing, Natalie Aguilera who suggested to write this book on global social change and who has supported the preparation of the manuscript with many valuable comments. My special thanks go to the section *Development Sociology and Social Anthropology* of the German Sociological Association. At their conferences in the last years, I could give talks on these topics in individual sessions or plenaries. I would like to especially thank the publishers Sage, Routledge, and Lit that kindly authorized me to take some parts of individual theoretical chapters of my books published mostly in English in an earlier, largely modified version. I would also like to thank the Research Committee 09 *Sociology of Development and Social Transformations* of the International Sociological Association that I have been honoured to chair for a number of years. The Research Committee's sessions organized at conferences in Brisbane (Australia 2002), Durban (South Africa 2006), Barcelona (Spain 2008), Gothenburg (Sweden 2010), Buenos Aires (Argentina 2012), Yokohama (Japan 2014), and Vienna (Austria 2016), and on the occasion of World Congresses of the International Institute of Sociology (IIS) in Krakow (Poland 2001), Beijing (China 2004), and Stockholm (Sweden 2005) helped to prepare the various edited books that I have published in recent years on issues of social change and globalization possible. Thanks also to the many conference participants, the young students, and experienced colleagues who have contributed with their case studies to these volumes, which have become resources for some short case studies in individual chapters of this book. My thanks also go to my colleagues at the *École des Hautes Études en Sciences Sociales*, Paris and to those from the German-speaking universities that have contributed to this research on global-local aspects of societies. Furthermore, l would like to thank my students at the EHESS in the master program *Étude comparative du développement* and the PhD program *Sociétés Territoires Développement* who have commented on the various chapters and the individual topics of this book with their enthusiasm that has contributed to improve my understanding of these research fields. For many years, I have greatly enjoyed teaching and research with these groups working on similar topics.

Finally, I want to thank the anonymous reviewers for their valuable comments on my book proposal and the first chapters of this book at Sage. They have ensured that some of my ideas could develop in a most productive way. Last but not least, I am responsible for any remaining shortcomings that were hard to avoid in the breadth of the tackled topics.

I dedicate this book to my late mother who always supported my projects and ideas throughout my career. I have to thank her for her continuous understanding of my objectives.

Paris, August 2016

ACKNOWLEDGEMENTS

Chapter 3: Transformations of Local Socio-economic Practices in a Global World, Copyright © 2008 From *Globalization and Transformations of Local Socio-Economic Practices* by Ulrike Schuerkens (ed). Reproduced by permission of Taylor and Francis Group, LLC, a division of Informa plc.

Introduction and Chapter 4 Copyright © 2010 From Theoretical and Empirical Introduction, Globalization and Transformations of Social Inequality, *Globalization and Transformations of Social Inequality* by Ulrike Schuerkens (ed). Reproduced by permission of Taylor and Francis Group, LLC, a division of Informa plc.

Chapter 6: Introduction: Socio-economic Outcomes of the Global Financial Crisis – Theoretical Overview and Some Empirical Observations, Copyright © 2012 *Socioeconomic Outcomes of the Global Financial Crisis: Theoretical Discussion and Empirical Case Studies* by Ulrike Schuerkens. Reproduced by permission of Taylor and Francis Group, LLC, a division of Informa plc.

INTRODUCTION

This introduction to the field of social transformations and social change in a global world discusses the current state of research and questions the main issues. The first chapter is a short historical overview of the problem, followed by a theoretical discussion that puts the subject in the general scientific context but also links it to issues in related disciplines such as political science, economics, and social anthropology.

In the following chapters, questions are discussed which the research on social transformations and social change in a global world is engaged with today. Such issues include the definition of this area compared to fields such as globalization, social inequality, poverty, socio-economic practices, transnational migrations, the crisis of neoliberalism, and the transition to a multipolar world. Brief country and regional case studies in each chapter illustrate the arguments and prepare them for a critical reception by students.

The author of this book has edited and published articles and books in recent years, on most of the aforementioned areas which have been a valuable source for case studies and thus the concrete development of this book's arguments. The state of research has been updated in each case, so that the present volume is based on broad research efforts and a large spectrum of case studies.

TO UNDERSTAND SOCIAL TRANSFORMATIONS AND SOCIAL CHANGE IN A GLOBAL WORLD

This book differs from others in this field of research by putting development(s) in the broad context of globalization, the consequences of which have had an impact on social transformations and social changes in the global world in the last decades. Today's social transformations are characterized by a new form of international integration, whether in the form of trade, finance, communication, migration, or other forms of human activities. Recent strong links between social transformations, development(s), and globalization are thus examined.

By the complex and often unquestioned nature of social transformations and changes illuminated in this book, I show how different theoretical approaches have become a product of special traditions, political and philosophical positions, academic disciplines, or discourses. It can be shown how social transformations and changes are connected to issues of power and political influence. For example, a close connection must be drawn between the gender issue and educational programs for women, to reproductive health issues, cultural norms and values of different societies, poverty, and inequality.

Another aspect of this book relates to the consideration of different transformation paths in various regions and cultures. If one raises the question of long-term and historical trends in different regions, there is the possibility to show many different social transformations and changes, pointing out that they are the product of multiple processes and actions. This volume provides an outline for different forms of social transformations and changes, which must be seen in the plural and not - as was usual in the Western tradition and in the sociology of transformations - in the singular. A brief outline of the respective social transformation processes will be given, indicating controversially-viewed perceptions of origins by scholars and thus the roots of this tendency in the European Enlightenment and the Age of Enlightenment in the eighteenth century. The ideas of modernity, progress, and rationalization have influenced social transformations and social changes and thus the entire field to be considered here. Being modern has been viewed as a goal to be realized after a process of social transformations. Science, capitalism, and industrialization have been associated with these concepts.

Although social transformations and social changes only acquired global importance after the Second World War, today, the global South is an extremely heterogeneous entity. Post-development theorists (e.g. Escobar, 1995b) argue that development is associated with knowledge and power which both force the countries of the South to accept economic development models that have little to do with their resources and needs. Some scholars argue that the mere deconstruction of developments does not mean that an improvement in living conditions has occurred (see Ferguson, 1990). The idea of development has enabled international institutions, such as the World Bank and the International Monetary Fund, together with national elites, to intervene in these societies and to change them most often gradually. Some radical authors consequently see development as a form of Western imperialism that magnifies the power of the North and marginalizes the interests of the people of the South[1]. In this sense, development is potentially a universal project that can be used against local diversities and pluralistic developments. Today, however − so the argument of the book − one should speak on global trends and processes, the need to accept local diversities simultaneously, which means that humanity is characterized in its various forms by certain global structures in the economic, political, and cultural fields. This book will thus argue that processes of change constitute fundamental aspects of the development of societies all over the world.

Today, it is assumed that social transformations and social changes affect both the South and the North. The growing importance of Asia in the international economy shows that we are on the way to a multipolar world order that is no longer solely determined by the countries of the Triad (USA, EU, Japan). Western cultural identity poses a growing threat to the authenticity of cultures in different world regions, especially in the global South. This process follows different paths of social transformations in various societies and cultures of the globe. It is thus important to understand these transformation processes conceptually and empirically. This is one of the objectives of this book.

Is there an alternative to social transformations and social changes in the age of globalization? Social change is considered in this book as a process that has taken place in the past, takes place in the present and will take place in the future. Although post-development critics question the concept of development, they have not suggested any practical alternative, so that this topic continues to be on the agenda of the international community. The problems treated in this book are embedded in historical processes which have to be adapted to changing conditions.

THE ARGUMENT OF THIS BOOK

The relationship between social changes and globalization is complex and not always clearly defined. The various chapters of this book are intended to illustrate and demonstrate that transformation processes are associated with issues of power. To understand various global development paths, I argue that the relationship between development(s), structural and global factors, local contexts and conditions has to be analyzed. Only in this way, the historical nature of changes, cultural values, colonial heritages, and political approaches can be understood. At this point, the plural nature of transformations becomes visible, with development paths and strategies that are the results of numerous processes and interventions by many actors. In short, there are different and multiple forms of change, taking place in parallel. This book represents the increasingly accepted argument that transformations must be understood in the plural[2]. In addition, it will be shown that an understanding of these complex processes requires us to adopt an interdisciplinary approach on transformations and change and to accept fruitful insights from other disciplines.

It is argued that transformations also challenge our concept of globalization. Is it a project or a historical process? This book argues for the connection of these two approaches and shows the type of interactions between these processes and specific societies. Only then is it possible to show the plurality of transformations. It is assumed in this book that the ever-expanding global economy is accompanied by a growing worldwide acceptance of the market economy and the neoliberal economic approach. If one supports this model, to which currently, despite the sometimes justified criticism, there are no alternatives, one can point out that the growth of world trade has also led to rising incomes and better material living standards in the developing world of the South, where poverty has declined in recent years (see Bhagwati, 2004; Wolf, 2004). These two authors argue that countries like China and South Korea have experienced economic growth with rising wealth levels for formerly poorer groups. But this also means that economic disparities between countries and regions are reduced in part, so that some economies of East Asia and Latin America increasingly resemble the economies of the industrialized countries of the North.

The perspective of the globalizers underlines that greater global economic interdependence was achieved through the shifting of productions to the South. Higher production costs and higher wage levels in the North and the relative simplicity of this relocation process due to sophisticated communication technologies have supported this trend. Thus, an incipient new international division of labour and the transfer of the manufacturing industry from the North to the newly industrialized countries in East Asia and Latin America characterize the global economy today. This is associated with the expansion of the service sector in the North, but also in the South, such as Bangalore in South India (Schifferes, 2007) where banks, insurance companies, and transport companies use information technology for billing and other activities. These processes make it clear that North–South relations have been changed by globalization and have been called into question.

On the other hand, the argument of the critics of globalization that transnational corporations use unfair and unethical practices in countries where the International Labour Organization has little opportunity to combat low labour standards and difficult working conditions cannot be overlooked. Especially in Africa, countries exist whose infrastructures and capacities do not allow them to diversify their economies and develop the processing industry and services, so that they continue to rely on producing raw materials and local agricultural goods.

This book is not only interested in the sociology of transformations and changes, but in phenomena that concern many people who are influenced by globalization: tourists, immigrants, the critical global civil society, and political activists who are interested in individual phenomena discussed in the different chapters. The book may bring the reader to think in another way about North–South issues and to better understand the global interdependence of many problems. The current difficulty in creating enthusiasm for Third World topics is related to this displacement of the problem.

This book will have achieved its goal when the understanding of the relationship between globalization and transformations is considered to be complex and controversial. Our understanding will be favoured by concrete empirical studies that are context-specific and take into account historical developments. These studies illustrate the different and unequal ways that globalization takes in transformation processes in regions and societies throughout the world.

NOTES

1   The term 'North' refers to countries that are most often classified as 'developed', while the term 'South' refers to those classified as 'developing'. The North includes Europe, North America, Australia, New Zealand, and Japan. These terms do not express a judgment on the level reached by a particular country in the development process.

2   See the discussion of Eisenstadt's multiple modernity approach in Chapter 1.

1

SOCIAL TRANSFORMATIONS AND DEVELOPMENT(S) IN A GLOBALIZED WORLD

Summary

The chapter presents the current theoretical state of research on the subject of transformations and development. In addition to a brief historical overview, the central theoretical approaches are presented such as modernization theory, dependency theories, structural-functionalist theories, multiple modernities, and the theory of entangled modernities. As such, the chapter prepares the reader to understand the following chapters which deal with empirical transformation fields.

INTRODUCTION

The reconstruction of social change in societies has to take various factors into account and has to combine synchronic and diachronic elements. Today, if one analyzes the main theories of social change, dependency theory, the theories of evolution and structural-functionalist variants, one has to look for approaches that overcome their incompleteness. It seems currently consensual that evolutionary theories and structural-functionalist approaches cannot adequately explain social transformations and development(s) because of their epistemological structure (Helbling, 1984: 84). Among scholars defending evolutions, these are understood as the development of human societies in a succession of necessary and non-reversible societal types. Structural functionalism tries to explain society – including its history – through structures and functions that maintain the stability of the social system. Recent anthropological and sociological approaches argue that the explanation of social changes and diachronic aspects must also consider synchronous processes. However, a succession of predefined types of society cannot be presumed.

I agree with Helbling (1984: 95) that a social process and social change can only be explained by isolating particularly significant elements that make up a given social structure and by analyzing the relationships between them. By focusing on certain elements and their interrelations, a specific point of a transformation process can be shown. The transformation of a given social structure or two different structures indicates different periods of the history of a social system. Without the concept of structural processes, social change cannot be explained and demonstrated.

THEORETICAL APPROACHES TO SOCIAL CHANGE

The theoretical approaches that underlie the entire analytical framework of social change are surprisingly diverse. This diversity began in the 1960s with modernization theories of mainly Anglo-Saxon origin; in the 1970s, theories of dependency theories followed, mainly promoted by Latin American intellectuals. At the same time and at a higher level of abstraction, theories of structural change were developed. In the 1980s, approaches were widespread that supported an endogenous development, promoted by UNESCO; the decoupling perspective of the Southern countries was also discussed (S. Amin). In the 1990s, globalization theorists began to examine social developments. Among them, one could find many sociologists, who were inspired by theories of modernization and pointed out a growing convergence of societies due to the globalization of cultural, economic, and political systems. Some of these scholars deny that distinct modernities can be identified nowadays. The world-system approach underlined that developments in the various regions of the world could only be described as Western copies or its deviations influenced by postcolonial developments.

MULTIPLE MODERNITIES

In recent years, the approach of multiple modernities of S. Eisenstadt reached a certain influence among sociologists. According to this paradigm, development options are not understood as a failure or deficiency of a general model, but as a singular form of modernity. The observed variations are considered by this approach as typical for an overarching framework of modernity. The publications of these theorists assume that, on the one hand, one can determine a common core of societies (Antweiler, 2011), which characterizes a modernity in the singular and, on the other, one can determine other historical legacies in different regions, primarily based on major religious communities (Christianity, Hinduism, etc.). Eisenstadt (2006) claimed that the content core of modernity is not fixed but reacts dynamically so that many varieties can be found in the global world.

This cultural-historical approach, however, is not considered sufficient by its critics (e.g. Berger, 2006 and Schmidt, 2006). According to them, the newer variant of research on capitalism, democracies, or cultural systems is pointing in the right direction, but an overall synthesizing macro-sociological perspective is still largely missing, similar to that presented by research on modernization. It is now assumed that there will be no convergence of countries and regions in the direction of one modernity pattern because the same institutional solutions are not found every-where. The concept of path dependency, which was emphasized and studied in recent years, interests many scholars (Goldstone, 1998; Mahoney, 2000; Beyer, 2005). It draws attention to contingent histories and questions the development of gen-eralizable relationships. According to Parsons' understanding, this argument relates mainly to the uni-linear evolutionism.

Shalini Randeria (1999, 2000) has further developed the model of Eisenstadt and speaks in contrast to this research program of 'entangled modernities' or inter-woven forms. She proposes to abandon the idea of parallel versions of modernity and instead to speak of a model of interwoven forms that has arisen in the course of world history. Today, institutional similarities can be found in different countries; they are the result of imitations and mutual learning.

GLOCALIZATION

It can be assumed that new cultural forms can more easily be adopted than single cultural or philosophical aspects. Modernity is therefore, according to S. Randeria, a global arena that constantly forces societal aspects together but which will neces-sarily lead to convergent developments. Meanwhile, a variety of studies – some of them are described in the individual chapters of this book – shows that some forms of Western modernity are not only copied, but connect themselves to new *glocal* units with local forms that often have a specific character and may have similarities in form, structure, and function across regions and countries (Schuerkens, 2003, 2005, 2008, 2010, 2012, and 2014a). Thus, Hall and Soskice's (2001: 60) claim vari-ants of capitalist development does not stand in opposition to the world market, but unfold in and with it. However, it should be noted that these global processes still remain under-analyzed. This book is therefore in its different chapters an analysis of various social dimensions (inequality, economy, culture, etc.) in different regions of the world showing the current state of research. The result will allow arguing that one can no longer speak of a change of institutions towards a global pattern. Instead, one can find transnational processes that should be further investigated in globalization studies in order to demonstrate transnational connections of indi-viduals, organizations, societies, or countries that have grown in importance in the last three decades. States have thus expanded their ability to check populations in transnational spaces (Interpol, NSA). Interactions, ideologies, institutions, the hier-archies of gender, ethnicity, and class are no longer only supported within nations, but have gained significance across nations. Transnational spaces that are composed of virtual and real social spaces exist in individual nation-states. Individuals, groups, and organizations act in such spaces (Boccagni, 2012).

EMPIRICAL FINDINGS

Today, it cannot be denied that empirical findings on individual measurable indicators such as GDP, life expectancy, and literacy rates suggest a convergence, as Berger (2006) and Schmidt (2006) emphasized. Nevertheless, behind these similar figures, different institutions and systems, in short, qualitative differences exist that cannot be overlooked. One can for example point out the different forms of capitalism in Western Europe, Japan, and China, as respective cultural schemes that assure specific expressions (e.g. on the dimension of individualism-collectivism or in accordance to ethical requirements). One can also refer to social globalization, through measurable personal contacts (tourism, street market, foreign residence), information flows (Internet users, the number of television stations, the number of newspapers) and cultural similarities, such as the number of McDonalds restaurants, Ikea stores, and the book trade (Dreher, 2006; Dreher et al., 2008). One might think that these measurements threaten given cultures. This could even more apply in the West than the South. But in fact, can social aspects of globalization be measured? It seems as if transnational networks or people who live as migrants in other regions can be described, so that our focus on the study of transnational networks in parts of this book should permit an answer.

DIFFERENTIATION THEORY

These considerations lead me to introduce a differentiation theory that can further develop cultural and structural comparisons in order to identify different constellations of institutions and their relationships to each other. The importance of culture is weighted in a different way during a transformation of structures. In today's global society, culture plays a role that is responsible for different dynamics. These are characterized by certain types of societies in the North and the South, or within a society between different cultural milieus. In this sense, it seems to me as if the multiple modernity approach to civilizations is given too much preference, so that some aspects of the *glocalization* debate with its different levels (nations, regions, and local contexts) should be fruitfully introduced. This would then lead to social actions that should be examined in complex institutions – as I will show in the individual chapters of this book – in which culture plays an important role. Eisenstadt's approach is interesting in terms of collective identities of geographical regions, such as Latin America or sub-Saharan Africa, where the respective national societies struggle to develop distinctive identities, which have been characterized by common colonial and postcolonial political influences. These regions struggle to resist the transnational forces that brought them together. Examples are today's economic unions, such as Mercosur (*Mercado Común del Sur*) or ECOWAS (*Economic Community of West African States*). The recent cycles of globalization can thus only be understood by the study of the growth of transnational flows, such as those in the Andean Community or in the ASEAN (*Association of Southeast Asian Nations*). These regions combine various states into an entity characterized by transnational flows and a partially shared history.

Sanjay Subrahmanyam (1997, 2005) has spoken in this regard of connected histories, and Michael Werner and Bénédicte Zimmermann (2002, 2006) have coined the term *histoire croisée*. This view allows taking mutual influences and resistances, new combinations and transformations into account. These interactions point to a network of dynamic relationships, defined by certain connections with each other. A transnational perspective that exceeds migration processes is thus needed in the research and development of transformations. The discussions in the various chapters of this book concretize this perspective and show that a societal analysis must transcend national boundaries. Today, we realize more and more that international groupings and agreements spring up like mushrooms. They are welcomed as they provide new skills and exercise power that responds to global requirements. Thus, the concepts of globalization and transnationalism refer to similar strands of research that coexist. Practices that are introduced across borders, social networks that exist or have existed prior to the globalization of the last 30 years, as well as the movement of ideas and people make it possible to analyze the processes that form collective identities. Such a perspective allows us to understand how the cultural history of macro-regions is connected to collective identities and affects power, meaning, and the character of social, political, and cultural forces of a society.

A THEORETICAL APPROACH OF THE ANALYSIS OF SOCIAL TRANSFORMATIONS AND SOCIAL CHANGES

The theoretical approach used in this book builds upon a theory of social change that was developed by Teune and Mlinar (1978). According to the authors, specific properties of all social systems make them develop and change. Change is defined as a growth of social differentiation, a parallel increase in the number of elements, and the integration of new elements. The analysis of social structures allows defining important factors of social transformations. In addition, the special type of conflicts and frictions characteristic for a given process and period has to be determined. Consequences of individual events of an endogenous and exogenous or, better, a global and local nature can be detected and possibilities of developing a certain type of society can then be suggested.

Social transformations can be explained by an analysis of written materials, the use of quantitative and qualitative methods, and the comparison of different periods of a society. The dynamics of a given society are thus different from other social entities, but due to the current interdependence of societies there are certain common processes. An analysis of social changes must take into account social relations among the concerned populations, the impact of globalized social structures on the local populations, and the phenomenon of change that results from the interaction of different social systems. The analysis of the transformation of a society is characterized by extreme diversity. Only an investigation that takes into account these three aspects can show the complex character of these social relations and the specific nature of these transformations.

A THEORY OF SOCIAL TRANSFORMATIONS

This general framework leads me to clarify the subject of the theory of social transformations (see also Kollmorgen, 1999). In general, scholars try to use these approaches in order to explain causes, forms, and possible directions of social change. The anthropological and sociological explanations of transformations refer to the structure of a society in transition and to factors causing this change. The analysis of the transformation of a society permits to show conditions and describe elements that lead a society from a characteristic situation to another one.

It seems of interest in the analysis of transformations and developments to focus on the concepts of structure and time and to highlight particular aspects with regard to different categories of countries (Crow and Heath, 2002; Evans, 2003). The structural and temporal aspects of development concern both global and local social structures that interact with each other. Due to the European colonial expansion of the last centuries, the countries of the geographical South in Latin America, Africa, and parts of Asia continued to stay in close contact to Europe, so that local economic, political, or cultural structures could gradually change. A basic assumption of this approach is that particular structures were internationalized, leading to a more or less conscious acceptance of global models or at least parts of them by more or less large population groups in the respective regions. These processes led to situations in these regions which made it possible to detect a specific mix of indigenous local and Western (global) models. Colonization thus led to a certain degree of structural changes in colonized regions. The growing interactions between colonial powers and local populations consisted e.g. in the introduction of wage labour, a formal educational system, and a bureaucratic administrative system. Thus, the direction of change was determined by a politically implanted outside structural model which had to adapt to a certain degree to local cultural structures that could permit functional societal changes. One can argue that the resulting frictions, contradictions, and mixtures were considered development problems by Western elites and their counterparts in the South since the 1960s.

DIVERSITY OF LOCAL CULTURES

Despite the diversity of local cultures, the socio-economic and cultural elements that were brought from the outside into these social systems were limited. In a first phase, local elites or groups that were chosen for this purpose introduced the proposed innovations. Therefore, one could find a similarity of developments in certain closely linked geographic spaces. Changes introduced from the outside were then extended to other population groups, often involving coercion and violence. This integration of new structural elements into existing social systems took place in gradual and successive processes, so that the principal influences grew over time. For sub-Saharan Africa – the region I know the best - this meant several successive developments and a process of modernization in the 1960s (the introduction of mass media, democratic structures, and urbanization); a dependency and debt crisis in the

1980s; and, finally, the acceptance of certain elements of global structural models in the 1990s and after the turn of the millennium (through the introduction of political parties and democratic electoral processes; the promotion of the participation of girls and women in schools, universities, and the wider society; and the expansion of formal and informal employment). Today, these processes influence all population groups globally: immigrants from remote rural areas of southern regions bring information from the North to the South by means of videos, webcams, the Internet, and smartphones. Today, one rarely meets groups that are still unaffected by any global structural features. The type of change depends on the particular local cultural systems, which react differently to these elements coming from the outside of a given society. Actors of these local social systems have shown resistance and have challenged the increasing influence of structures originating in the global development model. These local societies have accepted the coexistence of very different cultural models (e.g. the culture of poverty or that of the elites). These models have formed new relations with elements of global social structures, which have been imported from outside and have led to ambivalent new social systems.

At this point, the time factor is a tool for analyzing the changes that have taken place in these societies. Since a change in a social system never affects all elements at the same time, individual elements mostly convert in a first phase and initiate the change of other elements until the moment when the emergence of another structural model is identified. In many regions of the world, structural transformation processes can be observed that are more or less dependent on given local social systems of populations so that parts of these systems continue to exist for years.

The problems of social transformations and development(s) are thus linked to analyses on the interactions of different cultural models. These processes are long term ones and require a diachronic description so that the different periods can be described in a chronological order that takes phenomena resulting from the increased interaction into account.

DIFFERENT RESEARCH METHODS

An approach that would respect these different aspects requires a significant analysis of their developments and the use of different research methods. To show discords, fractures, and frictions within the societies of the North, the South, or the East, it seems essential to compare elements of the interaction of indigenous or autochthonous local societies to elements of global cultures and societies. The last decade has seen an increasing number of studies that have gone in this direction. Nevertheless, they often do not represent a detailed overview of the problem, as they investigate transformations and their mechanisms in parts of local societies, without locating the problem within a larger theoretical framework. The brief overview of theoretical perspectives of transformation problems at the beginning of this chapter has shown that development processes can only be considered adequately when the transformation of local societies is incorporated into global transformation processes and structures.

THE CONCEPT OF STRUCTURE IN EXPLAINING SOCIAL TRANSFORMATIONS AND DEVELOPMENT(S)

If one considers that powerful actors most often form the structures of a society, these structures can be regarded as rules that regulate the lives of the majority of individuals. These rules can be known or unknown. During an interaction, social actors can either make use of them as a resource for a specific targeted action or don't use them, if they do not know their existence. The structure of a society is a factor that gives the system stability and continuity. The social actors who know the functioning of this structure can use their knowledge to realize their intentions. In this way, they are included in a process that involves the structure and the interactions between both. The social actor who does not know the functioning of this structure rather suffers its consequences and rarely has the opportunity to influence their functioning. The distinction between intended and unintended actions becomes important at this point. Analytically, both types of actions must be considered, as they often coexist in the lives of the actors. The actions of individuals are shaped by macro-societal structures and various elements, which have served as mechanisms to influence these social actions.

At the macro-societal level, these differences also have a meaning. At this level, power reveals its importance as an important social aggregate that permits the structuration of social actions. Often, only minor parts of social groups have the power to establish and transform structures. A powerful group, for example, will try to impose its value system. This may go so far as to support powerful ideological systems, such as socialism or capitalism in the time of the Cold War, or, in times of globalization, neoliberalism as an economic system. Powerful social actors recourse to macro-cultural societal structures and plans to institutionalize certain structures or the meaning of structures they want to change. I will show in the following how these actors influence these processes and the transformation of the structure in question in order to achieve their goals. Since a societal structure only exists in the moment when an interaction between different groups takes place, an analysis of the changes that have taken place over longer periods permits to show different temporal aspects of these structures.

A MACRO-SOCIETAL ANALYSIS

The advantage of a macro-societal analysis lies in the analysis of the formation of structures, the proof of their existence, and their stability or instability. A single actor – even if they belong to the group of powerful people – does not necessarily know the effects of, or the reasons for his/her actions. An individual of a disadvantaged social group often lives these phenomena, without knowing the mechanisms underlying their functioning (Foucault, 1975).

It seems to be particularly useful to study the interaction that takes place between individuals, groups, and societal structures in a process of structural change. Life stories can then be viewed as an expression of the conflict between two structures. The actions of individuals orientate themselves in a structural transformation process towards two different and incompatible social systems (e.g. during the colonial period in the South between indigenous social systems and Western social structures). They reflect the frictions and ruptures between these two value systems. The analysis of a transformation process is based on the fact that any given structure at a particular time may no longer be based on an acceptable value system. This structure proves then to be no longer adapted to social reality. If the action system changes, structures that are no longer favoured become problematic. Before the actors are involved and realize this type of change, a given structure can already have undergone a change and have become a dominant structure.

When analyzing transformation processes of societies, this phenomenon can be striking. Thus, for example, colonization - seen as a gradual process of transformations over time and the development project of a powerful exterior group – led in a relatively short time period to a fundamental restructuring of social systems of African, Asian, and Latin American societies. French colonization – which I know the best – can be taken as an example for this type of transformation process. The systematic introduction of economic, political, social, and cultural systems that were different from those of the indigenous local societies implied that the colonial power could succeed to gradually enforce Western structures and to realize some of its goals (Schuerkens, 2001a).

Since the analysis of social change must take into account social systems of the indigenous peoples, the influence of Western cultures on these social systems, and the phenomenon of change that results from the interaction between both, it appears to be extremely complex and goes beyond modernization theories that privilege a development towards a Western model, without regarding the specific elements of a given society, and also further than dependency theory, which tried to explain this change by influences coming from an unequal world system. Only an analysis that takes into account these three dimensions will allow to highlight the totality of social relations and the specific nature of change during the colonial period and its impact on current processes of development.

As this approach resembles a research program, I'm going to emphasize some individual phenomena in this book after the presentation of the theoretical model in this chapter. This brings me to the subject of what is considered a theory of social change.

A COMPLEX APPROACH

In general, social scientists try to analyze reasons, forms, and possible directions of social change. In part, this practice reflects the interests of the members of a society to gather knowledge about the past, the present, and the future while considering the fact that it is rarely possible to fully explain history or future events better than by giving some general conditions. The anthropological and sociological explanation of transformations refers to the structure of a society in transition and to factors causing this change. The analysis of the transformations of a society permits to identify conditions and elements that lead a society from one characteristic state to another one.

It seems of interest here to focus on the concepts of structure and time and to highlight particular aspects with regard to different categories of countries. If you look at developments from a structural and temporal aspect, the question arises of how global and local social structures interact with each other. A basic assumption of this approach is that there was an internationalization of some particular structures and a more or less conscious acceptance of global models or at least parts of them by large population groups in the respective regions. These processes then led to the fact that in these regions situations occurred which made it possible to detect a specific mix of indigenous local and Western (global) models. Colonization thus implanted a partially planned structural change in colonized regions. The increase in interactions between colonial powers and local populations consisted e.g. in the fact that a structural model coming from the outside was introduced, which had to adapt to local cultural systems in order to introduce a functional change.

These processes concern all population groups in today's global age: immigrants from the remote rural areas of southern regions bring information from the North back to the South. Today, one can hardly meet groups that are unaffected by individual global structural features. The type of change certainly depends on the particular local cultural systems which react differently to these elements coming from outside their social structures. The actors in these local social systems have shown resistance in one or the other way and have developed certain important aspects for their survival, parallel to the increasing influence of structures created by the global development model.

At this point, the time factor is a tool for analyzing the changes that have taken place in these societies. Since a change in a social system never affects all elements at the same time, individual elements convert mostly in a first phase and trigger the change of other elements up to a moment when the emergence of another model structure is observed. In many regions of the world, structural transformation processes can be observed that are more or less dependent on given social systems and the concerned population groups.

INTERACTION OF DIFFERENT CULTURAL MODELS

The problems of social transformations and development(s) are thus bound to analyses concerning the existing interactions of different cultural models. These processes proceed in the long term and require a diachronic description so that different temporal situations can be described in a chronological order that must take into account new phenomena resulting from increased interactions.

Processes can be represented by individual structural characteristics, which represent a sequence of events over time. A social process can only be explained by isolating significant empirical elements found which form a given structure and by analyzing their relationships with each other. A specific moment of a transformation process can be illustrated by the connection of individual elements and the relationships between them. The transformation of a given structure or the emergence of two different structures may represent different periods of social history. Without the concept of structure, social processes, and thus history as a special kind of long-term development, cannot be understood.

Analyzing the structures of a society allows the identification of elements and events that are important for a historical development; particular conflicts and contradictions within a given process; the outcomes of individual events – whether endogenous or exogenous – that occur within a social system or the possibilities of development, which a certain type of society allows. The historical time of a social system is thus nothing more than the result of the combination of different parts of a system and its different times. To define the characteristics of a transformation process, the outcomes of different processes at different moments of social history must be reconstructed.

THE APPROACH OF TEUNE AND MLINAR

The approach of Teune and Mlinar, which influenced my research in the last years, has attempted to apply this framework to a theory of social transformations. Since this conceptual design can be considered being a heuristic framework, I present here some essential aspects for the subject of this book. Both social scientists claim that they have proposed a theory that applies not only to highly industrialized societies but also to societies of the South, their past, present, and future (1978: 9). In their understanding, development is a feature of all social systems. It is defined by a growing diversity of system components and the subsequent integration of these or other components. Social development thus takes place between the two poles of diversity and integration (Lockwood, 1964): the extreme point of integration means that the stability of the various system components is so high that a continuous development due to the rigidity of the structure is no longer possible. On the other hand, a high degree of diversity leads to a progressive change. The development of a system is thus dependent on the interaction between diversity and integration.

A no longer acceptable degree of integration determines, according to the authors, the degree of probability of a change in the characteristics of a particular system element (Teune and Mlinar, 1978: 43). Diversity is the opposite pole on this continuum between integration and diversity. Social development, according to Teune and Mlinar, is a process that combines new levels of integration and diversity (1978: 44). The change of these levels indicates the direction of social development. Possibilities of disintegration (high diversity) or stagnation (high integration) are not excluded.

The transformation of a system is realized at the moment in which a system reaches its limits of diversity and integration. At this moment, a new integration principle of society and its characteristic structures appears. The development form is also dependent on the number of system elements, i.e. a higher variation in the elements of a system allows a greater change. This process can be considered in the following manner: a new element is introduced into a system at a given time; this element increases the diversity of the system but reduces its level of integration; the individual components of the system accept the new element. The probability that a new item is created increases, and once this element exists, the process described here begins again (1978: 72). Consequently, each new element reduces the degree of integration of the system and increases at the same time the total number of its elements. The new element must be integrated into the system and thus changes the relationships that the elements have established among themselves. The degree of integration can also increase in proportion to the degree of development of the system (1978: 74ff.).

I return to the temporal factor that is of great interest in this field: the diachronic process. Only by observing the structure of a given society and its specific transformations, can sociologists and social anthropologists determine the characteristics of a social and cultural system. Often, this analysis is only possible with the aid of a theoretical and empirical approach that includes the time factor. In fact, this analysis refers to a specific location and a specific moment of social history. However, the most important theoretical aspect is the process of the construction of social elements rather than place-specific transformations or the historical moment that is taken into consideration.

THE CONCEPT OF TIME IN THE ANALYSIS OF SOCIAL CHANGE

The second notion I would like to discuss is the concept of time that is linked in two ways to the discussion of the concept of structure: it is a notion that is closely related, on the one hand, to a structural change, as it can only take place in time, and, on the other hand, to one that represents a set of values that are particular for a certain type of society. Since a change can only be recognized by the comparison of different time intervals, the specificity of a structural change is based on the temporal distance that exists between the past, the present, and the future. The past structures the present, since a later moment is linked in one or the other way to an earlier moment. A future structure can only be realized if it represents individual and social values that are compatible with existing social systems and which do not form breaks or frictions with other values. Powerful groups often initiate structural transformations. In some countries of the South (e.g. sub-Saharan Africa), the groups that came to power went through European educational institutions. These groups initially accepted certain new values. Educational institutions (e.g. mission schools, overseas universities) and mass media legitimized them. These social actors, who created new cultural systems and who were acculturated by these systems, had to spread these values in a second phase to ensure the survival of the system that they represented. The distribution of these values was assured according to existing social layers. Since a disadvantaged social class can rarely introduce a structural change, in most cases, a dominant group has elaborated the structural change that took place in the countries of the South. This group carried out the formal implantation of this structure, introduced new values, and managed to have them accepted and valorized by groups that were more and more interested in possessing these values (including goods) and also in benefitting from their utilization. These new social values could thus become preliminary conditions to participate in important new social systems (e.g. school and university education, and obtaining qualifications for certain professions).

COLONIAL DEVELOPMENT POLICY

In the case of large parts of the countries of the geographical South, these transformations were first introduced by colonial powers that influenced these regions with their colonial development policy and economic exchange. The formation of a difference came from outside of the social system of the indigenous populations and had to be incorporated into the existing social system. All this was done with the explicit goal to initiate a process of transformation that was viewed as irreversible. If one considers that the societies in sub-Saharan Africa were confronted with societal structures that significantly differed from their own, one can imagine how much effort was needed from these societies to maintain their values in a functional state, derived from two cultural systems that were based on different structures. The resulting fractures and frictions are expressed in what is referred to as development problems since the 1960s.

THE UTILIZATION OF THE CONCEPTS OF STRUCTURE AND TIME IN THE ANALYSIS OF SOCIAL CHANGE

A structural analysis that takes into account the diachronic factor combines structural conditions that follow one on another in time. They can exist in a more or less balanced form depending on significant features of both structural systems so that critical elements are accepted, expressing the asynchrony between both social systems. The disharmony that should challenge the stability of a system can only be overcome when integration levels are reached that are functional for a given social system. An in-depth analysis makes thus clear the specific way of the connection of elements and allows clarifying the inconsistency and incompatibility of values of different origins.

STRUCTURAL CONFLICTS

This understanding of the problem offers a first possibility to overcome a structural conflict. A structure can be formed that depends on the functioning of the system and on specific objectives of social actions. The selectivity of the structure is then conditioned and adapted in terms of their duration. Limited opportunities make it possible that the system works according to some new criteria that do not favour the acceptance of so-called traditional and modern values. The new structure can then offer previously unknown action possibilities and allows, through a process that takes into account different events, the selection of other options that can lead to a structural change. Each new element then puts the interaction over time – past, present, and future – in a relationship that is different from the previous ones. The concept of time makes it thus possible to determine the differences between the earlier and the later events. However, this temporal dimension of future events shows that the new element is always a transitory factor, which also depends on time and its historic character.

The various elements of social structures in our contemporary societies and their integration into a functioning system are constantly changing in the world system. This requires special efforts not only from powerful groups, but also from poorer population groups that are more or less affected by these structural transformations. The persistence of change if it is not accepted in a positive way can create disharmonies, ranging from the general structures of a society to the characteristic local structures: interactive groups, labour relations, and friendship relations. The possibility of a change can be limited to the creation of relatively stable structures. The structure that is suitable for social change is then stabilized or replaced by a structure that was nonconformist in view of given options.

The realization of a structure requires a consensus on common values and allows a re-orientation of social expectations and selected options. It is thus clear that transformation in this sense is the acceptance of different states of a social system, without being always sure what type follows next, what is a desirable development, and what is adapted to the specific situation at a specific time. A social system can learn to react through these different options. Neither the repertoire of existing values, nor updated actions make it possible to define the nature and the characteristics of an intentional change. A stabilization of social expectations is guaranteed by any legal system. The conformity of an action with the existing development opportunities is then assured. However, the legal system is also obliged to ensure its own survival. An action that follows another one must remain a latent possibility: only the choices made can be evaluated. Structural changes are taking place continuously, even without the awareness of social agents. When structures have become obsolete, the social actor is aware of this and re-updates the changes.

Scholars usually make a distinction between two forms of change: one that can be characterized by its teleological aspect and another by its non-deliberate, non-predictable transformation process that is limited and permits a functional relationship with its previous state (Luhmann, 1984: 485 ff.). This last type is certainly the one that includes most frequently an aspect of apparent randomness.

MORPHOGENETIC PROCESSES

These morphogenetic processes (Archer, 1985) depend on elements located outside of the system and on the reduced possibilities of a system to initiate its own change. This type of transformation requires special attention since it appears risky to adopt constant transformation processes without a detailed analysis. Research on intentional actions in sociology and social anthropology provides significant insights on certain processes. The proposed analysis of transformations and developments – including intended objectives – has therefore a teleological character without being a fully planned action and can point out transformation processes in order to achieve social expectations and cumulative conditions that allow structural changes without challenging the social system. Wolfgang Zapf's definition that referred to transformation processes in East Germany and Eastern Europe is similar to the concept proposed here. He wrote:

> Transformation and transition are modernization processes that differ from open modernization processes of evolutionary innovation in *that the objective is known*: The acquisition, construction, incorporation of modern institutions which are democratic, and based on the market economy and the rule of law. (1994: 138; translation; emphasis in the original)

IMPLICATIONS FOR THE STUDY OF SOCIAL CHANGES

This more or less theoretical discussion insists on certain necessary elements of an analysis of transformation processes that take place in the countries of the South and the North. It seems as if an analysis that uses the terminology of the approaches of the 1960s up to the 1990s is no longer possible.

My remarks underline that an approach adapted to the problem of change cannot avoid the recourse to the concept of structure and in particular the transformation of a structure over time. In the case of the societies of the South but also increasingly those of the North, this means that there are actual transformation processes that can only be explained by the interaction of two social structures that have confronted each other more and more since the beginning of the European colonial period and later on in the globalization processes of the last 30 years. This interaction has meant that two or more very different structural systems interact. In this situation, it is easily understood that the structures of dominant groups are easier to implant. However, they are in opposition to social structures of other populations that may resist and create divergent reactions. It is an empirical question whether the coexistence of two or more structures is possible despite their differences and what the developing transformation would look like. Gradually, dominant structures of a powerful model may be implanted. They may encounter less powerful structures that have to respond. In most cases, the survival of these social systems depends on historical situations and given possibilities, so that the social actors themselves may be quite unconscious of the diminishing importance of some elements, or even the possibility that these elements challenge the functioning of the entire social system. When disharmonies become obvious, one begins to speak of mixtures, glocal situations, or hybridization. However, these terms set out the facts without revealing the real causes linked to overall transformation processes in the global world.

GENESIS AND FUNCTIONALITY

I have shown here that transformation problems must be observed in other terms so that problems can be explained while respecting their genesis and their functionality, so that it is possible to overcome a situation that is often considered to be dramatic. This presentation of the problem is a first reflection in theoretical terms that I try to specify in the book so that concrete situations can be analyzed - which will be carried out using numerous examples of different societal sub-fields – and empirical problems are chosen, which make it possible to substantiate the validity of such an approach and to point out current problems of the global world through an analytical choice. This also means that global and local cultures need to be taken into account in transformation and transition processes, their influences on global changes that no longer appear to be reversible, and that allow the various world societies to develop in a peaceful way.

In this book, therefore, I emphasize the divergence of global changes and the limited universality of certain structures that have emerged from social structures of world populations in interaction. The diversity of transformations is realized in a specific place and in a specific solution of wanted, accepted, or rejected interactions. However, the diversity of cultures will continue; a fact that does not trigger the same variety of possible developments. Transformations in an interactive world must accept local variations, but should in no case be reversed to put an emphasis on the authenticity of a given culture. However, the current trends underline that differences are orientated to processes of glocalization that I try to summarize in this book.

DISCUSSION QUESTIONS

1. What are the primary differences between modernization theory and dependency theories?
2. What is the benefit of an approach including time and structure?
3. What are the advantages of the approach of entangled modernities?
4. How would you start research on global change?
5. What is the main purpose of an analysis of change under global conditions?

ANNOTATED FURTHER READINGS

Hopper, P. (2012) *Understanding Development: Issues and Debates*. **Cambridge: Polity.**
Understanding Development is an introduction to the major issues and critical debates about development in the contemporary world. Drawing on a wide range of case studies from across the globe, the book explores the contested and plural nature of the field and takes full account of the impact of globalization.

Kollmorgen, R., Merkel, W. and Wagener, H.-J. (eds) (2015) *Handbuch Transformationsforschung*. **Wiesbaden: Springer VS.**
Topics of the book are fields, theories, and methods of social science research on transformations. The volume begins with the three major paradigms of transformation research: system, institutions, and actors. Prominent research approaches follow, among others, modernization theory, structuralism, development economics, and political economy. Another part is devoted to methods. This manual integrates perspectives of political science, sociology, and economics.

Rist, G. (2014) *The History of Development: From Western Origin to Global Faith*. **(Fourth edition). London: Zed Books.**
The History of Development is a classic development text, which provides an interesting overview of what the idea of development has meant throughout history. Rist traces it from its origins in the Western view of history, through the early stages of the world system and the supposed triumph of third-worldism, through to new concerns about the environment and globalization.

Websites

http://www.ids.ac.uk/
Website of the Institute of Development Studies, United Kingdom.

http://rodrik.typepad.com/
Dani Rodrik's weblog on economic development and globalization.

http://blogs.adb.org/blog/
Asian development blog.

http://blogs.worldbank.org/developmenttalk/
A blog of the World Bank.

http://csd.columbia.edu/blog/
Website of the Center for Sustainable Development of the Earth Institute Columbia University.

http://www.isa-sociology.org/rc09.htm
Website of the Research Committee 09 Social Transformations and Sociology of Development of the International Sociological Association.

http://www.asanet.org/asa-communities/sections/development
Website of the Sociology of Development Section of the American Sociological Association.

(all websites accessed 27 September 2016)

2

THE SOCIOLOGICAL AND ANTHROPOLOGICAL STUDY OF GLOBALIZATION AND LOCALIZATION

Summary

This chapter sketches the development of the topic of globalization and localization within sociology and social anthropology during the last 20 years and summarizes research findings. It is argued that global cultural flows have been successfully mapped in the last years and that systematic procedures have been introduced in many scientific disciplines. This has led to a more differentiated assessment of global cultural homogenization. The chapter tackles the problems of cultural convergence, non-Western globalization, and alternative modernities. Cultural exchanges from the South to the North, and the South to the South have received increasing attention during the last years. A cross-culturally valid notion of modernity is discussed. Finally, the question whether humanity is gaining or losing in the globalization process calls for further investigation.

INTRODUCTION

Consider the following two snapshots:

Snapshot One: In Bangalore, more than 100 women are sitting before computers and are entering the data from approximately 300,000 tickets of an airline from 2015 onwards. One floor down, many women work as 'decision-makers' and enter data on medical claims in the processing system of one of the largest insurance companies in Germany. One woman's fingers fly over the keyboard and the frenetic clicks of the buttons fill a large, cool room where women with MP3 players are working in eight-hour shifts in front of computer monitors: they are listening to the latest Indian pop music or raga rock.

Snapshot Two: In France, women from Tunisia have come together for a wedding in a suburb of Marseille. Most women sit on low cushions along the wall at one end of the rented space. Older women wear long, very shiny Tunisian dresses made of polyester and are decorated with golden girdles. Some younger women are dressed in similar traditional outfits, while others wear athletic pants or miniskirts and jewellery, such as geometric earrings or necklaces with miniatures in pastel colours. Some women have flown in from Tunisia for the wedding, while others come from Paris or Lyon. Arab music is the background of this wedding celebration.

GLOBALIZATION IN SOCIAL ANTHROPOLOGY AND SOCIOLOGY

I begin with these snapshots because they illustrate very obviously on a general level what is now commonly known as globalization in anthropological and sociological circles. This term refers to the intensification of global networking, to a world full of movement and mixtures, contacts and bonds, as well as ongoing cultural interactions and exchanges. In other words, these images make it possible to show the complex interactions and mobility that characterize the world today. The images of these snapshots show an increasingly connected world. It is a world that is porous at the borders, so that more and more people and cultures relate to each other in an intense and direct contact.

I start with these snapshots because each highlights exceptional mobility or cultural trends – of capital, people, goods, images, and ideologies – showing that the various regions of the world are increasingly intertwined. For example, take the case of Bangalore. The scene shows how data communication technologies transport data and that data are more and more mobile. In an effort to reduce production costs, enterprises are more and more moving labour-intensive industrial production and service operations in the USA, Japan, and Western Europe to new low-wage countries and to locations around the globe. Places like Bangalore become nodes in the rapidly developing and increasingly dense network of global cities, which have become the epitome of the modern world.

Or take the case of France. The women in the suburb of Marseille are part of the extensive post-war migrations of populations from less affluent parts of the world into the major urban centres of Northern and Southern countries. The result is that peoples and cultures that previously remained in different parts of the world live now in the same areas of the North where many different and sometimes incommensurable cultures coexist. This intensification of global mobility and networking in regions such as France results in exposing groups to a wide variety of others in spaces in which they meet, clash, and fight each other inside different cultures. These cultures often coexist under conditions of radical inequality.

PANORAMIC VIEW ON THE WORLD OF GLOBALIZATION

I begin with these images because they allow us a panoramic view on the world of globalization. This is a world of movements and complex relationships. Here global cities and their inhabitants cross national borders almost effortlessly; more and more areas are involved in these dense networks of social and financial links; people come together; they easily cross national boundaries and turn countless areas to areas where different cultures converge and meet. Raw materials are rapidly transported from one place to another; people encounter culturally distant others; images flicker rapidly from one screen to another; people with resources migrate; new ways of being in the world are created; ideologies spread quickly through ever-increasing circuits; and struggles for cultural authenticity against foreign influences are formulated. These images describe a world in which a plurality of processes on a global scale across national boundaries constantly create integration processes, so that cultures and communities connect everything in the world of reality in new space-time combinations, so that experiences tie together (see Hall, 1984). I speak here of an intensely networked world – where people, goods, images, and ideologies from around the world join in rapid capital flows that compress our understanding of time and space, making the world smaller and distances shorter. This is the world of globalization.

Nevertheless, a few words of caution: there is no doubt that the world experiences shrinks as a whole. The innovations of the twentieth century in technology – particularly in transports and communications – have made it easier and faster for people and things to get around in the world. It is not that the world is shrinking for all and in all places. The experience of globalization is a rather non-uniform process. While some people possess, for example, political and economic resources around the world, many have little or no access to transport and communication tools: the price of a ticket or a call is just too high for them. And generally, in the widely open spaces of the planet only a few people are connected in worldwide networks even if a few places have still-insufficient networks that connect them to the world via satellites. What is important here is the contrast: while the world is full of complex mobilities and connections, there are still a number of people and places that are more or less excluded from these communication movements and which do not participate in the same way in the interconnectedness that permeates the world. And this is also the world of globalization.

THE SOCIOLOGICAL AND ANTHROPOLOGICAL ANALYSIS OF GLOBALIZATION AND LOCALIZATION

Below I draw on the theme of globalization and localization in sociology and social anthropology in the last two or three decades. It can be argued that the allocation of global cultural flows is still a vibrant research field. This has led to a differentiated assessment of global cultural homogenization. My topics here are problems of cultural convergence, non-Western globalization, and alternative modernity. Cultural exchange and the circumvention of 'the West' have received increasing attention in the last years. Finally, the question whether humanity wins or loses in the process of globalization is analyzed.

SOCIAL TRANSFORMATIONS BETWEEN PROCESSES OF GLOBALIZATION AND DIFFERENTIATION

The expectation that modernization would mean a world of increasing homogeneity has led to the suggestion that the countries of the South should disengage from the capitalist world economy and turn to the resurgence of alternative cultural agenda. Wallerstein's historical research on the position of Europe as the centre of the development of capitalism (1979) shows that processes of globalization have very close links with processes of Westernization. The simple explanation of modernization theory that social progress is equal to the spread of Western institutions and norms contained, as Hettne (1995) showed, a 'Euro-centric bias' in the thinking about development. This has led to the development of research strands which reconsider this basic understanding. In the West, the extended contact with other cultures through globalization has an influence on certainties that suggest the idea of Western superiority, so that it becomes increasingly difficult to specify what actually is the 'West'. It seems to be a fact that the processes of globalization and Westernization are closely related. But the link from globalization to Westernization makes it difficult to identify the progressively blurring geographical boundaries of the West, where people and ideas cross these frontiers. One of the most important effects of globalization is that social relations are less bound by spatial positions. Accordingly, it was accepted that the connection of local and global social relations is problematic, so that the idea of societies as discrete entities is no longer tenable. While the movement of globalization can be understood in one direction as Westernization – the exporting of Western values and ways of life – globalization also includes processes that import the encounter with the postcolonial reality into Western societies. Just think of labour migration, refugees, and the many restaurants from different regions of the world in Northern global cities.

GLOBALIZATION VS. WESTERNIZATION

Globalization could be regarded as synonymous with Westernization in the sense that it has its historical origins in the West, but it is not a process that promotes global homogeneity through the imposed reproduction of Western patterns elsewhere in the world. The countries of the South have not mechanically imitated the North. At the same time, numerous ideas and practices 'from the rest of the world' (Hannerz, 1989a) exist in the West. There are theorists for whom it is important to see capitalism as the driving force within globalization. Sklair (2001) argued that the role of transnational capitalism has been reinforced by the spread of transnational corporations and the globalization of mass media: both processes have promoted consumption as a central part of modern global culture. This allows a distinction between 'capitalist development' and alternative definitions of development in terms of economic growth, the distribution of social wealth, democratic politics, and the elimination of inequalities based on class, gender, and ethnicity. In the analysis of enterprises in the South, far-reaching concepts, such as postcolonialism and post-development (Escobar, 1995b) exist. These ideas are linked to postmodernism and the assertion that a transition from modernity has taken place. Postmodernism as a theoretical approach also attempts to predict the future.

'DISTANCE EFFECT'

One of the most important aspects of globalization is that it is based on the 'distance effect'. The post-traditional society is the first global society. Until recently, most parts of the world remained in an almost segmental state in which large enclaves of traditionalism existed. The local population is still strong. A global world is a world that cannot avoid existing traditions and contacts not only with others but also with many alternative ways of life. For the same reason, globalization is characterized by the fact that the 'other' can no longer be treated as inactive. It is important that not only the other 'answers back' (Hannerz, 1992), but that mutual interrogation is possible. In a post-traditional order, we see the formation of a cosmopolitan conversation of mankind. If there is no dialogue, this tradition changes to fundamentalism. Fundamentalism can be understood as an assertion of a truth regardless of its consequences. This counter-flow originated in return from the blending of Western behaviours and traditional attitudes. Nations that are structurally at the lower end of the international stratification system are dominated by Western and Westernized countries. On the other hand, the assertion that cultural diversity is the final form of the world as an absolute doctrine or absolute goal, is certainly naive and unrealistic. The Western world has become a living standard, a lifestyle, and a symbol of behaviour that attracts people of other nations. It is likely that this power structure will be irresistible in the long run.

DESTRUCTION OF LOCAL COMMUNITIES

The destruction of local communities in developed societies is important, as Giddens (1984) showed. Traditions that have survived increasingly succumb to the forces of cultural evacuation. The world of 'traditional society' is a world in which cultural pluralism in the form of several customs and traditions consists in separate spaces. The post-traditional society is very different. It is located in an intensely globalized world. The post-traditional order no longer consists of cultural pluralism in the form of separate forms of power. With the intensification of globalization processes, these traditions are being undermined. Traditions have to justify themselves. Giddens has suggested that traditions only exist insofar that they can justify themselves and are ready to engage in an open dialogue not only with other traditions but with alternative forms (Giddens, 1984).

NEW FORMS OF INTERDEPENDENCE

The post-traditional society is characterized by global aspects and new forms of dependence. In this sense, modernity is discussed by sociologists in theoretical debates because all over the world traditional societal aspects are questioned. Individuals are linked to changes in local societies which originate in global inputs. Actions take place without personal contacts from across the global networks of mass media, the phone, and the computer. Thus, the structures of communities do no longer rely on the local level, but are built by organizations that are far away. Social groups are increasingly characterized by a common local history, common relations, and a common worldview. Abstract systems, values, and symbols define the daily social reality. Local groups need to distinguish between face-to-face relationships and connections through impersonal symbols sent over the Internet. New social systems are created that are affected by global and local aspects in their transformation processes, processes that were and have been initiated by colonialism and neo-colonialism (Schuerkens, 2001a).

Further empirical research on these processes is required in order to determine the pattern of the mechanism that links local and global social elements in everyday activities. I have tried in recent publications to fill this gap (Schuerkens, 2003; 2005; 2008; 2010; 2012; 2014a). Connections between global and local patterns are displayed and emerge as new cultural forms in different countries of the South. Social anthropologists and sociologists who examine social developments in the countries of the South and the North need to understand local responses to global patterns in a changing international world. The traditions that we find in southern and northern societies are not static. They must be adapted by each new generation. Thus, the social sciences do not examine a stable social world, but need to understand a world that is influenced by aspects of knowledge from all over the globe. Several decades ago, social anthropologists argued that their objects were static. Today, sociologists and social anthropologists examine societies of the South and the North and find continual processes of change. Societies respond to global elements; consequently, anthropological and sociological studies need to investigate processes that affect the life-changing patterns of social groups. If we accept the definition of Giddens, we should not look at the populations of the world as victims of global processes, but document their experiences and actions. The study of dependencies between groups within nations and between nations around the world must therefore be reinforced.

THE TWENTY-FIRST CENTURY'S INTERDEPENDENCE OF THE WORLD

One of the main trends of the twenty-first century is the interdependence of the world regarding transnational relations, processes, and trends. Hannerz (1996: 17) wrote about the increasing interconnectedness across nations and continents. These connections across borders have led to a restructuring of spaces. A growing process of delimitations can mean the disappearance of solid frontiers of people in cities, villages, and nations. Today, activities and social relationships of individuals and societies are created across national borders. Relatively short spatial distances make the world a common area. If one thinks in periods, one can find more intense processes of globalization in the last 30 years, processes that have been characterized as an 'accelerated phase of globalization' (Waters, 1995: 36). During this time, a global network of streams, processes, and connections across boundaries was formed. The European colonization and the global expansion of capitalism in the nineteenth and twentieth centuries had already meant an extension of global networks. In this chapter, the processes of the last 20 to 30 years are discussed.

TRANSNATIONAL NETWORKS

Transnational networks contribute to the establishment and strengthening of global processes and demonstrate how these global processes are connected to multiple streams of cultural cross-border elements. From the perspective of local (national or subnational) units, this means an increasing integration into global and transnational contexts and growing contacts with 'external' cultural elements. External cultural elements are those that transcend national and 'cultural' borders to localize in a new context. These external elements may become local elements if they can be integrated in their new cultural context. Featherstone (1995: 8) wrote that in a global world, many people are involved with more than the traditional unique culture. Even if these local outcomes could also be found in previous cross-border relationships and activities, they are much more important in the current era of globalization. Due to the increase and the intensification of transnational processes in recent decades, the importance of these processes at the local level has increased in comparison to previous years. To paraphrase the words of Hannerz, we can say that the intensification and scope of global relationships had an increasing impact on the life and cultures of the peoples of the world. Hannerz (1987: 555) wrote: 'From First World metropolis to Third World village, through education and popular culture, by way of missionaries, consultants, critical intellectuals, and small-town storytellers a conversation between cultures goes on.'

CONTACTS ACROSS BORDERS

With respect to a local perspective, these connections and contacts across borders mean that the local habitat is important (Hannerz, 1996: 22-23). It increasingly contains external meanings and cultural forms for the group and the individual. Here one can discover interesting questions with regard to the cultural consequences and impacts of these increasing flows of external cultural elements at the local level. In the following paragraphs, I will analyze how local elements react when confronted with external global cultural elements. In particular, I will ask whether a global cultural homogenization is emerging and what local processes are opposed to this development.

GLOBALIZATION AND THE PROSPECT OF A GLOBAL CULTURAL HOMOGENIZATION

In social and cultural studies, various authors consider processes of globalization and the flow of cultural elements across borders as a global cultural homogenization, as 'Westernization' or 'Americanization.' For example, Nederveen Pieterse wrote (1993: 1): 'The most common interpretations of globalization are the idea that the world is becoming more uniform and standardized, through a technological, commercial and cultural synchronization emanating from the West.'

CORE COUNTRIES VS. PERIPHERAL COUNTRIES

This perspective is based on the fact that cultural flows across borders are dominated by Western industrialized nations, such as the United States. According to these scientists, the global spread of cultural forms and meanings takes place along a one-way street from the core countries to the peripheral countries. Hannerz (1992: 219) wrote: 'When the center speaks, the periphery listens, and mostly does not talk back.' Mass media, products from mass media and (material) consumption goods are considered elements that further the cultural homogenization on a worldwide scale. The distribution of these goods from core countries implies an increasing trend of consumption in societies that favour the Western model. Mlinar (1992b: 21) speaks of 'cocacolisation,' Appadurai (1995: 295) of 'commodization', and Hannerz (1996: 24) of a global 'takeover by giant cultural commodity merchants.' However, these predictions can be justified not only by a Western dominance in the global circulation of cultural elements. This idea emphasizes that Western cultural elements are uncritically absorbed in the countries of the South. In addition, in accordance with this theory, cultural inflows suppress existing local meanings and forms. Through processes of saturation and other tributaries of Western cultural elements, the thesis has been put forward that 'the center cumulatively colonizes the minds of the periphery with a corresponding institutionalization of its forms […] that soon enough there is no real opportunity for choice' (Hannerz, 1992: 236).

In most cases, however, this type of scenario is supported by superficial and anecdotal examples that can rarely be justified by scientific methods. Detailed empirical analyses of local reactions and interpretations with respect to the inflowing cultural elements and a detailed study of the interactions between local cultures and global cultural flows have been only created in recent years (see for theory: Hannerz, 1989a: 207 and Tomlinson, 1991: 38-44; and for more recent case studies, among others Schuerkens (ed.) 2003; 2005; 2008; 2010; 2012; 2014a). Often the early writings reflected fears of its authors or critical assessments of their own cultures. In some coastal regions, scholars have studied the long-term effects of contacts over several centuries (e.g. Gruzinski, 2004).

Hannerz points out:

> There has been time to absorb foreign influences, to modify the modifications in turn, and to fit shifting cultural forms to developing social structures, to situations and emerging audiences. This is not a scene where the peripheral culture is utterly defenseless, but rather one where locally evolving alternatives to imports are available, and where there are people at hand to perform innovative acts of cultural brokerages. (1992: 242)

ACTIVE ROLE OF LOCAL COMMUNITIES

Scholars - if they are not anthropologists - often ignore the existence of local cultural alternatives and the active influence of local populations on incoming elements. They do not consider the fact that inflowing cultural forms and meanings do not encounter a cultural tabula rasa, but existing local meanings and cultural forms. Newly added cultural elements enter into a dialogue with these local forms and meanings, these perspectives and experiences of the local population. Local groups in the countries of the South are not only passive consumers and uncritical recipients of Western culture. Often, these groups play an active and creative role in the transformation of their own culture in relation to the inflowing cultural elements. The local treatment of these elements is neither an imitation nor an uncritical acceptance as Hannerz (1989a: 212) argued. On the other hand, one cannot deny that the growth of cultural flows across borders in various fields means the creation of a comprehensive and global cultural approach (mass media, Internet). This is certainly true for some consumption patterns and preferences, and for some values and perceptions. Based on this insight, many authors have emphasized that on the one hand, a combination of increasing global cultural approaches exist and, on the other hand, a prolonged global cultural heterogeneity and differentiation. Appadurai (1995: 295) states, for example: 'The central problem of today's global interactions is the tension between cultural homogenization and cultural heterogenization.' Some authors emphasize that the globalization of material forms in addition to a global differentiation of cultural forms can be found, but differs in meaning and content.

GLOBALIZATION AND THE PROBLEM OF GLOBAL CULTURAL DIVERSITY

Currently, the processes of local absorptions of global cultural flows and the mix between global and local cultural elements are frequently examined. It has been shown that the global cannot exist without the local. The local is the space, 'in which a variety of influences come together, acted out perhaps in a unique combination, under those special conditions' (Hannerz, 1996: 27).

'FORM-OF-LIFE CONTEXT': HANNERZ

The essential elements of the local can be found in the local daily life-world. Hannerz called it the 'form-of-life context'. This framework includes daily activities at home, at work, and in the neighbourhood, daily emotional face-to-face relationships with other people in the region, daily uses of symbolic forms, in short, all those elements that last long and are part of the local life (Hannerz, 1996: 28). These events and experiences of local everyday life are considered to be direct and genuine. Often, these elements have a great impact on people's lives. The local daily life is regarded as the central area of the organization, production, and dissemination of culture. Here we find a constant circulation of meanings, including any person participating in local life, each consumer, and each worker. Hannerz (1996: 73) wrote: 'It is by way of people's attentions to one another in situations within the form-of-life frame [...] that meanings are most continuously and precisely constructed.'

This means that the central role of the life framework influenced by external cultural inflows must be negotiated with local daily actions and interactions. A cultural inflow is filtered by local human experiences that allow the adoption, rejection, interpretation, and transformation of actions and forms. Long wrote:

> In fact globalization itself can only be meaningful to actors if the new experiences it simultaneously engenders are made meaningful by reference to existing experiences and cultural understandings. (1996: 50)

THE RECEPTION OF EXTERNAL CULTURAL ELEMENTS

What is the central role of globalization in the construction of meanings and in the reception of external cultural elements? Because of this cultural power of the local, the opportunity for global culture to influence everyday culture is strongly limited. But this local living environment will change; it is limited in time so that an unchanged cultural continuity cannot be guaranteed. New cultural elements are introduced by TV series, Western consumer goods, and values of migrants; they may become elements of the local everyday life, often in changed forms and adapted to the local conditions. Hannerz (1996: 27) thus considers the local as an area 'where the global, or what has been local somewhere else, also has some chance of making itself at home.' Families are the most important places of cultural reproduction and transmission of traditions of immense external influences through processes of globalization. A trans-generational continuity of attitudes, beliefs, and desires is thus more and more undermined or put in question.

LOCAL DAILY LIFE

The local culture and the local daily life can no longer be considered as a space where practices and dispositions are transmitted (Appadurai, 1990: 18). The life and the cultural identity of a people are becoming less constructed according to a traditional setting. This means that 'the standard cultural production [...] is now an endangered activity' (Appadurai, 1991: 199). Due to mass media and other aspects of globalization, numerous possible lifestyles and identification models are currently used by different actors in local dimensions. They represent ideas, fantasies, and inspire perspectives that are not the same as traditional local representations and lifestyles. Imagination and tentative adaptation play an increasingly important role in the creation of an individual life. Appadurai (1991: 205) pointed out: 'Lives today are as much acts of projection and imagination as they are enactments of known scripts or predictable outcomes.' Individual lifestyles, values, and behaviours of people thus diverge more and more from local cultural traditions.

The mutual influence of the local and the global was described by Long:

'Local' situations are transformed by becoming part of the wider 'global' arenas and processes, while 'global' dimensions are made meaningful in relation to specific 'local' conditions and through the understandings and strategies of 'local' actors. (1996: 47)

Thus, there is a continuous interaction of local cultural elements and global cultural influences in the local cultural construction of local meanings and cultural forms.

GLOBALIZATION AND THE EMPHASIS ON LOCAL CULTURES

I have already discussed global connections and the extension of the human frame of reference and thus 'the possibility of being exposed [...] to the whole infinity of places, persons, things, ideas' (Strassoldo, 1992: 46). Parallel to global integration and the increasing importance of transnational levels, we find an intensification of local cultural traditions that has to be considered as a counter-trend in the current global world as Macleod (1991: 11) rightly underlined. We can find such an intensification of local characteristics and differentiation so that Buell (1994: 9) argued: 'Tighter integration has thus paradoxically meant, and continues to mean, proliferation of asserted differences.'

INTEGRATION PROCESSES

Integration processes can be found in numerous societal fields: in economics, politics, environmental movements, cultural values, etc. They can be an expression of enrichment, revitalizing, and reinventing local cultural identities and traditions, taking into account common ethnic, social, or religious elements. Several factors explain the appearance of these trends: global connections and their influence on local elements that may be interpreted as an attack on vague fears in the face of their own culture. The speed and extent of global change and the complexity of global systems may also help to strengthen the desire for stability and continuity. Strassoldo (1992: 46) argued that this new sort of localism permits the establishment of a refuge from the difficult larger world and thus the acceptance of this feared influence. References to local communities and local values, the revitalization of traditional cultures and an emphasis on local cultural identities may permit a feeling of stability and confidence in the face of globalization processes. Beyer (1994: 62) argued: 'To the extent that relativizing forces make themselves felt, individuals seek to orient themselves in our impersonal global society through identification with a particular group and its specific culture.'

FEARED EFFECTS OF PROCESSES OF GLOBALIZATION

From this perspective, the focus is not directed at the conflict between one's own culture and another real culture – even if groups who are concerned often emphasize this factor – but against the feared effects of processes of globalization. At the same time, in Western countries the emphasis on local cultures may mean the opposition to globalization processes and their origin. Bright and Geyer (1987: 69–70) wrote: '(T)he assertion of local and particular claims over global and general ones […] is rather an effort to establish the terms for self-determining and self-controlled participation in the processes of global integration and the struggle for planetary order.'

CULTURAL SELF-CONSCIOUSNESS

Another trend needs to be considered here: the worldwide development of a new cultural self-consciousness. This cultural self-awareness is growing due to the global spread of ideas and values and the worldwide recognition of culture and cultural elements as a universal value. A global recognition of the right to one's own culture and cultural self-determination accompanies these processes. As the idea of landscapes studied by Appadurai (1996) shows, the global spread of ideas and values is part of the current globalization processes. The fact that more and more groups consider their culture and lifestyle to be a political right lets them put an emphasis on their own culture. Today, due to mass media and global migration flows, global cultural differences are thus easier to determine and find out.

CONCLUDING REMARKS

In conclusion, we can state that many of the inflowing cultural elements are transformed during the processes of integration and embedding in new local environments. In particular, they are interpreted by local populations in terms of local cultures and experiences. They are accepted with the help of local requirements and are filled with appropriate contents and functions. Hannerz (1992: 238) showed that this process takes its time in reshaping the global culture. But these processes of local appropriation and transformation of cultural elements allow the emergence – due to the mixture of local and imported cultural elements – of something new and unique. The local clash of different cultural elements leads to a creation of new cultural forms, new lifestyles, and new representations. According to a global perspective, this means a global cultural diversity: but a diversity resulting from the current global cultural relations, from the cultural appropriation of external elements by local populations and from the creative mixture of 'global' elements with local cultural meanings and forms.

THE NEW GLOBAL CULTURAL DIVERSITY

Hannerz describes this process in the following manner:

> The world system, rather than creating massive cultural homogeneity on a global level, is replacing one diversity with another; and the new diversity is based relatively more on interrelations and less on autonomy. Yet meanings and modes of expressing them can be born in the interrelations. We must be aware that openness to foreign cultural influences need not involve only an impoverishment of local and national culture. It may give people access to technological and symbolic resources for dealing with their own ideas, managing their own culture, in new ways. (Hannerz, 1987: 555)

The global culture is certainly not a one-way street, but may rightly be interpreted as 'a global intercultural interplay,' as Nederveen Pieterse (1993: 9) described it. The countries of the South export, for example, their music, their literature, their spirituality, or healing methods to the countries of the northern hemisphere. These trends are not new, but due to processes of globalization, their importance increases: migrants and the media, tourists and scientists are constantly looking for innovations in other cultures and are interested in 'exotic' and 'authentic' cultures.

DISCUSSION QUESTIONS

1. Why do people defend their own culture? Is it an act of pride, or one of power and violence?

2. Can cultures learn from one another and are they able to understand differences? If so, how?

3. How can you describe the process of accepting global elements in local cultures?

4. What does it mean that 'cultures answer back' (Hannerz)?

5. Please explain the *glocalization* of global cultural flows.

ANNOTATED FURTHER READINGS

Appadurai, A. (1996) *Modernity at Large: Cultural Dimensions of Globalization.* **Minneapolis: University of Minnesota Press.**
This book by a leading cultural theorist offers a framework for the cultural study of globalization and places the challenges of contemporary life in a global perspective. The book offers a path to move beyond traditional oppositions between culture and power, tradition and modernity, global and local.

Hannerz, U. (1996) *Transnational Connections: Cultures, People, Places.* **London: Routledge.**
This book contains a few well-known pieces, notably 'Cosmopolitans and locals in world culture'. Hannerz emphasizes that globalization does not imply that persons acquire a global identity, but rather that cultural diversity is being organized in new ways. He reminds the reader that globalization and creolization are the products of world capitalism and colonialism.

Miller, D. (ed.) (1995a) *Worlds Apart: Modernity through the Prism of the Local.* **London and New York: Routledge.**
Worlds Apart is concerned with new global and local forms. Several of the chapters are written by anthropologists who examine television and mass commodities. The book also considers the ways in which people are increasingly not creating these images, but consuming them.

Nederveen Pieterse, J. (2003) *Globalization and Culture: Global Mélange.* **Lanham, MD: Rowman and Littlefield.**
While most assessments of globalization are confined to a short time period, Nederveen Pieterse argues that globalization belongs to a deep shift of civilizational centres with ongoing intercultural exchanges.

Websites

http://www.worldvaluessurvey.org
The World Values Survey is a global network of social scientists studying changing values and their impact on social and political life, led by an international team of scholars, with the WVS association and secretariat headquartered in Stockholm, Sweden.

https://www.ucl.ac.uk/anthropology/about/material-culture
UCL Anthropology is the world's leading centre for Material culture studies. Drawing on long-term fieldwork and through creative ethnographic engagement, the starting point is the empirical study of how people make, exchange, and consume objects.

https://www.ethnologue.com/world
Overview of languages in the world.

http://subcultureslist.com/
A list of subcultures and some information on theoretical approaches.

http://www.newworldencyclopedia.org/entry/Counterculture
An encyclopedia definition of countercultures.

(all websites accessed 28 September 2016)

3

TRANSFORMATIONS OF LOCAL SOCIO-ECONOMIC PRACTICES IN A GLOBAL WORLD

Summary

This chapter provides a comprehensive overview of the transformation of socio-economic practices in the global economy. It offers analytical and comparative insights at the world level, with regard to current socio-economic practices as well as an assessment of the overall economic globalization phenomenon in the global world. Through empirical case studies of different civilizations or cultures that describe situations where local socio-economic practices and global economic modernity intertwine, this chapter assesses the overall situation in the world, looking at the world as an economic system where some countries act as winners, others as losers, and some as both winners and losers of economic globalization.

INTRODUCTION

In countries of the global South with underdeveloped democratic institutions, processes of international competition have played a less important role than ethnic conflicts since the end of the global competition that was characteristic of the Cold War era. With the spread of globalization during the last decades, the collapse of most of the communist states, and the spread of the neoliberal credo, the concept of competition emerged as a prominent theme in understanding socio-economic development in a globalized world. A discussion arose on whether the common economic ideology introduced by modern global capitalism would have an impact on countries that were very different in social and cultural terms from the Western countries in the North. Since then, there seems to be no real alternative to the Western economic competition ideal, so that economists and sociologists have asked which institutions contribute to integrate competitive economic markets into social, cultural, and economic systems in Asia, Latin America, and Africa. In various regions of the world, the answer has mainly depended on the socio-structural characteristics of societies. Obviously, some societies are better positioned than others and can therefore be more active participants in global modernity. Maybe such a position would be best conceptualized by the concept of cultural communities rather than socio-economic and political constellations. If so, then a reflection on the cultural construction of social environments in the global modernity seems to be a prerequisite for the analysis of discourses and practices of economic globalization in non-Western civilizations. Global players exert pressure on local and regional cultures and ask them to adapt. The world market defines competitive capitalism. Private ownership and the virtue of individualism have become the dominant principles of colonial and postcolonial societies, principles that began to be introduced in the last centuries, and especially in recent decades in parts of Africa, Asia, and Latin America. Global players define civilizations and their global economic processes by referring to their adaptability. Culture as a given system has become a selection criterion for investment and capital. According to global players, competition may classify social systems that enable the highest profits by relying on cultural values. Societies that are able to easily adopt market principles are valued more highly than societies that resist changes required by capitalist logic.

APPROACH THAT TRIES TO UNITE ECONOMIC INTERESTS, CULTURAL PREFERENCES, AND POLITICAL INSTITUTIONS

This briefly sketched approach that tries to unite economic interests, cultural preferences, and political institutions in one logical system allows us to analyze why some societies are better able to endure global pressure and accept global market conditions. Within this theoretical framework, I present empirical case studies of local socio-economic practices in different cultures of the global world.

ECONOMIC GLOBALIZATION IN HISTORY

The analysis of the causes and consequences of economic globalization currently represents one of the most important debates in the social sciences. French historian Serge Gruzinski (2004) argues that economic globalization has its roots in the great discoveries in the East and West in the early 16th century when Asia, Africa, Europe, and America began to be connected by extensive communication flows. According to him, the period 1480 to 1520 should be considered as the first phase of globalization. For Williamson and O'Rourke (2002), however, the first global century did not begin until 1820 and lasted until 1913. It was connected to the gold standard under the free trade imperialism of the British Empire. In this global century, a global commodity market and increased international labour migration existed. According to Williamson and O'Rourke, the second global century began in 1950 and corresponded to the worldwide acceptance of the dollar. The time after 1985, with the fall of the Iron Curtain, the opening up of Eastern markets, and the decline of national controls of the economy can thus be regarded as belonging to a much longer trend.

The viewpoints of Gruzinski, Williamson, and O'Rourke are very different in terms of cultural and economic issues. For Williamson and O'Rourke, globalization is a form of economic integration through intensive economic exchanges. After 1492, Williamson and O'Rourke argue, tariffs, trade monopolies, war, and non-economic exchanges were the driving forces of global processes. Gruzinski, on the other hand, is mainly interested in examining cultural exchanges.

There are even more differences among scholars with regard to the different waves of globalization. For Richard Baldwin and Philippe Martin (1999), the first wave of globalization begins in 1870 in connection with the expansion of trade from Europe to the rest of the world. O'Rourke (2002) has chosen to define the beginning of globalization at about 1820 due to the higher growth rate of world trade at this time, compared to previous centuries. The interwar period of the twentieth century presented for many countries a global disintegration with the dissolution of external links. The liberalization of financial markets in Europe, the decline of national sovereignty in different policy areas, and the growing importance of markets and international institutions in the 1980s are often associated with the current phase of globalization. Other scholars underline the Bretton Woods agreement and the reduction of tariffs under the General Agreement on Tariffs and Trade (GATT) as the institutional infrastructure for the re-emergence of industrial capitalism and changes in financial and banking institutions, thus a time of globalization that has led to transformations in the fields of culture, communications, politics, and global institutions.

According to this discourse, globalization began as a movement that dominated most of the last 150 years. This development was related to processes that began 500 years ago. The logic of globalization encompasses more than Marx's logic of capital as it relates to economic, political, and cultural dimensions. Politicians, scientists, and opponents of globalization have helped to reify this phenomenon. One could argue that today's globalization is a reinvention of international capitalism that was politically compromised. But globalization has also been promoted by social actors – such as the non-governmental sector – with large impacts on individuals and the rules of competition. Globalization represents a risk and a possibility that governments and national elites underline when implanting reforms. It is firstly a hopeful slogan and secondly - for certain social categories and/or social groups in developing and in developed countries alike - a process that creates anxiety.

ECONOMIC GLOBALIZATION AND STRUCTURAL INFLUENCES ON SOCIETY

The commercial penetration of most regions of the world does not imply a unilateral extension of capitalism. Sub-Saharan Africa receives more aid than the Far East.

However, the African continent remains of little interest to private foreign capital with the exception of South Africa and some oil producing countries. Countries in the Middle East or in North Africa with oil deposits do not really industrialize. The multilateral aid from the International Monetary Fund (IMF) and the World Bank is disbursed with the conditionality to develop a *free* market economy in receiving countries and thus to contribute to the development of capitalism in these regions. Multilateral institutions finance productive and/or collective projects that promise profits in the long run. They often contribute to the restructuring of economic sectors such as agriculture, the energy sector, and communication (Adda, 2006: 132). The primary goal of these programs has been the systematic introduction of market mechanisms into these economies by using external exchanges and the financial system. This applies also to traditional sectors such as agriculture. The creation of these institutional conditions of capitalism has laid the ground for further economic processes linked to globalization.

HOW DO SOCIETIES RESHAPE THEIR PARTICULAR FORM OF CAPITALISM?

The question is how these societies internalize, appropriate, and reshape their particular form of capitalism. It is obvious that cultures react differently to these processes. In some societies, capital may enter and propagate a given material culture and consumption styles, although capitalism as a system based on competition may be barely developed (such as in parts of sub-Saharan Africa). Loans, public investments (China, India), and only a few private investments are thus the predominant forms of penetration of foreign capital, which are found in regions such as sub-Saharan Africa, the Middle East, and Central and South Asia.

In three other regions, economies have more easily adopted and implemented capitalist structures: Eastern Europe, Latin America, and the Far East. To a large extent, the first two regions were able to found their development on groups which came from Europe (refugees and migrants). The Far East was able to support global capitalism by focusing on three elements in its national development projects: the expansion of the education system, the existence of a local middle class, and an economic growth organized by the state. The state served as a market leader, securing the functioning of public bureaucracy (Evans, 1995), a condition that was more or less missing in most African and Latin American countries (Adda, 2006: 141).

NOTIONS OF WORLD REGIONS

The empirical facts that have been created in various regions of the world challenge the notions 'North-South,' 'centre-periphery,' 'First, Second, and Third World'. Braudel (1998) pointed out several decades ago that stable cultural realities represent structural constraints in different civilizations. The developmental discourse of recent decades forgot these findings under rather unpopular elites who founded their empirical measures on an understanding of development as an improvement of socio-economic conditions in each country. Adda (2006) expressed the opinion that 'the specific characteristics of these regions explain the manner of insertion in the global economy, as well as their capacity to profit from the globalization process' (2006: 164, translation by the author). This means that there are winners and losers even among those who are in between, such as Eastern Europe, which could base its economic success on its industrial culture that had emerged under the communist regimes. However, the question remains whether these societies are able to assimilate the Western capitalist logics. The new periphery in the global world seems to be sub-Saharan Africa, the Arab world, and Central and South Asia. In these regions, we find widespread poverty, structural unemployment, low salaries, and high fecundity rates, coupled with weak political structures, and often ethnic or religious violence.

THE INTERNATIONAL POLITICAL ECONOMY: A CULTURE OF COMPETITION

Our contemporary world is composed of three regions that claim a largely Western civilization, namely North America, Western Europe, and that part of Asia that developed from Japan, such as South Korea. These three regions spread over the rest of the world common development principles that support something that one could name *global modernity*. This kind of globalization is defined by the integration of different areas according to Western ideas and Western power logics. It is undisputed that a common dynamic exists, which is characterized by a certain political and economic unit, so that regions from around the world have tried to integrate into this common global system.

MULTIPLICITY OF GLOBALIZATIONS

CHINA

Currently, some scholars insist that there is a multiplicity of globalizations (Chang, 2007). The Chinese case is taken as an example of a civilization that imposed itself on the whole region of East Asia. China's ability to build on a written language, highly differentiated values, and a unique social and political system seems to establish the Chinese world as an alternative to the Western world. The political and economic events in China since the first half of the nineteenth century, and the impossibility for China to challenge European and North American modernity in the 1970s have not reduced China to a nation-state that has submitted to Western globalization. Sanjuan (2004: 123) emphasized that the Chinese world defends three forms of globalization: 1. an imperial model that designed China as a political, cultural, and cosmological factor, which is based in the north of China; 2. a network model, which refers to the networks of the Diaspora; and 3. a coastal city model, which links the great cities of the coast, such as Shanghai and Hong Kong, to major places in the world system.

    These globalization models have begun to be transformed by Western globalization, but in turn they also transform Western globalization as China has continued to redefine its relations with its neighbours, other countries of Asia, and the rest of the world. China has become the European Union's second largest trading partner behind the United States; the European Union is China's largest trading partner. EU imports from China are dominated by industrial and consumer goods. EU exports to China are concentrated on machinery and equipment, motor vehicles, aircraft, and chemicals.[1]

These facts indicate that China's political and intellectual elites try to strengthen the economic and political power of China in the world, even if they view globalization as a hierarchy of territories and peoples. The current political elite seems to be convinced that the power of China has to be considered in the world based on its fast-growing economy and not because of its culture or politics, as it was the rule in the Empire or under Mao. Since the opening up of China in 1978, the country has restored its global status. Chinese know that their nation is not the only superpower trying to reorganize the world. When it seems necessary, China's elites accept the North American model to strengthen the place of China in East Asia and in opposition to Japan, Southeast Asia, and India. According to Sanjuan (2004), the rivalry between China and the United States is not conceived according to the same notions. Chinese globalization builds on a regional power in Asia, and is rather uninterested in far-away conflicts in the Middle East or in Africa, even though China has enlarged its economic relations with Africa in the last decade. China does not attempt to transfer her model to other regions or to change the West. Chinese try to adapt to the current state of the world pragmatically and realistically in order to use it for their power project. Globalization, according to Beijing, can only be multipolar. The Chinese world is indeed global, as Chinese diasporas are spread over the five continents, trying to increase their transnational solidarity. Beijing has pursued a politics directed to the Chinese diasporas asking them to develop China by investments and industrial relocations, and by the promotion of Chinese products and the dissemination of Chinese cultural heritage. Chinese communities in Southeast Asia and in Western Chinatowns belong to a larger community with a global reach. Chinese towns have to display the success of these reforms in China and an international modernity with urban practices and leisure, architectural silhouettes, and new urban public spaces, foreign banks, and tourism. The Olympic Games in Beijing in 2008 and the World Expo in Shanghai in 2010 accentuated these processes.

SOCIO-ECONOMIC RESTRUCTURING IN CHINA

CASE STUDY

Thierry Pairault asks in his study if Western capitalism has transformed China into a neoliberal paradise. He underlines that some groups in China are excluded from economic change, such as ethnic minorities, migrant workers, and people from the countryside. State participation and economic growth are

(Continued)

(Continued)

not mutually opposed, according to him. China has seen economic growth without applying the policy rules of the World Bank and the International Monetary Fund. As the country did not accept the uniform policy of the IMF and the WB that has been applied in many countries, China could respect her local socio-economic situations, by basing her development on cultural roots, such as those provided by Confucius. Chinese leaders have only accepted advice coming from outside when they regarded it as appropriate and committed to a cultural tradition that they could find in the ideas of Confucius.

The success was of a mixed type: growth rates were rather high in the last years, but have been accompanied by growing social inequality. China has become the second largest economy of the world by nominal GDP and the world's largest economy by purchasing power parity. China's integration into the global economy is important for the local public opinion, which is optimistic and believes that the Chinese economy can withstand international competition. If the political elite redistributes economic achievements, this may have social consequences on economic growth. Pairault then discusses the social problems of the country and in particular high social inequality, the growth of the middle class, and the reduction of absolute poverty that have been found in recent years.

Pairault, T. (2008) 'China's response to globalization: Manufacturing confucian values,' in U. Schuerkens (ed.) *Globalization and Transformations of Local Socioeconomic Practices*. London and New York: Routledge. pp. 99–119.

These different elements underline the special integration of China into the community of developed countries and reaffirm her place as a dynamic actor of globalization. This does not only mean a reformulation of Chinese globalization, but also a reformulation of globalization in accordance to Chinese interests in a global order. China is now inviting other countries in the world and the global community to reinterpret globalization by taking into account some of her own interests.

EASTERN EUROPE

Beside this particular form of globalization that will probably change our understanding of the world in the coming years, the current Western form of globalization tried to increase its influence after the collapse of the Iron Curtain in Eastern Europe and in those parts of Central Asia that were formerly under the influence of the Soviet Union. Cultural products and their defenders originating from Western countries (including consumption patterns, ideas and concepts – such as psychoanalysis or management), have methodically targeted these regions after the fall of the

Iron Curtain. Huge financial support was given to these regions in order to favour economic developments and systemic changes of political, economic, and social systems. The discourse of globalization was introduced by the international financial assistance system. Business people and international experts were sent to various regions and supported newly introduced economic rules by using local experts in the implementation of programs of state institutions before they were formally adopted by national parliaments and presidents.

In fact, the United States took advantage of huge financial, economic, and human measures to accelerate the integration of Central Asia in global processes (Poujol, 2004: 146). They privileged bilateral contracts in important areas such as defence, economic investment, and participation in the oil business. The United States promoted democracy, the *free* market, political stability; and they supported private enterprises and educational programs. All in all, a complex program that built on the integration of new countries into the global economic system. Thousands of Americans and Europeans had the task to present and to implement a model as a universal framework of a global orientation. They worked as democracy specialists, members of the Peace Corps, or in international non-governmental organizations (NGOs) that tackled the entire socio-political space. USAID has been one of the most important organizations to spread the idea of globalization. The United States was considered to be more or less the only global player. Chinese, Japanese, Indian, and even Russian projects were regarded as based on bilateral efforts so that they favoured a national orientation and not a global one (Poujol, 2004: 148).

The rapid spread of these policies in order to integrate these countries into new economic, financial, and strategic networks was done with the intention to prevent the former Russian power from establishing new ties with its former Soviet satellites. The new partners of these countries sought to integrate a population of 50 million inhabitants into Western globalization. The peoples of these regions had to reconsider their own place in history and the future. They showed ambivalent feelings and an apparent submission in order to please money lenders. Often, large parts of the population rejected global cultural models that denied national peculiarities. But the political options of this region differed from anti-globalization movements since its leaders were trying to strengthen their respective countries while accepting large aspects of globalization. However, continuing political unrest in the region let appear that this is still a highly disputed political and economic field (e.g. Ukraine crisis, Crimea, Georgia).

AFRICA

Globalization refers to intense economic, political, social, and cultural relations across international borders. Barriers in the fields of culture, economy, and communication have been broken down. Economic *free* market ideas, liberal democracy, and good governance have become universal values for states, even if the respective local characteristics were different. The collapse of the Soviet bloc in the late 1980s and early 1990s led to the emergence of a global economy that has been influenced by the interests of mainly Western countries, increasing the integration of most economies in this global economy. Currently, capitalism as an economic system dominates the globe. The interdependence of national economies in a global market for goods and services characterizes present-day globalization. This globalization also affects the international division of labour: developed countries have specialized in high-skill manufacturing and services, and developing countries – whose labour force is most often less qualified - in low-skill intensive manufacturing. This asymmetry has had a serious impact on African countries, which mainly supply raw materials for industries in developed countries, which in turn sell finished goods to developing countries (Grégoire, 2002; Ajayi, 2003; Brunel, 2005; Rugumamu, 2005).

CAPITALISM AND MARGINALIZATION

The African continent is currently characterized by marginalization. Already in 1996, Africa's share in world exports had dropped to a meagre one per cent. If South Africa and the oil-producing states are excluded, the percentage is close to nil (Hugon, 2016). At the end of the last century, growth in the African countries slowed down to one per cent, while official aid was less than \$20 per head annually (Akindele et al., 2002). Despite the current economic growth in Africa (3 per cent in 2015)[2], poverty prevails on the continent. Scholars like Nigel C. Gibson have underlined the unequal world system since the beginning of the industrial revolution in connection with the exploitation of coloured and black people. According to Gibson, 'political power has been employed to gain advantages, exploit inequalities, and crush competition' (2004: 5). Africa, because of its centrality during the triangular trade between this continent, the Americas, and Europe, became marginalized according to him. European colonialism shaped modern Africa, but Africans also contributed to the rising power of Europe.

Africa was linked to other regions, such as China, India, and the Middle East by trade as early as the second century of our era (Beaujard, 2005). In the early sixteenth century, Portuguese colonization contributed to the partial destruction of African mercantilism in modern Mozambique. Some African economies remained in trade with Europe until the period of European colonization in the nineteenth century. For nearly 350 years (1519-1867), the far-reaching slave trade took place: it had a strong impact on the population structure of the African and American continents. Walter Rodney famously wrote (in Gibson, 2004: 6) that 'the development of America meant the underdevelopment of Africa.' Other authors, such as Akindele et al. (2002) underline the opinion that globalization is the latest form of dissemination of capitalism in Africa. The continent was opened up in the 1980s by structural adjustment plans, privatization, and the policies of the World Bank and the International Monetary Fund. The result was that Africa's consumers and productive forces increasingly accepted various aspects of Western capitalism.

GLOBALIZATION AND LABOUR PRODUCTIVITY

For most African countries, the first period of independence did not lead to the realization of the political objectives of the anti-colonial struggles. Often, African economies functioned more or less successfully by loading the largest share of the burden on the peasantry that produced agricultural goods for low renumeration. Cheap capital loans led to a high burden of debts while the prices for agricultural products declined. Since the 1980s, African countries were obliged to accept the rules of the international economic system by opening up their national economies to world-market competition. The free movement of capital was in search of new markets and cheap labour. Since the 1960s, there has been a constant migration of redundant workers from rural areas to the overcrowded towns. These men and women may have worked from time to time, but they have often been unemployed, part-time, or occasional workers. Export processing zones (EPZs), which specialized in the assembly of goods, have been created in 25 African countries, but they are only important in Tunisia, Egypt, and Mauritius. They have been successful in Mauritius, where they account for 65 per cent of exports (Gibson, 2004: 10). The rest of the continent is not a source of semiskilled workers from the point of view of international capitalism, so that, for example, Chinese enterprises bring their own workers to Africa, instead of using their plants as job and training opportunities for Africans. Since the 1960s, a significant brain drain of African elites (including doctors, computer specialists, and nurses) into Western countries has occurred. They are usually recruited through bilateral agreements due to the shortage of some skilled professional groups in the North. The result is a growing shortage of skilled workers in the South, particularly in the health sector. Another special element of the continent in terms of globalization is that women not only contribute through their unpaid work as small farmers to national economies, but can attain a degree of autonomy and independence, which does not exist in other continents (Berger, 2016).

Since 11 September 2001, there is a renewed interest in raw materials from Africa, especially oil. China, Brazil, India, and traditionally Western Europe and North America all mingle here, though in recent years China's influence has largely increased to the detriment of Western countries. Globalization as a myth is only affordable to an elite minority of Africans, while most other people are suffering from unemployment, illness, and starvation. As a result of structural adjustment programs and the debt regime, the majority of the African population is now faced with a situation that means a lack of opportunities for the youth, conflicts about resources, as well as social and political movements against globalization and some Western countries, especially in the Sahel region.

GLOBALIZATION AND A NATIONAL LEADERSHIP

Africa's populations have been looking for good governance, but have often been ruled by political elites who have tended to think more about their own privileges than about how they could improve the situation of these populations. In fact, world markets have contributed to the declining power of the nation-state and its elites. Political elites are less and less able to control their national economy. International organizations such as the International Monetary Fund or the World Bank are more important than national governments. Countries like Nigeria and South Africa have played dominant regional roles, but most other countries have been politically and economically weak. This low political autonomy represents a challenge for African elites. Yet the current situation in Africa could mean a turning point. Many types of crises are emerging: civil wars, ethnic and/or political conflicts, and high crime rates. The youth feels like a 'lost generation' and has nothing to lose, so they have been embarking on political upsets, religious fundamentalism, or cultural chauvinism (Sommers, 2015). The high rate of youth unemployment is a major challenge for the coming years and has already led to various socio-political movements in the second decade of the second millennium in North Africa (e.g. Tunisia, Egypt, and Morocco).

GLOBALIZATION: IMPACTS ON THE SOCIETIES OF THE SOUTH

Globalization influences local cultures, labour standards, productivity, and other elements of societies. Liberal economic policy has argued that trade would result in economic prosperity for the participating countries. After World War II, the General Agreement on Tariffs and Trade (GATT) played an important role in the reduction of tariffs for developed countries, the elimination of certain trade barriers and subsidies, the extension of the GATT principles to sectors such as services and investments, and applying of more rules to the agricultural trade. Long-term rules were established and national policies that hindered access to the market were reduced in both the North and the South. Since 1995, the World Trade Organization currently works with 164 countries (as of July 2016) that have accepted its free trade rules. The worldwide movements of capital and labour have become easier, so that today the poorer regions often have rural migrants who send money back from their region of residence and spend their holidays in their region of origin. But the evidence is mixed whether globalization has been beneficial to most countries. There are scholars who argue that poorer countries are marginalized in the globalization process, except those that can attract transnational subcontracting corporations. Global enterprises are concentrated in the global North, and international trade is dominated by this same category of countries. However, trade between countries of the South has begun to increase, and the share of BRICS (Brazil, Russia, India, China, and South Africa) in world trade now equals that of developed countries (see UNDP, 2013).

LEAST DEVELOPED COUNTRIES

On the other hand, some scholars think that the Least Developed Countries gain from engaging in global interactions. In fact, they gain access to larger markets and consumers get access to a larger variety of goods and services. The local industry, to the extent it exists, may thus have the possibility of serving global markets, and domestic producers may obtain lower-priced goods and products. Another argument is that these Least Developed Countries may improve their level of technology without the high costs of research and development, a tactic that has been chosen by China. At best, these countries can import capital goods, which increase their production capacity. These results can then trigger a future growth with higher domestic savings and/or international loans. South Korea has successfully improved its industrial production by providing a better education of its population. Another argument to follow international economic policies is that countries who insist on maintaining their policies and do not accept the market risk may no longer receive international investments, except those of migrants. The negative outcomes of this trend are growing inequality, rural depopulation, poor urban suburbs, and the rise of the informal sector.

TRADE-ORIENTED NATIONS

History suggests that the wealthiest nations of the world have been trade-oriented (Western Europe, the USA, Japan, South Korea, and Singapore). In contrast, the poorest regions of the world, such as some South Asian countries and sub-Saharan Africa have remained more or less absent from international foreign trade. Countries such as India, China, and Poland that have opened up their economies could strongly improve their standards of living for parts of their populations. The current policy of the BRICS countries with huge investments in poorer Southern countries seems thus to resemble a kind of Marshall Plan so that some negative economic and social aspects of globalization in some countries of the South could be tackled. The investments of China, India, and Brazil in Africa show their interests in local raw materials, but also new possibilities of international influences in times when the West and in particular Europe is struggling with internal economic problems. New forms of interdependence, such as land grabbing have created new development relations where huge parts of land belong to foreign states or transnational enterprises (from the US, China, the United Arab Emirates, India, or Brazil) which use the land as a financial security in times of financial crises but also as land to be cultivated for the benefit of home markets, hungry populations, and as a substitute to petroleum (see Sassen, 2014).

ECONOMIC GLOBALIZATION IN LATIN AMERICA

Corporate relations in Latin America have historical roots that are particular for the region. In the current global economy, most firms of Latin American origin are unknown outside the region. Most of the local groups are 'under the control of families and friendship cliques' (Conaghan and Malloy, 1994: 16). Only a few economic groups are important, but these 'groups are horizontally and/or vertically diversified industrial and financial powers' (Cordey, 2005: 79). The particular characteristics of power elites in Latin America are that horizontal networks link them: economic elites are in informal contacts via club memberships or meetings with political elites so that they may defend common interests.

THE *HACIENDA*

Economic power concentration has its traditional roots in groups that based their power on land and the enslavement of the population in the nineteenth century. These families maintained their power until the 1930s. Since the 1920s, new elite groups in the Central Andes began 'to articulate ideologies and economic programs that assigned a leading role in economic development to the state' (Conaghan and Malloy, 1994: 19). The *hacienda* was no longer an important economic factor: instead, state-run industries and new private enterprises appeared. In the following decades, military governments came to power. They sought an alliance with economic elites and gave them the ability to influence the decision-making processes. The masses were excluded from political processes. The absence of formal possibilities of inter-action between domestic economic elites and military governments contributed to a growing unease of the bourgeoisie, who looked for political and economic models better adapted to their own visions. From the 1980s, business groups began to support democratization in order to open up political processes to the masses (Conaghan and Malloy, 1994: 5). The state began to withdraw from state-owned enterprises and reaffirmed the private sector, so that the market power of corporations grew with their acquisition of state-owned enterprises (Cordey, 2005: 82). But economic elites continued to be closely linked to political power. These domestic elites tried to enrich themselves and were regarded as inefficient, but they had success in structural adjustment processes by underlining national realities of the different countries (Conaghan and Malloy, 1994: 219). The majority of the population was more or less excluded from these debates. The economy was an 'elite affair' (Cordey, 2005: 83). The special structure of state and business links in several Latin American countries and the interaction of economic and political elites have thus a particular character, which differed from other continents.

TRANSNATIONAL ENTERPRISES

With the globalization processes of the 1990s, transnational enterprises began to get involved in Latin America but they pursued another strategy from the one employed in Asia. They tried to acquire large domestic enterprises and national banks. These acquisitions allowed them to remove competitors and to have access to a distribution network, the local know-how, and the necessary social connections (Cordey, 2005: 122). The aim was to improve their strategic position on national, regional, and global markets (Cordey, 2005: 122). Some business groups from the region managed to become regional transnational corporations (TNCs), but most of the other TNCs came from the US, Europe, and Japan. Local groups built joint ventures with enterprises from these regions. These big TNCs have had a significant impact on the development of the economies, even if their investment has some-times corresponded to a marginal role in their global strategies. Cordey argued that developing countries had 'virtually no bargaining options and no alternative but to open up their economies' (2005: 123). The transnational era of Latin American economies began thus in the 1990s.

STRATEGIC ALLIANCE BETWEEN POLITICAL AND BUSINESS ELITES

The result of this strategic alliance between political and business elites has led to a wave of strikes and protests by the populations during the last decade. Some charismatic leaders like Chávez had tried to introduce political measures that favoured those groups that had become marginalized and impoverished in the preceding decades. Neoliberal policies and indirect taxation had often created small, privileged groups that favoured the TNCs in conjunction with governments, presidents, and some remaining domestic economic groups. The populations of these countries have become sceptical in the presence of corrup-tion and economic models favoured by political elites. Even after the shift to the left in recent years, there have still been – as in Brazil (from 2013 to 2016) and Chile (2013 and 2016) – mass protests.

COMPETITION IN ENTERPRISES IN DIFFERENT CIVILIZATIONS

ASIAN SOCIETIES

Let's start with the Chinese case. According to Paulmier (2004: 185), the Chinese argue in terms of flows; they try to circulate capital as quickly as possible. The control of these flows is more important than possessing this capital (Wong, 1997; Rocca, 2006). The market is characterized by small, highly competitive enterprises. Markets are conquered progressively. First, according to the Chinese, they should be developed at the periphery. Then leaders should try to get access to key markets. Accordingly, South Korean and Chinese groups have penetrated industries and high technology by conquering markets in Latin America, Africa, and Asia (Paulmier, 2004: 187) (e.g. the strategy of Samsung). This type of economy has favoured the development of a merchant mentality looking for rapid profits. The enterprise has often been a family project, controlled by the family head and managed by children, nephews, or brothers-in-law. This sort of administration means small businesses financed by the family. Industrial firms, however, have often been managed as a state-owned or state administered entity.

Japanese, Korean, and Chinese businessmen try to diversify their activities and their markets and to enlarge their economic possibilities. They demonstrate an economic mentality that is particularly adapted to capitalism (Huang, 1998). Just think of the many small restaurants of these groups in Western towns. Asian cultures have thus been particularly well adapted to current economic transformations of capitalism.

AFRICAN SOCIETIES

In Africa, the situation looks different. The failure of many enterprises in the modern industrial and service sectors in African countries is caused by business systems that are not adapted to the social context. Their main characteristics are that they find it difficult to shape the link between the individual and the group (Henry, 2004: 199). Nevertheless, there are some examples of success. Some firms have invented management books that describe all necessary procedures for the functioning of enterprises. These books offer an objective guideline for actions to be undertaken by economic actors and staff. Another example that Henry evokes is the development of software for the management of economic processes. This possibility is developed for example by banks, so that the counter staff can forward customers they know to other colleagues. Close social links prevent the staff being put in a tight spot.

A different understanding of economic competition is that of Morocco (Mezouar and Sémériva, 2004). In this country, the behaviour and settings of modern industrial economies were not really accepted. The daily life of the world seems very malleable, so that it can be interpreted by anyone according to their own opinion. Another problem is that the direct and central hierarchy is not recognized and is therefore illegitimate. At the same time, the positive written legal right characterizes the role of directors and the customary law that is based on oral practice is the foundation of social relations. People who are entrepreneurs were marginalized in the past. But a new generation of French-Moroccon binationals have recently decided to return to the country of their parents with the intention to obtain a better professional situation for them in opposition to the numerous discriminations they had to endure in France (see Bassi and Bertossi, 2010).

According to the social anthropological tradition in Africa, social facts cannot be reduced to individual phenomena. The rational economic actor of the Western culture seems to be particular to societies that are regulated by the market. Some scholars emphasize that Western rationality is incongruent with African social representations (see Engelhard, 1998; Latouche, 1998). In most parts of the continent, an economic action is often secondary to exchange relations based on symbolic and social values. However, according to orthodox economic thinking, economic agents everywhere respond to prices and individual calculations. But in Africa, local groups and state pressures contribute to undermine rationalized development processes. Rationalized economic actions are atypical, which has led to the opposition between the *Homo economicus* and the *Homo africanus* of Hugon. Hugon has stressed that Africans try to minimize risks that depend on social positions (2006: 58). Under uncertain conditions, these social actors prefer the short run over intergenerational investments. Insecurity and precarious situations let people choose the short-term perspective rather than long-term economic conditions. In connection with feeble states, social identities are forcibly based on community rules, even if these latter are also exposed to transformations.

THE CREATION OF THE MICROFINANCE SECTOR IN CAMEROON

CASE STUDY

In the early 1990s, microfinance institutions in Cameroon emerged from two major crises. First, the global crisis experienced by the dismantling of the coffee market combined with the crisis of the banking sector resulting in the closure of banks and the dismissals of several bank managers. These events led these unemployed professionals to the microfinance sector. The endorsement of Law No. 90/053 of 19 December 1990 concerning the freedom of association and the Law No. 92/006 of 14 August 1992 on cooperatives and common initiative groups led them to create new institutions in the field of savings and credit activities. Until the late 1990s, these microfinance institutions were linked to the Ministry of Agriculture and Rural Development (Minader). Some years later, the Ministry of Finance (MINFI) became responsible by the Decree No. 2001/023/PM of January 2001 for strengthening the supervision and regulation of the sector after many dysfunctions were noticed such as regarding the securing of savers' deposits, an excessive lending practice that generated doubtful loans, the over-indebtedness of customers, and a lack of liquidity. As an outcome of the crisis and because of the diversity and complexity of microfinance institutions, a regulation law was adopted in the countries of the Central African sub-region on 13 April 2002. The Central African Banking Commission (COBAC) counts approximately 500 microfinance institutions in Cameroon to date, of which 52 per cent are in urban, the other 48 per cent in rural areas. In 2012, according to the Bank of Central African States (BEAC), Cameroon provided 65 per cent of the total number of microfinance institutions, 70 per cent of total beneficiaries, 68 per cent of the deposits, and 75 per cent of credit loans in the region. Despite the growth and expansion of microfinance activities in the country for two decades, there have been dysfunctions in the sector, mainly due to bad governance. Microfinance stakeholders have encountered difficulties in meeting the requirements endorsed by BEAC on the regulation of these institutions. The crisis of the microfinance sector has generated a sceptical and critical public

(Continued)

(Continued)

opinion of microfinance. Understanding microfinance means analyzing its multifactorial dimension: supply, expectations, opportunities, and possibilities. There is not one microfinance crisis but rather a plurality of crises. Ethical difficulties were found, such as usurious high interest rates, complacency credits to microfinance leaders for their own profit and their personal needs, leading them to financial embezzlement.

In the 1960s, after the decolonization movements in Africa, most of the newly independent states were concerned about political and economic reconstruction. The issue of the integration of women in socio-economic life was considered less relevant. It was in the wake of global conferences on women in Mexico, then Nairobi, followed by Copenhagen, and ultimately Beijing in 1995, that the leading role of African women in development was recognized. The World Bank, NGOs, and public authorities became interested in the role of women beyond their domestic sphere, mainly in farming on the continent. In the wake of these events, in many African countries, Ministries of Women and specialized offices and departments were created. In Cameroon, the Ministry of Social Affairs was created in 1975. In 1984, a law was endorsed that created a Ministry specially dedicated to women. The Minister of Women and Social Affairs, Yaou Aissatou (1984-2000) decided to help households, mainly women, that were hit by their husbands' unemployment caused by the closure of public companies. The minister considered microfinance devices an innovative solution for women. In partnership with the Canadian Development Cooperation through its organization for Solidarity and Development (OCSD), a Micro-productive project for women (MPPF) emerged, was implemented, and led to the creation of CEC-Prom Mature, a women's cooperative for savings and credit microfinance institution that has given credits to many experienced businesswomen.

After 20 years of existence of the cooperative, my field survey (participant observation and a qualitative survey) in April 2015 in the Douala branch office showed that the non-recovery of debts is the 'Achilles' heel' of this women's cooperative. I could notice the following dysfunctions: deviance regarding the cooperative mission on the side of the promoters, low morality standards among the borrowers, and refusal to reimburse. The over-indebtedness of the borrowers reflects inappropriate financial products and services regarding the needs of the customers and a lack of professionalism on the side of the staff. The shortcomings in terms of governance and professionalization are also due to an ignorance of the regulations of the microfinance sector.

Despite the turbulences of the microfinance sector, it is clear that microfinance services are important and vital tools for the life conditions of the groups that are excluded from the banking system. With a low bankarization rate approaching 20 per cent and a high entrepreneurial potential, it is more than ever necessary not to eliminate microfinance services but to rethink, redefine, and reorganize the sector in terms of a social economy that can reconcile socio-economic and socio-political life in Cameroon. This implies fostering local development, citizenship education, and building adequate infrastructure for health, education, security, and justice.

Source: Clotilde Ekoka is preparing a PhD at the École des Hautes Études en Sciences Sociales, Paris on the topic of micro-credit in Cameroon under the supervision of Ulrike Schuerkens.

However, there are some constant variables: in Africa, a higher salary may mean that people decide to work less because they don't need more in order to survive. As far as salaries are considered necessary for social relationships (dowry, funerals, etc.), 'to work' can, for some people, mean to accept a job for a short time. In Africa, economic exchanges (e.g. gifts, reciprocal aid) influence labour relations. Therefore, social capital and social links are more important than the accumulation of goods. Despite widespread poverty, markets continue to be well furnished because of functioning distributive mechanisms, even if some rare actors are excluded from these community networks. They permit poor people to survive and elites to transfer capital outside their countries (see Schuerkens, 2010: 261–80).

African enterprises are also influenced by relationships based on community links. Economic efficiency is not a priority and an entrepreneurial drive that comes from within the African social system seems only slightly present. It is characteristic for the dynamics of enterprises in Africa that social networks influence the balance of power and the logic of redistribution. Although foreign enterprises emphasize elements such as profitability, they have to deal with weak and poor states that are not able to provide collective goods and services (e.g. infrastructure, energy). In Africa, public enterprises have become regulators of unemployment, as emphasized by Hugon (2006: 63–65), with low possibilities to change efficiency rules.

In recent decades, the crisis of African economies has led to their informality. Public contracts are rare and the private sector is more or less non-existent so that the informal economy continues to play an important role. Dominant characteristics are small economic units with little capital. These organizations are not characterized by wage relations, but by the community group and power relations. Today, most Africans aspire to meet their basic needs: food, housing, clothing, learning, and health care. The informal economy structure includes female activities such as preparing food, providing human and material benefits, and caregiving; male activities are repairing, recycling of industrial goods, the organization of transport, and production (Hugon, 2006: 65).

Often, the head of the business unit is a young person who has used personal savings to start their individual business, which is based on simple technology. Frequently, no distinction between the productive and the reproductive parts of an enterprise are made. When it comes to profit taking, the head of the unit tries to diversify their activities. These informal activities seem set to remain the main economic activities in the near future as they allow economic actors to survive. It may be that some enterprises function according to other criteria but the informal sector is, according to Hugon, the foundation of corporate governance in Africa.

LATIN AMERICAN SOCIETIES

What about Latin American societies? Following Inglehart et al. (1998: 15), competitive and economic successes are not priorities of social actors in the region. Brazil, Chile, and Peru try to change these economic understandings but results are not always obvious. On the other side, one can find projects in Venezuela, Nicaragua, and Argentina that are not based on economic progress but on social factors. Therefore, an industrial and economic development as it is understood in Northern countries is not promoted. A basic social stability can be found, which is considered an obstacle to the development of differentiation and economic change. The upper classes have been interested in preserving their privileges and have co-opted the *nouveaux riches* who have accepted their rules. These groups have the potential to modernize the region, but they are often only interested in short-term successes. The ethics of saving is not widely shared and there is a lacking interest in investments. Despite centuries of a more or less common history and a common culture, regional geographic integration trends in several Latin American societies have remained weak. Economic, social, and political inequalities have remained high. Market-based ideas and actions have been introduced but social conditions (an economic development based on agricultural products) have revealed that they are rather inadequate for the region. Training and entrepreneurship are not highly esteemed values as social connections determine economic and social positions. What is still largely missing is a group that favours modern economic values. Unlike in Asia, a reassessment of traditional values and norms in order to lead to a stronger market economy development seems not to take place. Only some of the larger countries in the region possess enterprises that promote productivity; indigenous and local enterprises that are able to compete with them and which are able to innovate are rather rare. The technical culture is developed but a market-based education has been neglected.

Because cultural transfers from outside the region have been viewed as uniform and powerful, intellectual elites have focused on self-discovery processes and the refusal of external influences. The result of this denial of the economic development in the North has been a technical and industrial time lag that has prevented the formation of groups favouring industrial development. External reasons were said to have caused regional and national underdevelopment (dependency theories). This policy has prevented the formation of groups that support industrial developments. Recent political changes in some Latin American countries have shown that political and economic elites have limited visions and strategies for their societies. Different political crises show that the social and political pressure from below forces politicians and upper classes to change their social projects. Impulses that come from other countries in the region, China and India, or from the North appear to be necessary to implement social and economic transformations. It may be just a matter of time whether or not these societies will be ready to take over some Western attitudes and consumption styles with corresponding economic, political, and social changes. Some countries such as Chile (HDI rank in 2015: 42) and Argentina (HDI rank in 2015: 40) are already classified as very high-developed countries. Chile and Mexico have moreover become OECD member countries.

In recent years, regional economies have been experiencing low growth averages far from the expansion of 2003-2012 at rates of over 5 per cent. Commodity prices are now decreasing and investments are shrinking. The region's growth average is characterized by a slowdown in important economies, such as Argentina and Brazil. In the last decade, Latin America managed to lift more than 70 million people out of poverty.[3] Better-quality education and healthcare services have become the core demands of rising middle classes.

WORLD COMMUNITY AND ECONOMIC MODELS

It seems as if today we are witnessing the creation of a world community that builds a different world from various civilizations. In today's world, there are groups of people who do not need to meet physically, but share behaviours that define a kind of global culture. These people know that they belong to a common universe, that they form a group with the same consciousness. Sociologists such as L. Sklair (2001), M. Hartmann (2016), or J.A. Scholte (2005) have studied these groups.

'Civilization' in the singular seems to be the culture of the present, which spread around the globe since the last quarter of the twentieth century. Networks of science and technology characterize this global civilization, as Schäfer (2004: 79) argued. In this sense, globalization is happening to societies culturally different from the core of the West, the American culture. Global networks, human rights, music, and world markets spread the individualistic capitalist lifestyle. This trend interests many people. In this sense, a cultural model is assumed even if cultures with alternative symbolic systems exist. Local cultures are thus embedded in a global civilization which includes large parts of the population, even if whole groups of disadvantaged people continue to be excluded.

Globalization seems to represent the triumph of market competition and its principles throughout the world. Past studies have shown that in earlier times the state had been trying to help enterprises adapt to different economic structures. In our current world, transnational corporations try to introduce a global economy where a lack of social rules can be found. Since the collapse of the bipolar world order (East-West), financial crises and social movements have shown that new rules are needed. Critical intellectuals and politicians have begun to discuss these issues, even if governments who want to maintain global capitalism seldom follow them. The recent social movements in many countries (Greece, Portugal, Spain, etc.) have shown that large social groups challenge the global economic competition.

This chapter has examined the transformations of socio-economic practices in a world that is characterized by globalization. The case studies show an understanding of the world that is not as commercialized as economists often think, but where socio-economic aspects are abundant and no longer hidden. Often, former production systems have been destroyed or have been revitalized in the process of globalization. In this sense, the case studies are not presented as being ethnographic evidence of socio-economic practices, but their value is to allow an investigation within a specific social context.

In the case studies economic markets are considered as social phenomena. This concept makes it possible to obtain information about the conditions imposed on socio-economic practices. Capitalism as a neoliberal global phenomenon characterizes identities and defines values. Globalization produces wishes and expectations, but a reduced job security. Current globalization instead promotes precariousness, outsourcing, and the hiring of cheap labour (women and immigrants). It increases social and economic differences between rich and poor regions.

THE CULTURE OF THE NEOLIBERAL ECONOMY

The culture of the neoliberal economy is consumer consumption in a global market. Some of these consumers construct their identity less through their local cultural history than through consumer goods which they can buy. Even in countries such as China, people had contacts with the media and advertising for several decades. New consumption patterns have thus appeared next to an unprecedented level of inequality between the Chinese coast and the impoverished hinterland. The growth of non-traditional exports has accompanied changes in the economic policies of the countries of the South. These markets reunite a range of global relations, symbols, and work processes, which include bankers, local producers, and bureaucracies. In China, the consumer culture was spread by the media, which permitted the population to acquire wishes, even if initially the majority of goods was not available in the regions in which TV programs created a yearning for these products, which were elements of a distant culture. Since the approval of advertisements in

Chinese television programs in the late 1970s, the culture industry created a huge group of 'consumers-in-training' (Zhang et al., 2012) that wished to participate in the global culture of capitalism.

CROSS-BORDER STYLE OF CONSUMPTION

The current cross-border style of consumption is only available to a small proportion of the population in the geographic South. Some scholars estimated this share to only 20 or 30 per cent of the population (Mattelart, 1983). With e-commerce, the Internet, diasporas, international tourists, and transnational consumer contacts using legal or illegal channels, this share has seen an increase in the South even if these flows continue to be more important in the northern part of the globe (Appadurai, 2013). This fact requires an explanation. The global social hierarchy is part of an ethnic and cultural order that is more applicable in some countries than in others. Cultural differences are therefore a key to economic inequality. In this sense, culture seems to be an obstacle to development in the twenty-first century, just as the differentiation according to the concept of race was in the colonial era. What else is important to know? Winners are people who invest much time and energy in economically productive activities and who meet their social obligations. Common social rules that emphasize egalitarian socio-economic practices may thus explain economic difficulties of entire groups. The neoliberal credo and individual success, however, can lead to the accusation of witchcraft for actors that do not accept social rules of redistribution, a phenomenon that is widespread in sub-Saharan African countries (Geschiere, 1997).

The two case studies above emphasize the extent to which Southern societies are already affected by the market-stereotype. The authors show how actors move in and out of the market. They point to changes in socio-economic practices in societies, referred more or less as 'anthropological' societies, which are dominated by reciprocity and giving. The results show that it is becoming increasingly difficult to be 'pre-modern', which remains an obstacle to economic development.

The case studies of this chapter suggest that the peoples of the Southern regions but also of Southern Europe are not helpless victims of the neoliberal credo, but that they are able to make creative interventions in socio-economic 'globalized' practices. In this way, these populations can continue to do what they have done for a long time, but only with other resources, so that it comes to a growth from below.

THE NOSTALGIC TRADITION OF AUTHENTICITY

Social anthropologists have often tried to project a utopian vision of a society that they studied. This nostalgic socio-anthropological tradition of authenticity stands in contrast to the transformations of socio-economic practices, which I imagine here. Many experiences of the current world can be considered instructive from a socio-economic perspective. The desire to be dependent on the market was first implanted in many parts of Africa in the early twentieth century and changed its character in recent decades. In the South, people are increasingly becoming consumers that are characterized by the global neoliberal credo of capitalism.

The case studies show that there are several varieties of neoliberal global capitalism. Local cultures also include global economies and try to adapt their seemingly neutral rules. This also means that current global markets depend on historical and concrete situations despite global elites that consider the neoliberal economic system as the only possible solution in our current world. It is obvious that the power of these groups is so important that only highly organized major movements have the potential to make a difference. But these movements are very disparate, as Fougier (2004) has shown in an interesting study. This has often meant a lack of effective counter-projects. Nevertheless, recent social movements in North Africa and parts of Europe as well as the movements at meetings such as the World Summit for Social Development gather so many people that politicians include aspects of these demands in political measures. Thereby, parts of the negative effects of the current neoliberal globalization process may be influenced and improved by political measures. Political reactions can also be seen in election results, which no longer favour the old established parties, but particular politicians on a 50/50 basis divide (e.g. in Germany and the USA). The peoples are no longer convinced that the political elites should be kept in power (see the 2016 presidential elections in the USA and its surprising results), leading to large numbers of non-voters in national elections or, alternatively, extreme right wing parties or outsiders gain large support from an electorate that is dissatisfied with its political elites.

NEW SOCIAL MOVEMENTS

In this political situation, new social movements represent a force. Their results will contribute to socio-economic inputs that combat injustice, inequality, and poverty. They aim to improve development opportunities offered by our current world and want to achieve greater responsibility in terms of social issues. Nevertheless, the most frequently underlined ideas of diversity and localism make them rarely accepted on a global scale.

Meanwhile, it is the creed of these groups to create alternative local spaces and change long-term values. Governments, political movements, and enterprises could then be asked to respect aspects or requirements that are formulated by these groups. According to this understanding, social, political, and cultural aspects have to be modified in order to be able to live in a human form of neoliberal capitalism in our contemporary societies. Current social movements could then contribute to changes that the economic sector and/or the political sector alone cannot introduce. In many countries, there is still an urgent need to take survival measures. In countries where only a quarter or half of the working-age population is more or less regularly occupied in commercial, public, or private entities, where neither the state nor the open market is sufficient to meet the needs of the population, more alternative economical solutions are necessary. Illegal or even criminal activities, difficult working conditions, trafficking in drugs or arms exist. These solutions are not recommended. The informal economy is one of the possible alternatives. But the question remains whether there is an alternative to the market. Although alternatives to the market exist (e.g. non-governmental organizations, public wealth), Caillé (2003) underlines that there are still no economic alternatives, other than more austerity implanted by public servants or subsidies for NGOs that are funded by taxpayers' money. Based on this assumption, Caillé thinks that there is an economic and not a quantitative problem. According to him, an economy based on solidarity could represent a systematic and automatically regulated alternative to capitalism. The socialist project in Eastern Europe, as an economic opportunity, no longer exists in countries like China, which for over twenty years got results with market principles that T. Pairault has described in his case study. In this sense, there are different ways to create solidarity, and social and political communities. As everyone knows, the family makes it possible to support economic relations with its rules different from the market mechanism. Village members, cultural groups, immigrants, workers, or the social sector can support more solidarity, reciprocity, and democracy, such as Jean-Louis Laville (2011) has emphasized.

RESEARCH INSIGHTS: EXPULSIONS: BRUTALITY AND COMPLEXITY IN THE GLOBAL ECONOMY: THE CASE OF THE SOUTHERN COUNTRIES OF THE EUROPEAN UNION

In her recent book *Expulsions*, Saskia Sassen explains disparate 'thick realities' that she sees as expressions of larger phenomena driven by the logic of inclusion/expulsion within the global world. As an empirical and theoretical sociologist, she argues e.g. on the shrinking of economic spaces in the European Union. She finds a system of inclusion into the global capitalist system, opposed to a system of expulsion and marginalization of the 'losers'. According to her, this inclusion/expulsion dynamic is often linked to complex mechanisms (such as financial instruments comprehensible by only a few) that lead to the logic of expulsion (e.g. mass unemployment, criminalization), a determination of what will be counted in economic indicators and who will not be counted and live at what Sassen calls the 'systemic edge'. Sassen identifies the latest shift in capitalist accumulation as in the 1980s. At this point, the economic space began to push out the marginalized, those who stopped to receive unemployment benefit, and those who were arrested. When one looks at the extreme case of Greece after the economic collapse of 2007, one can see these results of austerity measures imposed by the European Union. In fact, the Greek economy was declared to be recovering because the measures that were supposed to prove this recovery ignored the social collapse of the population which has survived due to family assistance and informal work. The economy of many countries in the European Union, as Sassen argues, exists today in a shrunk space, after social welfare related expenses. This can be found in countries subjected to austerity programs (e.g. Portugal, Spain). Youth unemployment is another phenomenon in the global North that is regulated in parts by out-migration to other world regions (well-educated French youth may go the United Kingdom; Spaniards may go to Latin America), or by the radicalization of parts of young people. Sassen's book describes the inclusion that the post-War period permitted in Europe and the new expulsions in all these forms, be they social or economic from the 1980s onwards. She names this systemic edge 'the space of expulsion', where those who are expelled survive. Her arguments discuss this shrinking space at the system's centre.

Source: Sassen, S. (2014) *Expulsions: Brutality and Complexity in the Global Economy.* Cambridge, MA: Harvard University Press:.

HOW TO IMPROVE GLOBAL CAPITALISM?

There seems to be an urgent need to take a look at the economy, taking into account ethical and political criteria and promoting an improvement that emphasizes not only economic factors. More and more economists share these ideas. They have come together in the PEKEA movement (Political and Ethical Knowledge on Economic Activities)[4], where famous scholars such as Alain Touraine, Jacques Sapir, Yves Berthelot, and Noam Chomsky are gathered around the members of the Scientific Advisory Board. This group defends the need to reorganize the market and the rules that make it possible to continue to assure social policies in a market economy.[5]

DISCUSSION QUESTIONS

1. Please explain the concept of Western economic competition.
2. Please describe the process of economic globalization in history.
3. How can you characterize the culture of competition of global neoliberal economies?
4. What does globalization mean for the marginalized global South in Africa?
5. What are the characteristics of economic globalization in South America and Asia?

ANNOTATED FURTHER READINGS

Benerìa, L., Berik, G. and Floro, M.S. (2016) *Gender, Development, and Globalization: Economics as if All People Mattered* **(Second edition). New York and London: Routledge.**
The book analyzes the extent to which globalization changed gender dynamics and women's conditions all over the world.

Schuerkens, U. (ed.) (2008) *Globalization and Local Socioeconomic Practices.* **London and New York: Routledge.**
This innovative volume provides a comprehensive overview of the transformation of socio-economic practices in the global economy. The contributors offer analytical and comparative insights at the world level, with regard to the current socio-economic practices as well as an assessment of the overall economic globalization phenomenon in the global world.

Sheppard, E. (2016) *Limits to Globalization: The Disruptive Geographies of Capitalist Development.* **Oxford: Oxford University Press.**
This book summarizes how globalizing capitalism – the economic system now presumed to dominate the global economy – can be understood from a geographical perspective.

Websites

http://www.pekea-fr.org/
A global network of thinking on the economy. PEKEA is an NGO with a special consultative status to the Economic and Social Council of the United Nations, granted in July 2006.

http://www.journaldumauss.net/?The-New-Economy-Movement
An article on the idea that we need a 'new economy' – that the entire economic system must be radically restructured if critical social and environmental goals are to be met.

http://www.unrisd.org/flagship2016-consultation
Policy Innovations for Transformative Change: UNRISD Flagship Report 2016.

http://www.worldbank.org/en/topic
The World Bank Group's Global Practices bring together knowledge and expertise in 14 sectors and 5 cross-cutting areas. The goal is to help developing countries find solutions to the global and local development challenges.

http://www.oecd.org/about/
The mission of the Organization for Economic Co-operation and Development (OECD) is to promote policies that will improve the economic and social wellbeing of people around the world.

(all websites accessed 1 October 2016)

NOTES

1   Available at http://ec.europa.eu/trade/policy/countries-and-regions/countries/china (accessed 24 October 2016).
2   http://www.worldbank.org/en/region/afr/overview (accessed 16 December 2016).
3   See http://www.worldbank.org/en/region/lac/overview (accessed 16 December 2016).
4   http://www.pekea-fr.org/ (accessed 24 October 2016).
5   See http://fr.pekea-fr.org/pages/FrLGCCall-08-05-19.pdf and http://www.pekea-fr.org/presentation.html (accessed 16 December 2016).

4

GLOBALIZATION AND THE TRANSFORMATION OF SOCIAL INEQUALITY

Summary

Social inequality is a worldwide phenomenon. Globalization has both exacerbated and alleviated inequality over the past 25 years. This chapter offers analytical and comparative insights from current case studies of social inequality within all the major regions of the world. The author provides an assessment of the overall social globalization phenomenon in the global world as well as an outlook of transformations of global social inequality in the future. This chapter contributes to our understanding of current transformations of social inequalities in different parts of the world and reveals regional, national, and local differences in inequality patterns and globalization impacts and the importance of political choices for inequality levels.

INTRODUCTION

In recent years, a number of publications have discussed the link between globalization and inequality (e.g. Wade, 2007; Milanovic, 2011b). So far, social inequality is measured within countries, between countries, and also globally among all populations of the world. Currently, a relative consensus seems to exist that insists on the fact that in-country inequality has increased almost everywhere over the past 20 years. International inequality has fallen since the late 1970s, when China and India were included (Held and Kaya, 2007: 5-6); when these countries – which together have more than one fifth of the world's population – are excluded, an increase in international income inequality can be found. Nevertheless, global inequality among nations, according to the Gini coefficient, is very high but decreasing: from 72 points in 1988 and 1993 to 70.5 points in 2008 or even 69 on a scale that goes to 100 for a more detailed sample (Held and Kaya, 2007: 5 and Milanovic, 2011b). The 2011 global Gini coefficient was 67, some 2 points lower than in 2008. This change has been driven by the high growth rates in China and India and for the last years by the absence of growth in Northern European countries and the USA. The USA mean income, for instance, was lower in 2011 than three years before.

GLOBAL INEQUALITY

However, global inequality is underestimated as the very rich are not included in surveys and if they are included, their incomes are underestimated. People move legally owned assets more easily in the global world and do not mention them when they fill out questionnaires. This means that the decline in global inequality would be less significant if the incomes of the very rich were to be included. Moreover, money in tax havens is included neither in fiscal nor in household survey data. According to Milanovic, the income 'parked' in tax havens by the global top 1 per cent could amount to 0.7–1 per cent of global GDP, so that it contributes to underestimating global inequality (Milanovic, 2011b). Another point is the reassessment of price levels in Asian countries in 2011 (Indonesia, India, and China). Higher real incomes in these countries have been translated into reduced global inequality. When global inequality is measured in 2011 $PPPs, the Gini coefficient is 'only' at a level of 64 (Milanovic, 2016).[1]

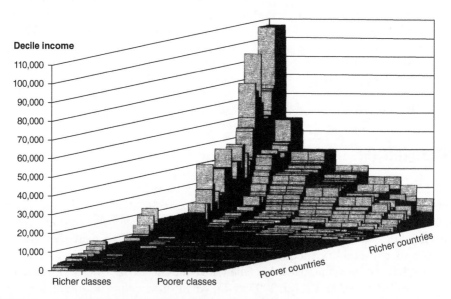

FIGURE 4.1   A VISUALIZATION OF GLOBAL INCOME DISTRIBUTION

Source: Sutcliffe (2005)

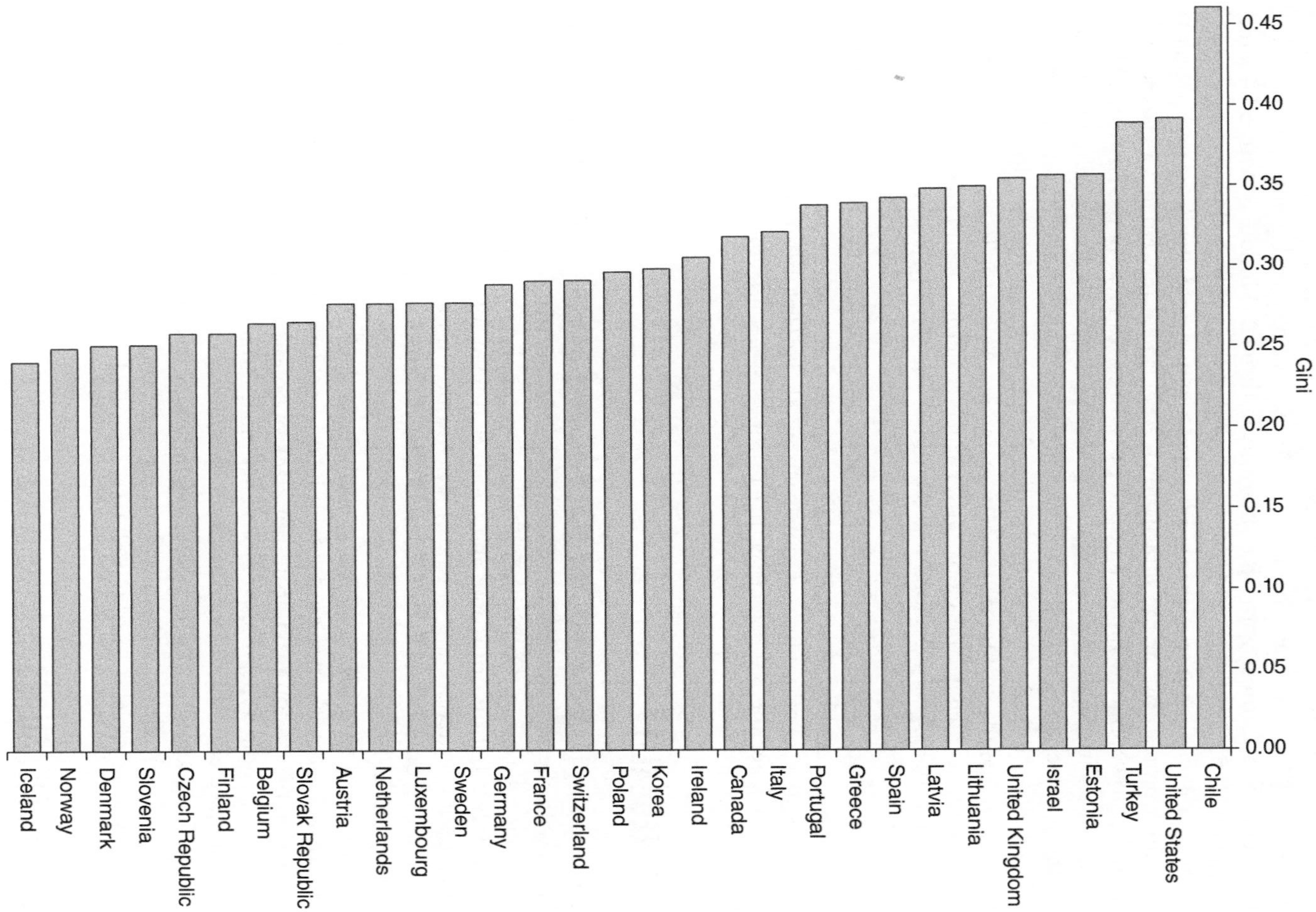

FIGURE 4.2   INCOME INEQUALITY

Since the 1980s, the gap between the richest and the poorest has been very large. Held and Kaya wrote in 2007: '[T]he world Gini coefficient is at a level [...] that now exceeds all (...) of the most unequal countries by several points' (2007: 6). In 2010, these were Zambia with 55.6, Lesotho with 54.2, Honduras with 53.4, and Columbia with 55.5. Such a high Gini coefficient (69 in 2008) within nations would mean for individual countries that governments would be destabilized and populations would protest. But at the international level, social movements are expected only rarely. However, new movements have begun to reappear in the last years. They target social realities within countries and are transnationally linked. The multiplicity of these movements in various world regions force us to reflect on their reasons which are often linked to populations that face poverty and unemployment on a national level (see the chapter on social movements). At the top level, elites currently react: they try to change the global governance structure in international institutions (such as the Doha Development Round of the World Trade Organization or the G20), which are responsible for global political and socio-economic measures. However, the high global Gini coefficient leads to the emergence of fundamentalist movements and attacks on tourists and foreigners from rich countries and in rich countries to attacks of symbols of globalization. This global inequality has also contributed to trigger the refugee crisis that Europe has been facing between summer 2015 and March 2016.

WAGE INEQUALITY

Wage inequality has increased in the global era, so that we can see from 1981 onward and thus with the beginning of neoliberal globalization, that inequality within countries as 'a global pattern' (Galbraith, 2008) has increased. As a result, in some countries, a public redistribution of income and wealth has been introduced, so that extreme poverty could be reduced (e.g. Brazil). The world's population living in extreme poverty (an income below 1.25 US\$ a day) has fallen from 32 per cent in 1990 to 16 per cent in 2010. Wade mentions one of the reasons for this policy: 'Inequality not only spurs social troubles, but it is also likely to be bad for the economy' (2007: 7). If one considers that the poor suffer from health problems, lack of education, lack of participation in decision making, in short, lack of opportunities in life, it may be useful to consider policy measures at global, national, and local levels and not to follow the neoliberal credo that the market alone should determine incomes and wealth. In this chapter, the above outlined theoretical and empirical ideas on transformations of social inequality in the global era will be discussed and the allegedly positive impact of the market on social inequality will be questioned.

POLITICAL MEASURES

In fact, politicians use various opportunities to influence important social and economic structures of the global era. Political elites and civil society possess instruments and can use policies to criticize social inequalities that are judged to be unjustified and that lead to discriminations against certain groups. A political focus on these instruments can influence inequality measures. These instruments include political activities of trade unions, national social redistribution measures, or remittances of transnational migrants. Thus numerous mechanisms to change unequal situations exist. However, concrete results are dependent on power relations and therefore eminently political decisions. The global financial crisis of 2007–2009 has made the importance and necessity of political actors in the post-neoliberal economy obvious. Banks and enterprises that had ruled out political interferences in what they understood as the *free* market, have begun to defend the position that the market alone cannot cause sufficient regulations of groups and their divergent interests. State and political elites have to persuade their electorate that they are responsible actors who defend the interests of citizens of their country if they want to be re-elected. In this sense, the last crisis appeared as an opportunity for the future of our global world. New players have emerged, such as the *Indignados* of Spain and similar movements that ask for new political measures in order to build a creative future in our global world. The outcomes of the activities of these new political forces are still in the making with *Podemos* in Spain and *Syriza* in Greece. However, they challenge long-running agreements on inequality and equality.

THEORIES EXPLAINING INEQUALITY

In the literature (Milanovic, 2005), two theoretical approaches on inequality are discussed. The *Individualists* promote a rational choice approach that studies inequality quantitatively and empirically, an approach that has been defended by governments and international organizations such as the World Bank and the International Monetary Fund. Politicians can often be found promoting this approach. In the past 30 years, much of the literature on poverty was committed to this approach.

Over the past decade, however, a different concept that has examined qualitative indicators of poverty has become predominant. Sociologists, economists, and some ethnologists have favoured this second structural approach. Often non-governmental organizations, civil society, trade unions, and left-wing parties support this approach. These structuralists argue that one should not only look for obvious empirical evidence of inequality, but should focus on research of the social structures that cause unequal social relations. For example, measurements show that life chances are distributed unequally which determine educational levels, health status, jobs, etc. Structuralists emphasize that poverty is based on an unjust distribution of resources, not just a lack of resources. Inequality can therefore be found in fields such as class, gender, race, ethnic origin, etc. and has multiple influences on life chances. This socio-economic approach examines structural aspects of inequality, e.g. why the poor are in poor health and attain lower educational and professional positions. Moreover, these status lines are often cumulative so that poor people may be in poor health, have attained only basic educational levels, and earn small salaries.

POVERTY

With regard to absolute poverty, it can be noted that '[a]ccording to the most recent estimates, in 2012, 12.7 per cent of the world's population lived at or below $1.90 a day. That's down from 37 per cent in 1990 and 44 per cent in 1981. This means that, in 2012, 896 million people lived on less than $1.90 a day, compared with 1.95 billion in 1990, and 1.99 billion in 1981.'[2]

Poverty rates have declined in all regions, but East Asia saw a reduction from 80 per cent in 1981 to 7.2 per cent in 2012. In South Asia, extreme poverty dropped from 58 per cent in 1981 to 18.7 per cent in 2012. Poverty in sub-Saharan Africa remained high with 42.6 per cent in 2012. In fact, about half of the world's population lives on less than 2 US$ a day. 'In 2012, just over 77.8 per cent of the extremely poor lived in South Asia (309 million) and Sub-Saharan Africa (388.7 million). In addition, 147 million lived in East Asia and Pacific. Two-thirds of the poor still live in Asia.'[3] Hundreds of millions of poor people have been lifted out of poverty in China and India. The sustained economic growth in Asia has changed the picture so that poverty is concentrated more and more on the African continent. Poverty could thus be reduced over the past decades so that the first Millennium Development Goal target – to cut the 1990 poverty rate in half by 2015 – was reached five years ahead of schedule, in 2010.

CASE STUDY

SOUTH AFRICA'S 'TOKENISTIC' SOCIAL POLICY

The immediate post-apartheid era, starting in 1994, should have offered the opportunity to decisively establish a generous South African welfare state. The adoption of what former Minister of Intelligence Ronnie Kasrils (2013) termed Nelson Mandela's 'Faustian Pacts' with big business had the opposite effect, rendering social policies *tokenistic* (Bond, 2014a). That word implies that the extension of most apartheid-era social policies – which had earlier been limited to white, 'Indian' and 'colored' South Africans – was pursued in a manner that stressed 'width not depth' and that fell far short of potential resource allocation. In contrast, during the mid-2016 election campaign, politicians ranging from the centre-right Democratic Alliance to the far-left Economic Freedom Fighters promised that if they had national power, they would *double* the size of the social grants to the poorest third of the country.

This case study assesses the government's existing standards and policies. These are not especially ambitious, as the 2012–30 National Development Plan seeks to lower inequality – measured as the Gini Coefficient (0 is least inequality, 1 is maximum) – from 0.69 to 0.60; i.e., the income share earned by the poorest 40 per cent will rise from 6 to just 10 per cent. Within 15 years of liberation, as

Mandela's 1994-99 government gave way to Thabo Mbeki's 1999-2008 presidency, the dilution of the African National Congress' (ANC) commitment to its radical 1955 Freedom Charter was confirmed: for example, the nationalization of mines, banks, and monopoly capital was off the agenda. South African social policy and state services suffered cutbacks in financial ambition – for example, the Lund Commission's 26 per cent reduction in the main child support grant in 1996 (from the then equivalent of $37 to $27/month) – even while many more people gained access. The number of South Africans receiving monthly grants soared from fewer than 3 million in 1994 to 17 million two decades later (out of 55 million residents). But measured in late 2015 exchange rates (following substantial currency depreciation), monthly grants were just $22/month for supporting each poor child under age 18. In addition, there was an $83/month pension for retirees over 60 years old and for the disabled. The size of these grants rose far more slowly than the inflation rate, especially the rate estimated for poor people.

In all cases, these grants were means-tested. Ironically, however, social grants spending was less progressive – i.e. less directed to the poorest South Africans – in 2006 than in 1995, by quite substantial amounts, according to Servaas van der Berg's (2009) modelling. Using a –1 value as the most progressive outcome in which all spending benefits the poorest, and +1 the most regressive, van der Berg argued that progressivity for social grants worsened from -0.371 in 2000 to -0.359 in 2006 (Van der Berg, 2009: 12).

As a result, after the first decade of liberation – from 1995 to 2005 – the slight positive impact of these grants and other social policies were unable to offset the general income deterioration that accompanied neoliberal economic policies. University of Cape Town researchers found that African households[4] lost 1.8 per cent of their overall income (including wages, salaries and unearned income), whereas white households gained 40.5 per cent (Bhorat et al., 2009: 8).

An update of the poverty line by Statistics South Africa (2015), drawing on 2011 data and with a line of approximately $1.50/day (in mid-2016 currency terms), estimated the poverty rate to be 53 per cent. However, Stats SA had adopted a controversial policy of rejecting certain data so Budlender et al. (2015) redid the calculations for the 'upper-bound poverty line' which includes food and essentials and found the rate to be 63 per cent, far higher than any 1994 poverty calculations. This was not surprising because even by official data, during the same period, the ratio of surplus in the economy given to labour versus that taken by business (i.e. wages to profits) shrunk by 5 per cent, so not just the poor but the formal working class were victims of the neoliberal era (Forslund, 2012). In contrast, by all accounts, market income inequality rose (to what the World Bank in 2014 measured as a Gini coefficient of 0.77) and so did unemployment: the official rate soared from 16 to 25 per cent from 1994-2015,

(Continued)

(Continued)

and adding those who gave up looking for jobs brought the rate to 35 per cent (Bond, 2014b). At the same time, extremely high increases in fees for consuming basic state services (especially electricity and water) began to kick in, creating the grounds for thousands of protests annually by the late 1990s.

Meanwhile, vast surpluses were allowed to escape social control. In spite of South Africa possessing the world's greatest mineral resource endowment, valued at peak by Citi Group at $2.5 trillion (Maia, 2012), the structure of multinational corporate control left very little reinvestment. Illicit Financial Flows (e.g. transfer pricing and tax avoidance schemes) were measured by Global Financial Integrity (2015) at $21 billion annually over the period 2004–13, while licit profit and dividend outflows regularly drove the current account deficit to -5 per cent. In 2014 and 2016, PricewaterhouseCoopers (2016) found South African corporates leading the world in corruption, with a 69 per cent economic crime rate. These factors may help explain South Africa's 2013 rating as the third most profitable country for corporations among major economies, according to the IMF (2013). As one example of the permission the South African capitalist class needed to wage class war by the state, recall the 2012 massacre of platinum mining workers at Marikana by Lonmin's allies in the police force, catalyzed by emails from a Lonmin 9 per cent shareholder – Cyril Ramaphosa – who became South Africa's deputy president in 2014. This allegiance to the side of capital in the class war appeared to take precedence over any residual social democratic instincts left in the liberation movement. Even if profit rates ultimately fell, it was because the gambles made by capital on continuing high Chinese demand for mining and smelting products went bust.

In turn, the suffering of the majority gave rise to disparate forces from the left, especially the Economic Freedom Fighters (who won 6 per cent of the vote in the 2014 election) and National Union of Metalworkers of South Africa (the country's largest union, which broke from the Congress of SA Trade Unions). The tenuous position of labour and communist forces within the ANC Alliance and the corruption-riddled character of the ANC leadership would, in due time, offset the popularity and historic prestige of the liberation movement that defeated apartheid. The ANC's last option is to shift to a genuine social policy (e.g. to include a National Health Insurance), but the party's internal forces demanding austerity – including substantial real cuts to social grants in the 2015–17 budgets – would prevent even minor progressive tinkering with tokenism.

Source: Patrick Bond (2014a) 'Tokenistic Social Policy in South Africa,' *Transformation* 86: 48–77 and some recent updates.

INCOME

WEALTH

To introduce a further inequality dimension, the Dutch researcher J. Nederveen Pieterse comments on the issue of wealth (2004b: 4). According to him, the richest 20 per cent of the world population received 70 per cent of income in 1960. Until 1991, this share has risen to 85 per cent. During the same period, the share of the bottom 20 per cent fell from 2.3 per cent to 1.4 per cent. The income ratio between the richest and the poorest has increased from 30:1 to 60:1 (Nederveen Pieterse, 2004b: 61). According to OXFAM (2014: 2), 'almost half of the world's wealth is now owned by just one per cent of the population. The wealth of the one per cent richest people in the world amounts to $110 trillion. That's 65 times the total wealth of the bottom half of the world's population. The bottom half of the world's population owns the same as the richest 85 people in the world.'[5] This unequal distribution of wealth suggests that something is wrong with the neoliberal version of the world economy.

Globally, the middle classes and the top 1 per cent have seen the largest gains in the last years. Lakner and Milancovic (2015) showed for the period 1998 to 2008 that the global median incomes in China and India and that of the top 1 per cent in the advanced economies experienced the largest gains. As a report from the IMF (Dabla-Norris et al., 2015: 10) showed: '[I]ncome gains rapidly decrease after the 50th percentile and become stagnant around the 80th–90th global percentiles.'[6]

HISTORICAL DEVELOPMENT OF GLOBAL SOCIAL INEQUALITY

In order to introduce an understanding of the *longue durée* (Braudel) on social inequality, let us make some brief remarks on the historical development of global social inequality. According to Milanovic, who examined long-term historical income statistics, international inequality rose in the years 1820-1870 (2005: 29). The same applies for the period from 1870 to 1913 although, after 1913 until 1938, it came to a decline, perhaps even to a stabilization between the two world wars. From 1938 to 1952, inequality rose again. The reason was that some rich countries (USA, Australia, Argentina, and New Zealand) had improved their individual development, while others got worse. Inequality, measured between nations according to the Gini coefficient, remained at the same level from 1952 to 1978. This period corresponds to the golden age of economic prosperity for the richer countries and to a policy of import substitution with a strong role of the state for the less developed countries. Towards the end of the 1970s, neoliberal policies led to a sharp rise in inequality. Thatcher's and Reagan's fiscal policies in the United Kingdom and the United States have been instrumental for the emergence of this trend. This tendency has since then continued, e.g. during the recent financial crisis.

Despite current regional disparities, which can be found in China and India between urban coastal regions and rural interior areas, the situation in South America and Africa has deteriorated. One may begin to speak of an 'Africanization of poverty', as Milanovic wrote (2005: 33).

UNEQUAL DISTRIBUTION OF INCOME

Another interesting figure: the proportion of total global income of 5 (or 10) per cent of the richest people in the world represents 33 (or 50) per cent; for the bottom 5 (or 10) per cent, this means that their share is 0.2 (respectively 0.7) per cent of the world's income (Milanovic, 2005: 39). These figures show the extremely unequal distribution of income in our current world. The outcomes have even been magnified by the recent financial crises with an increase of incomes at the top and an impoverishment of the middle classes and the poor at the bottom. In the USA, 'the top 10 per cent now has an income close to nine times that of the bottom 10 per cent' (IMF, 2015: 11). The top 1 per cent accounts for nearly 10 per cent of total income in advanced economies (Alvadero et al., 2013). Even in countries such as China and India, the share of the top 1 per cent has grown. One of the reasons is the higher inequality in labour incomes but also growing capital incomes amongst the most fortunate. In many advanced countries, pre-tax incomes of middle class households have decreased (USA, UK, and Japan; contrary to Sweden, Australia, and Canada). This development means a declining share of labour income because average wages have increased more slowly than the productivity growth of enterprises. This is also linked to the weak bargaining power of labour unions among precarious jobbers in the service sector or among those working on a part-time basis.

ECONOMICALLY MORE DEVELOPED COUNTRIES

The situation is different for Economically More Developed Countries (EMDCs) with rising inequality that is driven 'by a shift in incomes of the "upper middle class to the upper class"' (page 11) (e.g. China and South Africa). Falling inequality in EMDCs that still have high inequality rates on a global level – such as Peru and Brazil – benefitted the bottom and the middle of the income distribution (Alvadero et al., 2013).

Another way to measure inequality lies in the comparison of the positions of people from different countries in the global income distribution. According to Milanovic: 'The poorest Frenchmen are actually richer than 72 per cent of the people in the world' (2005: 41). And he continues: 'Even the richest 5 per cent of people in rural India are poorer than the poorest 5 per cent of people in France' (2005: 41). In political terms, the transfers from richer countries to poor countries therefore need to reach the local poor, provided that their elites do not have other interests.

IS GLOBAL INEQUALITY A PROBLEM?

In the last few years, the question was discussed at length whether global inequality is a real problem (Wade, Milanovic). Some commentators argue that this idea is too abstract and that there is no world government that is interested in a decline in global inequality. But when one considers that globalization increases people's knowledge of one another and of differences in incomes through holidays and TV screens, one can hardly deny that global inequality triggers far-reaching questions. As September 11 has shown, poverty and inequality in other regions affect the populations in the North more than a few decades ago. One of the consequences of these inequalities are the growing terrorist acts in the North but also in selected southern countries (Turkey, Pakistan, Tunisia, etc.). With the world's high degree of global inequality, the richer world cannot choose the solution to become a fortress and close its borders to the poor. European and North American immigration policies have shown that this is almost impossible because of illegal immigrants who come by sea to the Southern Mediterranean countries, cross the EU borders in Eastern Europe, or cross the desert in the United States. Or reflect on the 'refugees' of 2015 coming from Eastern Europe to Western Europe: among Syrians, there were numerous economic migrants from North and West Africa or Asia. Images from Germany filled TV screens and the news in the South so that poor people from the South were rapidly attracted and followed the Syrian refugees leading to a major crisis in the European countries on the assistance to be given to these large groups.[7] Germany approved more than 140,000 asylum seekers, mainly from Syria. Global financial transfers, not just remittances of migrants have been asked for, similar to the socio-economic measures at the beginning of the twentieth century and after World War II in Europe to alleviate global inequalities and poverty. Turkey and Greece have received financial and political assistance in order to regulate the Syrian refugee problem at the frontiers of the Eurozone. Moreover, financial assistance from the EU member states to African countries to prevent high out-migration rates shows first success.[8]

THE OUTCOMES OF THE FINANCIAL CRISES

With the financial crisis 2007–2009, the development policies of the North and the richer countries changed: Western governments organized financial assistance programs for banks in order to protect financial institutions and the economy from the negative impacts of the crisis. These funds were no longer available for the global aid flows from the North to the South. In parallel, however, emerging countries such as China, India, and Brazil have invested in Africa and Latin America, above all in countries with large mineral deposits. China could thus take over roles that were originally possessed by former European colonial powers and could expand its contacts and economic interests. The refugee crisis of 2015 and the growing number of terrorist acts have shown that the North cannot maintain its socio-economic standard if it does not implement transfer policies directed towards southern countries.

Nowadays, liberal politicians still see inequality as a necessary condition of an economy that depends on the market and on competition, innovation, and an aspiration to obtain a given income in an unequal world. According to this liberal doctrine, governments should not worry about global inequality since income inequality is a result of market processes. As long as the liberal world order is not threatened, inequality has not been an issue for strictly liberal politicians.

However, these arguments can be questioned as the following explanations display. The impact of income inequality on other variables is now clearly outlined by extensive research. According to Wade (2007: 115), 'higher income inequality within countries goes with: (1) higher poverty […]; (2) higher unemployment; (3) higher crime; (4) lower average health; (5) weaker property rights; (6) more skewed access to public services (…); and (7) a slower transition to democratic regimes, and more fragile democracies.'

According to this scholar, who is professor at the London School of Economics, the possible impact of 'inequality at the national level supports the normative conclusion that income inequality above moderate levels should be reduced via public policy' (Wade, 2007: 118). What is interesting here is that Wade suggests that the 'economic growth during the 1990s - and presumably the 1980s as well – has benefitted mainly two categories of people: those in the upper half of the income distribution of the high-income states, and those who have made it into the swelling ranks of China's middle class' (2007: 124). According to Wade, those who are responsible for the perpetuation of the neoliberal economic model belong to the upper-strata groups who live in high-income states. Within-country inequality continues to increase at a global level as poorer groups have increasingly precarious jobs worldwide and parts of them lose their income (BIT, 2013; Sassen, 2014). On the contrary, global 'middle classes' are emerging: 29 per cent of the populations of the world belong to this group that controls 43 per cent of global income. According to the World Bank, populations with incomes above $PPP10 per day and less than $PPP50 per day belong to this group (Milanovic, 2016). In 1998, only 17 per cent of the world population was included in this category of middle classes. The distribution around the middle is different from the two peaks with high percentages of people among the extremely poor or the very rich. Nevertheless, the 'global median class' with incomes ranging from $PPP2 per capita per day to $PPP16 per capita per day has increased from 23 per cent to 40 per cent of the global population (Lakner and Milanovic, 2015: 23).

WHAT IS AN ACCEPTABLE LEVEL OF GLOBAL INEQUALITY?

Given the existing global inequality structure, the following question has to be asked: What is an acceptable level of global inequality? According to Wade, it should be one which gives sufficient income incentive to take sufficient risk to generate sufficient economic growth to provide sufficient opportunities for the poorer to become less poor. But not so much difference in income outcomes that the rich can translate their income differential into a political oligarchy which sets rules that continuously fortify these differentials and keeps social mobility at low levels. (2007: 126)

It is obvious that this conception of redistribution proposes priorities that cannot easily be brought into the political agenda so that difficulties to alter actual inequality levels in societies worldwide remain.

If one argues on inequality in political terms, one should also mention the view of the Commission for Africa (2005: 7) that described the contrast between the world's wealthy and the conditions of the poor in Africa as 'the greatest scandal of our age' (Greig et al., 2007: 1). The arguments of this chapter are similar to Amartya Sen's thinking that underlines that development should envision individual human advancement rather than national economic development. For Sen, development concerns people who are able to raise their *capabilities* so that they achieve a functioning they appreciate. According to Sen (1999), unequal social relations contribute to the marginalization of the poor and their social and political subordination. More powerful actors often block their advancement, people who favour their own privileged children so that the poor can never compete with them in the manner neoliberal economists promise.

LACK OF RESOURCES AND UNEQUAL SOCIAL RELATIONS

I agree with Sen that there is a huge difference between poverty as the lack of resources for the poorest, and poverty as the result of unequal social relations. If policy tries to change these relations with redistributive measures, this would mean a more equal society for all. In fact, numerous measures exist to reduce inequality: governments and civil societies have implemented a redistribution of economic resources in various societies worldwide and have passed social and political power to less well-off people (see the case study of Ivo and Laniado on Brazil in Chapter 6). It becomes obvious that in recent years the discussed changes have been implemented at local, national, and international levels in connection with the Millennium Development Goals in order to reduce poverty and promote social justice in the global world. People have learned to use their agency in order to challenge some of the influential structural constraints of globalization.

The UN's Millennium Development Goals (MDGs)[9] illustrate why it is morally unacceptable to ignore the destiny of the poor. As the very unequal distribution of wealth in the world lets us presume, it is difficult to believe that humanity does not possess the means necessary to decrease global inequality. Ramonet (2004: 127) gave an interesting argument in this sense: meeting the basic needs of the poorest in the world corresponds to the costs of Europe's annual consumption of perfume!

Moreover, the financial crisis from 2007–2009 was accompanied by voices that underlined that the amount of the US$750 billion program in the USA would have been sufficient to reach the Millennium Development Goal aimed at eradicating extreme poverty in the world by 2015.

INTERNATIONAL INSTITUTIONS

The current international system, based on democracy and the market, needs effective institutions that create opportunities for the poor, improve their conditions, and protect them against the negative outcomes of globalization in an interdependent world. This would mean for states to cooperate more and better, and develop mechanisms that go beyond national issues. Multilateral institutions, such as the United Nations, have improved their governance structure as well, as recent discussions on challenging global issues have already shown (Doha Round, G20, and the IMF). International governance will necessarily play an important role in determining whether globalization will benefit people and nations or not. Global governance challenges new democracies in the South, fragile states, and institutions with feeble civil societies and their smaller degree of citizen participation and interest expression. But it can no longer be assumed that globalization is neutral; it is a political phenomenon and only efficient political measures will assure that globalization is at the service of the people of the world. Contemporary religious fundamentalism in Asia and North Africa draws on the support of the losers of globalization, on those who have been excluded from the benefits of globalization. Strikes, bombs, and attacks against symbols of globalization show that life has become more insecure for many, so that there may be very few alternatives to some of the political measures on social inequality outlined in this chapter.

On the level of countries or regions, there are a number of instruments, whereas international instruments are still at their beginning. On a global level, instruments to decrease the high international Gini coefficient are hardly ever discussed. However, remittances have an impact on the development of poorer countries and affect inequalities inside these countries and in a smaller way among the different countries. Furthermore, the growing number of informal jobs in developing countries and part-time jobs in the developed world makes life-chances in the global post-neoliberal economy more precarious. Most countries have transfer measures in order to react against inequality in the form of taxes; in other regions, such as the USA, wealthy people contribute to philanthropic activities through foundations or donations.

The international governance structures of the International Monetary Fund and the World Bank are much biased and influenced by the powerful countries of the world, such as the G8. Since the recent financial crisis that displayed the interconnectedness of the world, countries such as China, South Korea, South Africa, and Brazil have been asked to contribute to international efforts destined to regulate financial institutions. This participation shows that the West can no longer maintain its economic and financial power in a world where emergent powerful nations such as China and India contribute to global policy measures.

The recent financial crisis also showed that governments and political elites must act as responsible actors who defend the interests of the citizens of their respective countries or their major political groupings such as the European Union. The importance of political actions has changed during the financial crisis in autumn 2008 – social phenomena such as inequality that have been regulated for a long time by the market according to the understanding of parts of global elites, have again become elements that political actors take into account in political programs. Although wealthier groups lost large proportions of their assets in the financial crisis, they could return to positive gains in the following years. However, parts of the poorer groups have been struggling after having lost their homes or their jobs. Thus inequality requiring political measures continues to matter.

EUROPEAN UNION WAGE INEQUALITY

In the years before the financial crisis of 2008, a reduction in EU wage inequality could be observed. This was the result of the economic convergence between richer and poorer EU Member States. In 2008, this trend was reversed and wage differentials between countries increased again. Enrique Fernández-Macias and Carlos Vacas-Soriano have presented an analysis that looks at wages from a pan-European perspective in their report 'Recent Developments in the Distribution of Wages from an EU Perspective'. The Gini coefficient for full-time equivalent EU wages in PPP was 0.346 in 2011. Most EU countries have lower values with some exceptions for the UK, Portugal, and Latvia, that have higher values. This value is also lower than the value of the USA (0.4 for full-time employees; Eurofund 2015). After 2008, between-countries' values did not reduce any longer while within-country inequality tended to increase. The 2004-2008 convergence resulted from a catch-up of Eastern European countries and wage stagnation in the UK and Germany (Fernández-Macias and Vacas-Soriano, 2015). After 2008, wage levels in Southern Europe dropped because of a massive destruction of employment, while German wages slowly began to increase. Wage inequality decreased from 2004-2011 in many Eastern European member states, while the opposite trend could be found in Austria, Belgium, and Denmark (Fernández-Macias and Vacas-Soriano, 2015).

Regarding the global trend of financialization, one could become optimistic insofar as major political actors challenge the financial activities of banks. This means that: 1) the high salaries of top executives in banks and enterprises are in question; and 2) the ethical responsibility of bank managers in the credit market is demanded. It should not be based any longer on profits and credit policy, but should be viewed as a challenge. Big losses, such as those of poor and the middle class families in the USA who had acquired houses under difficult credit conditions which meant they were not able to pay back these loans, have to be avoided. The public discussion on these issues shows that political groups that have defended poorer groups have had electoral successes (e.g. in Japan, Greece, and recently in the USA elections with Bernie Sanders, who became an important challenger to Hillary Clinton). First impressions also signal the appearance of growing right–wing nationalist parties that have been elected in national or regional governments in several European countries where populations are no longer supporting mainstream parties that have difficulties defining their political programs.

CASE STUDY

INEQUALITY IN EASTERN EUROPE

Nina Bandelj and Matthew Mahutga analyze rising income inequality in Central and Eastern Europe for the period between 1990 to 2000. As the authors underline, 'social inequality ([...] and income inequality [...]) [were] substantially lower during socialism than inequality in other systems at comparable levels of industrial development' (Bandelj and Mahutga, 2010b: 193). Since 1989 and the fall of the Berlin Wall, social inequality has increased throughout the region. For example, 'In 1989, the average Gini index was 22 across these countries, but increased to 34 only a dozen years later. The magnitude of this change becomes evident when we consider that the Gini index increased about 3 points in the United States, and declined slightly in a few West European countries during this same period' (Bandelj and Mahutga, 2010a: 2134). With regard to the levels of inequality in postsocialist countries, in 2001 Romania, Estonia, and Lithuania were close to the high levels we find in Anglo-Saxon countries like the USA or the UK. However, inequality levels in Slovakia, the Czech Republic, and Slovenia were closer to those of Scandinavian countries, with relatively equitable income distribution. Bandelj and Mahutga (2010b: 199) attempt to explain these differences and the role of globalization in generating them. They find that 'there is a clear positive association between income inequality and foreign capital penetration,' as there is an 'increasing wage inequality between management and labor within the foreign sector.' Another finding of the study is 'an expanding difference in average income between agricultural and non-agricultural sectors' and thus sector dualism. As some countries of the region are characterized by 'a cultural shift from a collectivist to a more individualistic orientation [...] the population declines,' so that the authors conclude 'poor families continue to live in traditional households and have more children so that wealth concentrates in the segment of households with more educated individuals from middle and upper class backgrounds who adopt new forms of living arrangements.' The differences in the countries of the region, according to Bandelj and Mahutga, are also linked to the fact that 'countries with weak labor market institutions

[...] have significantly higher income inequality.' The authors conclude by underlining that the inequality trends they find 'are related to social and cultural challenges that accompany the institutionalization of a market-based order' and do not form 'by-products of economic development.' Political choices of elites have thus been responsible for higher and lower levels of inequality in the region.

Ramos and Royuela (2014) report analyses that examine trends between 2007 and 2011, based on the European Union Survey on Income and Living Conditions (EU-SILC) to find that 'average inequality levels among new EU members and other European countries in 2007 was quite similar to the one observed in old EU members with an average of the Gini index close to 0.29.' Among the postsocialist countries Ramos and Royuela (2014) analyze, Slovenia and Slovakia have low levels of inequality, the Czech Republic and Hungary have intermediate levels, and the majority of postsocialist countries – Croatia, Estonia, Poland, Lithuania, Bulgaria, Romania, and Latvia – have high levels of inequality. In terms of change, however, Hungary and Slovakia have a high absolute change, with Gini coefficient increases of more than 1 point between 2007 and 2011. Still, during this same period, the Gini coefficient decreased in Romania, the Czech Republic, and Bulgaria. So far, we have little research that would provide a robust identification of factors that explain these variations in Central and Eastern Europe. Specifically, it is puzzling that levels of inequality in countries that have been severely hit by the economic crisis have somewhat declined in some countries and somewhat increased in others. Ramos and Royuela (2014: 17) who include 30 European countries in their analysis conclude: 'Overall we see inequality negatively associated with development (negatively associated with GDP and positively associated with higher shares in agriculture), positively associated with sectors opened to global competition (agriculture, commerce, transportation and tourism), higher in regions with higher value added services and highly educated workers and/or employed in science and technology, and conditioned by a list of institutions.'

Sources: Bandelj, N. and Mahutga, M. (2010a) 'How socio-economic changes shape income inequality in Central and Eastern Europe,' *Social Forces* 88(5): 2133–2161.

Bandelj, N. and Mahutga, M. (2010b) 'Rising income inequality in Central and Eastern Europe: The influence of economic globalization and other social forces', in Ulrike Schuerkens (ed.) *Globalization and Transformations of Social Inequality*. Routledge: London and New York. pp. 193–218.

Ramos, R. and Royuela, V. (2014) 'Income inequality in Europe. Analysis of recent trends at the regional level.' Research Institute of Applied Economics Working Paper 2014/25. Available at http://www.ub.edu/irea/working_papers/2014/201425.pdf (accessed 7 October 2016).

GLOBALIZATION: FASCINATION AT THE BEGINNING OF THE SECOND MILLENNIUM

In recent years, globalization has become an anthropological and sociological fascination, while the market and socio-economic issues dominated the debate during the 1980s and 1990s. As Anna Tsing commented, globalization is multi-referential: partly a corporate hype and a regulatory agenda, partly a cultural excitement, partly a social commentary that asks for protests (2000: 322). Often anthropologists have discussed globalization, and among other things, how subaltern groups creatively show resistance or how homogenizing influences have been imposed from above (e.g. advertising, soap operas, forms of work discipline, political ideologies) (see Graeber, 2002: 1223). Social anthropology thus contributes to the debate on global social inequality, social movements, popular campaigns and ideas that are central to the understanding of globalization and social change. In the late twentieth and at the beginning of the twenty-first century, cultural anthropologists and sociologists were more interested in methodological approaches that allowed an understanding of globalization and transnationalism (e.g. in work on mobility and migration).

METHODS TO FIGHT SOCIAL INEQUALITY

The political and social processes in different regions of the world show that there are different methods to fight social inequality. Economic globalization has spawned social movements (stronger in Latin America than in Africa). The former political focus on issues such as race, gender, and identity has been enhanced; corporate power and justice but also labour rights are discussed. These are dynamic and persistent processes, which pose a challenge to globalization and are more than irrational anti-global protests: they allow other developments and alternative scenarios. This widening struggle for different rights proves that this is part of the broader movement for global justice. Social anthropology and sociology can thus pose new research agendas that focus on activist networks and social movements in the socio-economic globalization. The last financial crisis has shown that more far-reaching policy measures are needed not only in financial terms, but also in welfare systems. Government spending on redistributive programs generated by market inequalities (Garrett, 2003) compensates for inequalities in some countries (Northern Europe). However, many governments have chosen austerity measures that exclude whole population groups (Sassen, 2014). In less wealthy countries (e.g. Romania), the consequences of neoliberal policies are facilitated by remittances of migrants that help to alleviate widespread poverty. Alternative development strategies are also possible, such as shown in Nicaragua (see the case study above) where major structural changes have been created in the social sector (e.g. health, community work). Such findings confirm the existing national differences in economic globalization.

Since the beginning of the financial crisis in 2007, alternatives to neoliberal globalization are increasingly discussed. Whether economic globalization homogenized labour standards, promoted gender equality, and increased social inequality is discussed passionately. What is new is that the defenders of economic globalization are forced to accept government interventions that may eventually lead to structural changes and create an era of post-neoliberalism.

PAY GAP, SOCIAL MOBILITY, AND WEALTH

The pay gap data for the 27 countries for which data exists show that Brazil, China, India, and the United States have the highest pay gaps between highest and lowest earners; the lowest level can be found in Belgium and the Nordic countries (ILO, 2008: 12). With regard to inequality and social mobility, training is one of the factors that allow the wealthier families to maintain their status position, so that segregation between income groups continues to exist. Thus, households are often linked to low income groups over several generations (ILO, 2008: 23).

As the globalization of financial markets and the resulting global financial crisis have highlighted, low-income households or those of the unemployed were particularly affected. It is also interesting to know that wealth inequality is higher than income inequality: the global Gini coefficient of wealth is 89.2 (ILO, 2008: 44) and thus substantially higher than the global Gini coefficient of income. To give some figures of the Gini coefficient of wealth in different countries for 2000: in the USA, it was 80.1; in Brazil 78.3; in Mexico 74.8; in Nigeria 73.5; in France 73.0; in Germany 67.1; in India 66.9; in China 55.0, and in Japan 54.7 (Davies et al., 2008, cited in ILO 2008: 59). The global top 1 per cent is dominated by the 'old' OECD countries that unite over 60 million people belonging to it. The richest 11 per cent of Americans are members of this group (Milanovic, 2016). In countries such as Germany, France, Japan, and Great Britain, 4 to 5 per cent of the richest people belong to the global top 1 per cent. Outside of this group of countries, only Chile and Taiwan have more than 1 per cent of their inhabitants in this group. According to Milanovic (2016), 'Brazil, South Africa, and Russia, each have their own top 1 percent also in the global top 1 percent, but not more than that.' According to an IMF report: 'Estimates suggest that almost half of the world's wealth is now owned by just 1 per cent of the population, amounting to $110 trillion – 65 times the total wealth of the bottom half of the world's population' (Fuentes Nieva and Galasso, 2014: 2).

LABOUR INSTITUTIONS AND EMPLOYMENT STRUCTURES

Recent decades have seen a significant decline in unionization triggered by the rise of precarious forms of work (informal work and part-time jobs). From the 1990s onwards, this new labour structure has reduced membership in trade unions that do not include these groups (ILO, 2008: 72). Redistributive policies were continued at a reduced level, with the exception of parts of Latin America (see the case studies of Muhr and Ivo/Laniado). The extent of atypical forms of employment has increased in most countries in the world. In high-income countries, part-time and temporary work increased; in Africa, Asia, and Latin America, informal employment is widespread. The remuneration for these jobs is usually less than that in standard jobs. In Latin America and India, informal temporary workers earn on average 45 per cent less than permanent employees (ILO, 2008: 115). Among women, part-time work is widespread in high-income countries (in Germany up to half of all women).[10] These trends contribute to the fact that trade unions no longer defend these populations and thus cannot play a role in the definition of the economic relation of employers and employees. In recent decades, enterprises had to face fierce competition in order to react to rapid changes so that they were reluctant to hire full-time and long-term workers and argued that salaries should not increase. However, in 2006, in Latin America, informal employment formed more than half of total employment (ILO, 2008: 120). Also in Africa, the majority of jobs are insecure and poorly paid and rarely include social benefits (health and old-age). Precariousness is increasing in Europe, combined with high unemployment figures mainly in Southern Europe.

TAXES AND SOCIAL TRANSFERS

Inequality can be influenced by a combination of social services, transfer payments, and taxes. But except in the Nordic countries, redistribution in developed economies could not stop the rising income inequality. According to the Luxembourg Income Study (ILO, 2008: 136), 'since the 1980s, the Gini coefficient on final income has risen almost as much as that on market income.' According to Mahler and Jesuit (2006: 491), transfers contribute 75 per cent of total fiscal distribution in OECD countries, compared to only 25 per cent from direct taxes. In some countries (e.g. China, Brazil, and Nicaragua), social policy measures play a major role. However, there still is a shortage of research on the impact of transfers and taxes in further countries of the world.

GENDER AND INEQUALITY

In most regions of the world, the chances for women to get into paid employment have risen, albeit with large regional variations. Often, these female employees earn less than their male counterparts. The promotion of gender equality in the world of work still requires policies that can only be enforced against oppositions. The desire of women to remain in the labour market is undervalued. Nevertheless, there are some positive results. In the last 20 years, the percentage of women in public offices in the countries of the geographical South and North increased. In some regions, women still make up a high proportion of non-employed persons: in the Middle East, North Africa, and Asia.

SOCIO-POLITICAL TRANSFORMATIONS AND INEQUALITY

The labour and income system creates a social dynamic and contributes to the explanation of social transformations. Political elites are trying – together with economic, cultural, and social elites – to prepare the future of our global world. These elites cannot act alone. They must respond to social, political, economic, and cultural processes in which the middle classes and poorer groups demand more influence. Conflicts between these groups may thus give rise to social developments affecting the future form not only of social inequalities, but also of the characteristics of global social, economic, and political systems (see Chapter 10 on social movements).

IMPLEMENTING FINDINGS OF SOCIAL ANTHROPOLOGISTS AND SOCIOLOGISTS

I would like to address another point, namely the challenge of implementing findings of cultural anthropologists and sociologists. When analyzing transformation processes, sociologists and anthropologists have the opportunity to initiate political projects of economic, social, and cultural elites and to take into account the needs of the poor (Escobar, 1995b and 1997). Since the mid-1970s, when development agencies began to be interested in cooperations with poorer groups and introduced cultural and social changes, anthropologists and sociologists have had more opportunities to contribute to the development of these processes. United Nations organizations have engaged social scientists and especially development anthropologists and sociologists as well as people who could help to reduce the negative impacts of ambiguous policies which cause inequality. This has meant that these professionals have introduced their knowledge into public arenas. Their activities include a moral commitment to current and critical issues, an attitude that Mead advocated decades ago. Later, Michael Horowitz (1994), David Gow (2002), John W. Bennett (1996), and sociologist Norman Long (2001) supported these views.

THEORY AND APPLIED RESEARCH

The polarization between theory and applied research that exists in Western academic institutions is not universal. Scientists who defend applied research are actively involved in policy debates, through topics they study by taking the methodological rules of their disciplines into account. Interested in the poor, they contribute to their increased visibility. This focus on the poor should contribute to a larger significance of disciplines such as sociology and cultural anthropology in political debates. The visions of these scientists constitute forms of power that control the systems; these views are intended to transform the conditions under which people live (Escobar, 1995a: 155-6). Obviously, there are major differences in terms of inequality in the neoliberal or post-neoliberal economy. The authors of the case studies in this chapter have studied complex social realities both in the centre and at the edges of global, transnational, and local processes. They are not blind to the ambiguities of their own research on power and inequality. Their commitment to the poor is to deliver an important message that sociology and cultural anthropology allow (see Escobar, 1997: 498).

SOLUTIONS TO IMPROVE UNEQUAL SITUATIONS

One may wonder how these scientists are aware of the consequences of their research on the groups or situations they study. An analysis of social transformations provides knowledge on how to combat inequalities of the present world order at the beginning of the twenty-first century after the recent financial crisis and inside the post-neoliberal globalization. Sociology and cultural anthropology question the neoliberal state and its administration of the poor. These disciplines examine the discourses and institutional practices that characterize inequalities in economic neoliberalism. Their knowledge is power: they suggest other solutions in order to improve morally unacceptable situations. These scholars explore 'the spaces between what we know and what can be done with that knowledge' (Chambers, 1987: 322). They are trained to understand empirical complexity. Their knowledge cannot be easily translated into political programs, but their findings are important. This chapter has collected evidence that can contribute to the reduction of poverty and inequality, a goal that the Millennium Development Goals of the United Nations have emphasized at the beginning of the second millennium. The 2030 Agenda for Sustainable Development with the Title *Transforming our World* involves 'changes in social structures and relations, including patterns of stratification related to class, gender, ethnicity, religion or location that can lock people (including future generations) into disadvantage and constrain their choices and agency' (UNRISD, 2016: 12). As this is a political project, diverging interests between groups and actors are challenged so that power relations may be changed in the long run. This also means questioning the current dominant growth paradigm which is associated with inequality and exclusion. Redistribution tackling vertical and horizontal inequalities, coverage of social protection systems, and minimum wage policies are thus becoming policy options that have to be implemented by collective actions of societies (UNRISD, 2016: 13). These measures also include changes in North–South power relations and in global governance institutions. In fact, the Sustainable Development Goals (SDGs) aim to leave no one behind (goal 10).

CASE STUDY

THE ALBA INITIATIVE IN NICARAGUA

In his article, T. Muhr (2010) focuses on the ALBA initiative in Nicaragua, which represents a powerful counter-hegemonic initiative in Latin America and the Caribbean. This movement is based on a moral legitimacy that intends to challenge global neoliberal capitalism. The social dimension of ALBA, which is relatively unknown outside the Hispanic world, underlines the increased social injustice that has shaped global capitalism over the past two decades. ALBA's important characteristics are solidarity, cooperation, and the rejection of capitalist profit. Instead, a direct participatory democracy is promoted in this region. The establishment of a Bank of the South should continue to ensure financial independence from the international financial institutions and represents the existence of a 'broad-based consensus on non-neo-liberal integration among the progressive LAC governments' (Muhr, 2010). One of the featured measures that Muhr analyzes is based on gasoline imports which have led to a substantial reduction in bus fares in Managua. Another important project relates to health care: Cuba and Venezuela have committed themselves to provide eye surgeries for six million citizens with low incomes throughout the region. Muhr writes that this project allows patients to be flown for operations to Cuba and Venezuela, where free surgery and postoperative treatment are carried out. This program covers travel expenses, visa costs, accommodation, food, and medicine as well as support provided by a family member in ten per cent of the cases. An interesting factor is that the project is based on the principle of political, ethnic, and religious neutrality. Another project has contributed to the fact that since 2009 Nicaragua has been illiteracy-free in accordance with UNESCO standards (95 per cent literacy). ALBA is thus a 'transnational bottom-up structure' (Muhr, 2010) and has a significant influence in the fight against social inequality in the region. The initiative contributes to the creation of a politically integrated region according to social, economic, and political rules that don't exist in many parts of the geographic South. So far, the increasing pressure from the USA and the European Union and the global financial crisis of 2007–2009 have not slowed down the dynamics of the ALBA initiative in Latin America.

Source: Muhr, T. (2010) 'Nicaragua: Constructing the Bolivarian Alliance for the Peoples of Our America (ALBA),' in U. Schuerkens, *Globalization and Transformation of Social Inequality.* London and New York: Routledge. pp. 115–34. and recent updates.

DISCUSSION QUESTIONS

1. Please describe the Gini coefficient for in-country inequality and for between-country inequality.

2. What are some of the political measures that can influence inequality?

3. Please explain the approaches of the Individualists and the Structuralists regarding inequality.

4. Can you describe the top 1 per cent and its link to taxes?

5. What do you think is an acceptable level of global inequality?

ANNOTATED FURTHER READINGS

Dabla-Norris, E., Kochhar, K., Suphaphiphat, N., Ricka, F. and Tsounta, E. (2015) *Causes and Consequences of Income Inequality: A Global Perspective.* **International Monetary Fund: Strategy, Policy, and Review Department.**
This paper analyzes the extent of income inequality from a global perspective, its drivers, and what to do about it. The article finds that increasing the income share of the poor and the middle class actually increases growth while a rising income share of the top 20 per cent results in lower growth – that is, when the rich get richer, benefits do not trickle down.

Lakner, C. and Milanovic, B. (2015) 'Global income distribution: From the fall of the Berlin Wall to the Great Recession,' *The World Bank Economic Review* **1-30. Available at https://www.gc.cuny.edu/CUNY_GC/media/ LISCenter/brankoData/wber_final.pdf (accessed 10 October 2016).**
The paper presents a database of national household surveys between 1988 and 2008. In 2008, the global Gini coefficient is around 70.5 per cent, having declined by approximately 2 Gini points over this 20-year period. When it is adjusted for the likely under-reporting of top incomes in surveys, the estimate is a much higher global Gini coefficient of almost 76 per cent. Tracking the evolution of individual country's deciles shows the underlying elements that drive the changes in the global distribution.

OECD (2015) *In It Together: Why Less Inequality Benefits All.* **Paris: OECD Publishing. Available at http://www.keepeek.com/Digital-Asset-Manage ment/oecd/employment/in-it-together-why-less-inequality-benefits- all_9789264235120-en (accessed 10 October 2016).**
This publication finds evidence that high inequality harms economic growth. The rise in inequality observed between 1985 and 2005 in 19 OECD countries knocked 4.7 percentage points off cumulative growth between 1990 and 2010 according to the OECD. And what matters for growth is not just the poorest falling behind but also inequality affecting lower middle and working class families. It is their loss of ground that blocks social mobility and brings down economic growth.

Websites

http://alba-tcp.org/public/documents/decimo/English/Management_report.pdf
ALBA-TCP (2014). 'ALBA-PTA Management Report 2004-2014. 10 Years Consolidating Solidarity and Integration Among the Peoples of Our America'.

http://www.onepercentshow.com/
1% Privilege in a Time of Global Inequality: A Photobook.

http://www.cgdev.org/blog/national-vices-global-virtue-world-becoming-more-equal
Milanovic's Center of Global Development Blog: 'National vices, global virtue: Is the world becoming more equal?'

http://glineq.blogspot.fr
Global Inequality blog (Branko Milanovic).

http://www.undp.org/content/undp/en/home/sdgoverview/mdg_goals.html
United Nations Development Program: Millennium Development Goals. (Includes links to various reports.)

http://www.un.org/sustainabledevelopment/sustainable-development-goals
The United Nations Sustainable Development Goals: 17 Goals to Transform our World. Adopted by countries around the world on 25 September 2015.

http://www.un.org/sustainabledevelopment/takeaction
The Lazy Person's Guide to Saving the World.

(all websites accessed 10 October 2016)

NOTES

1 PPPs are the rates of currency conversion that equalize the purchasing power of different currencies by eliminating the differences in price levels between countries.
2 Available at http://www.worldbank.org/en/topic/poverty/overview (accessed 24 October 2016).
3 Available at http://www.worldbank.org/en/topic/poverty/overview (accessed 24 October 2016).
4 'African' refers here to coloured populations in South Africa.
5 Available at https://www.oxfam.org/sites/www.oxfam.org/files/bp-working-for-few-political-capture-economic-inequality-200114-summ-en.pdf (accessed 24 October 2016).
6 Available at https://www.imf.org/external/pubs/ft/sdn/2015/sdn1513.pdf (accessed 24 October 2016).
7 See http://www.bbc.com/news/world-europe-34131911 (accessed 17 December 2016).
8 See http://ec.europa.eu/news/2016/10/20161018_en.htm (accessed 17 December 2016).
9 See http://www.unmillenniumproject.org/goals/ (accessed 17 December 2016).
10 Available at http://www.welt.de/wirtschaft/article114214467/Fast-die-Haelfte-aller-Frauen-arbeitet-Teilzeit.html (accessed 24 October 2016).

TRANSNATIONAL MIGRATIONS AND SOCIAL TRANSFORMATIONS

Summary

This chapter tackles the combined effects of transnational migrations and social transformations. During the last few years, it has become obvious that globalization brings with it more and more transnational migrations. New forms of interdependence, transnational societies, and regional cooperations transform the lives of millions of people, who are linking the future of states and societies. In the countries of the global South, international migrations contribute to the development of these societies by remittances of migrants from the North to the South, which play an important role in national and even international development plans. World system theory considers international migrations as a structural consequence of the extension of markets into a global political-hierarchical system. International migrations followed the creation of global links between primary goods, labour, and land. Some simple theses result from this: international migrations follow international capital movements, but in the opposite direction. The creation of ideological and material relations completes these migration processes: colonialism, common languages, commerce, transport, mass media, and travel links, and have linked different regions of the world, and have developed international migration flows. For many countries of the South, international migrations are one aspect of the social crisis that accompanies their integration into a global market.

INTRODUCTION

Mobility has led to human advancement throughout history. Migration has become an everyday reality in the twenty-first century so that human mobility substantially contributes to progress and development. Large-scale movements will continue if worldwide inequality patterns remain as sharp as they are now. One billion of the world's seven billion inhabitants are migrants. About 244 million (2015) are international and 740 million are internal migrants (2014).[1] This has brought humanity global labour markets, more diverse societies, and ever-denser transnational networks. There is thus an urgent necessity to understand migration dynamics in order to avoid cementing privileges and wasting talents and resources.

THE UNEVEN ECONOMIC DEVELOPMENT OF WORLD REGIONS

One of the main reasons for migration is, according to Hoffmann-Nowotny (1973), the uneven economic development of different regions or countries of the world. Rural exodus caused and causes a progressive urbanization of societies. During the nineteenth and early twentieth century, people in European countries, migrated not only to urban areas, but some groups migrated instead to overseas countries. This emigration was viewed as a result of differences in economic development in a market economy. In recent years, the decline in transport and communication costs has increased international migration. The construction of railways and roads as well as the use of telephone, radio, and television sets have led to an integration of the countries of the South in the international economic market. Personal networks in the South are increasingly linked with communication systems of developed economies abroad. Consequently, this development has made international migrations easier and cheaper but has also widened transnational migration flows linking different national spaces so that it becomes more and more difficult to speak about out-migration and immigration (see Wihtol de Wenden, 2016a).

EMIGRATION FROM COUNTRIES OF THE SOUTH

The emigration from countries of the South can be explained by the formation of a potential group of migrants due to capital, access to markets, and differences in economic development over time and space, and difficult political situations. In recent decades, each country and each region of the South has been exposed to migrations to developed economies. However, there are differences between countries in terms of the total amount of emigration: in the nineteenth century, France witnessed migrations at a fairly low level, while migrations were numerous in England. Today, citizens of Spain and Portugal migrate to Latin America because of language facilities and unemployment in their countries while young binational French citizens, whose parents' country of origin was a former colonial region, emigrate to these regions. Differences between countries, their access to the global economy, colonial relationships, technologies, and political factors determine the direction and extent of migrations. Economic relations between the countries of origin and destination are an important explanatory factor. Currently, there are not only South-North migrations (e.g. from Africa to Europe), but also South-South migrations (e.g. from Guinea to Senegal or Nigeria; from Nicaragua to Costa Rica; from Honduras and Guatemala to Mexico; from Bangladesh and Nepal to India; from Indonesia to Malaysia). Other migrations are based on difficult political (e.g. Syria, Afghanistan) or economic situations (e.g. migration to South Africa from Southern African countries or to Latin America from Spain and Portugal).

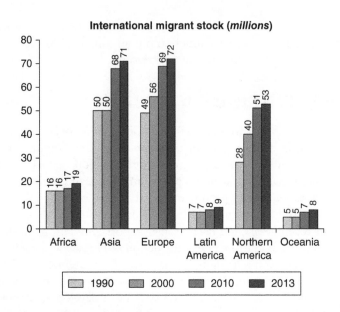

FIGURE 5.1   MIGRATION NUMBER BY REGIONS

Source: United Nations (2013) *Trends in International Migration Stock. The 2013 Revision.* Available at http://www.un.org/en/development/desa/population/migration/data/index.shtml (accessed 17 December 2016)

South–North migration is estimated to account for 35 per cent of the total, while South-South migrations represent 37 per cent and North-North migration amounts to a further 23 per cent, while North-South migrations accounts for 5 per cent (e.g. some 100,000 individuals from Portugal and Spain to Brazil and Argentina in 2008 and 2009 (Córdova Alcaraz, 2012; World Bank, 2015)). Portugal and Ireland are the countries that have the largest number of North-South emigrants. However, the majority of migrants live within their region of origin. Historical ties and social networks are important in shaping movements of people. There are specific migration corridors: between Mexico and the United States; Bangladesh and India; Turkey and Germany; India and the United Arab Emirates; and the Philippines and the United States (Ratha and Shaw, 2007).

THEORIES: MIGRATION AND DEVELOPMENT

This section addresses the question whether migration triggers development and/ or whether development triggers migration. Major international and internal differences in income were considered by sociological theory as the main factors explaining internal and/or international migration (e.g. Hoffmann–Nowotny, 1973). Hoffmann-Nowotny showed that migrants from poor countries migrate to richer countries. He studied this phenomenon in Switzerland and Canada in the 1970s.

My own study of the Republic of the Congo and Sudan (Schuerkens, 1981) was influenced by this approach. I found that regional economic, urban, and educational differences influenced the direction and the quantity of migrations. However, poorer regions supported internal migrations only to a small extent, while richer regions, which were characterized by a higher level of development, contributed more to internal or international migrations.

INEQUALITY AS A REASON FOR MIGRATION

What about inequality as a reason for migration today? An International Organization for Migrations' report underlined in 2013: 'Recent estimates suggest that about 9 per cent of the world population receives 50 per cent of global income, while the bottom half of the population, namely, the poorest 50 per cent – receive about 7 per cent (Milanovic, 2011b). Current levels of global inequality are said to be the highest in human history' (IOM, 2013: 25). Today, it is no longer self-evident that a rise in per capita income reduces migration, as Hoffmann-Nowotny and I suggested in our respective studies. The statement that the best migration policy is an increase in income is challenged today. But recent policy measures, such as the EU Emergency Trust Fund for Africa, offer several billion euros to African nations and Turkey in exchange of accepting migrants go in this direction. In fact, the argument is: if the economic situation in these regions improved, people would have less ambition to look for an uncertain future abroad, far away from family and friends.

RELATIONSHIP BETWEEN MIGRATION AND DEVELOPMENT

According to Fischer et al., the relationship between migration and development can be explained by the concept of a 'modified inverted U-curve'. They wrote: 'Development often first enhances and thereafter reduces the scope and incentives for migration, but the sequencing of enhancement and reduction is usually different for different types of migration' (1997: 92).

One of the simplest explanations of economic migration is that people migrate with the aim of improving their situation. Migration helps individuals and families to increase their incomes, develop new skills, improve their socio-economic situation, and more generally attain a better quality of life. At the international level, this would mean that large groups of migrants migrate from poor areas to rich regions. However, the total number of international migrants is rather small. International organizations such as the International Labour Organization, the International Organization for Migration, and the UN High Commissioner for Refugees evoke some 3.3 per cent of the world's population in 2015 or 244 million migrants worldwide (UN DESA, 2016a). Another important fact is that the importance of international migrations has changed over time. For example, sending countries become receiving countries: Italian immigrants arrived in Germany in the 1960s; in the 1990s, Italy had become an immigration country for African immigrants.

CONVERGENCE EFFECT OF MIGRATION

The convergence effect of migration can be shown if we differentiate the impact of migration on development according to short- or long-term consequences. In the short run, migration affects median wages in immigration countries as migrants are likely to accept lower wages. Migrants who send parts of their income to the country of origin influence the economy of their home countries and may improve the local socio-economic situation. Migrants also contribute to the financing of public social services (most of them are young and in good health) in the country of immigration, which in turn has an impact on welfare spending. The availability of labour can also lead to changes in the production structure (e.g. cheap immigrants who help maintain low prices for goods, such as clothes) and may influence trade conditions between both countries (e.g. fewer imports). The decrease of wages in the country of sojourn may have a negative outcome on poorer local groups who face unemployment or underemployment if no public measures such as tax incentives or an upgrading of educational measures are taken.

DIVERGENCE EFFECT OF MIGRATION

Marx, Hirschmann (1970), and Wallerstein (2004), all have argued that increased migration reduces worldwide differences in development. These scholars thought that technological progress cannot be spread from the Northern 'core' to the Southern 'periphery.' Fischer et al. argued in the following way. Wages will remain low in the disadvantaged region. The latter can only catch up by improving its technology and efficiency, which will become increasingly difficult once the production resources are beginning to leave the region. If, in the extreme case, all production resources were mobile and left, the situation would become increasingly difficult in the long run until the last turns off the light (Fischer et al., 1997: 116). However, recent developments have shown that parts of technology can be adapted to conditions in the South: smartphones and computers can be produced in the South with affordable prices for poorer populations. (See Chapter 7 in this book.)

EMPIRICAL CASE STUDIES

Empirical case studies have shown the coexistence of the convergence and divergence theses related to migration. Periods of economic development of regions and countries cause the divergence effects of migration. They can be followed by periods in which migration induces convergence effects. The actual connection between migration and development remains an empirical question and must be examined in concrete situations. For most countries, the impact of international migrations on development is positive, but this impact is essentially

TABLE 5.1   MIGRANT REMITTANCE OUTFLOWS

Migrant remittance outflows (US$ million)	1980	1985	1990	1995	2000	2005	2010	2014	2015
Algeria	165	131	31	..	..	27	28	53	..
Angola	..	79	150	209	266	215	714	1,299	..
Argentina	36	18	..	195	268	314	1,040	771	..
Australia	304	312	674	701	1,053	1,531	4,655	7,000	..
Austria	334	190	320	1,485	1,298	2,120	2,017	4,037	..
Azerbaijan	..	..	..	9	101	239	954	2,031	..
Bahrain	330	778	332	500	1,010	1,223	1,642	2,364	..
Belgium	..	..	..	..	..	2,427	4,185	4,497	..
Bolivia	2	3	8	9	37	67	102	189	..
Botswana	26	16	119	200	147	107	85	89	..
Brazil	152	6	12	347	366	374	1,024	1,539	1339.0869
Burkina Faso	52	41	81	..	45	84	112	160	..
Cambodia	..	..	..	52	104	128	171	219	..
Cameroon	102	139	111	22	30	56	54	..	..
Canada	..	..	..	..	..	3,318	5,290	5,393	..
China	..	3	5	..	789	1,817	1,455	4,155	..
Colombia	39	98	44	150	219	56	112	204	..
Costa Rica	..	1	..	36	142	209	259	419	..
Côte d'Ivoire	787	287	471	457	390	597	726	..	..
Cyprus	9	6	12	48	63	241	952	751	..
Czech Republic	..	..	..	100	605	1,163	1,497	822	..
Denmark	..	..	..	209	662	1,488	2,826	3,152	..
Dominican Republic	..	..	..	7	19	25	519	591	..
Ecuador	67	114	2	4	6	54	136	196	..
Egypt, Arab Rep.	..	..	27	223	32	57	305	351	..
El Salvador	9	3	3	..	20	24	22	51	..
Finland	15	12	16	54	100	266	721	835	..
France	5,070	4,170	6,956	4,941	3,770	9,475	12,029	13,835	..
Gabon	144	104	147	99	78	186	..	..	..
Germany	5,826	3,601	6,854	11,356	9,039	12,710	14,685	20,836	..
Greece	59	45	122	300	546	902	1,932	1,424	..
Guatemala	11	6	14	8	56	42	21	27	..
Guinea	..	..	20	10	27	60	41	..	..
Haiti	54	47	..	..	11	60	167	249	247.297664
Hong Kong SAR, China	..	..	..	..	225	348	483	711	..
Hungary	..	..	..	146	86	912	1,133	1,053	..
India	29	31	106	419	486	1,348	3,829	6,222	..
Indonesia	..	..	..	..	..	1,179	2,840	4,119	..

(Continued)

TABLE 5.1   (CONTINUED)

Migrant remittance outflows (US$ million)	1980	1985	1990	1995	2000	2005	2010	2014	2015
Ireland	..	62	165	173	181	1,441	2,267	1,960	..
Israel	31	410	850	1,410	3,260	2,206	3,727	5,155	4938.99981
Italy	428	606	3,764	1,823	2,582	7,546	12,886	11,154	..
Japan	220	..	..	1,820	3,169	1,150	4,366	4,215	..
Jordan	154	236	71	107	197	349	495	499	..
Kazakhstan	..	..	..	504	440	1,893	3,006	3,558	..
Korea, Rep.	58	27	1,026	2,062	3,651	6,667	9,123	9,571	8321.39981
Kosovo	..	..	..	..	..	162	127	100	..
Kuwait	692	1,040	770	1,350	1,730	2,648	11,864	18,129	..
Latvia	..	..	..	1	7	491	443	615	533.318692
Lebanon	..	..	..	..	..	4,012	4,390	5,604	..
Libya	1,050	859	446	222	463	914	1,609	..	..
Lithuania	..	..	..	1	38	259	552	905	..
Luxembourg	..	..	..	2,220	2,720	6,699	10,645	12,700	..
Malaysia	19	13	230	1,331	599	5,679	6,729	8,074	..
Mali	19	29	45	42	26	69	176	..	..
Malta	8	5	25	13	14	192	1,612	1,027	..
Mexico	11	..	..	..	..	..	..	1,002	..
Moldova	..	..	..	1	46	46	79	147	..
Mongolia	..	..	..	..	3	40	169	337	..
Morocco	77	21	16	20	29	35	62	..	..
Mozambique	25	25	25	21	156	24	54	194	..
Namibia	..	..	30	11	9	18	28	12	..
Netherlands	970	658	1,393	2,803	3,128	4,547	9,398	9,945	..
New Zealand	151	127	366	427	459	647	534	709	..
Niger	53	49	66	29	12	29	72	..	..
Nigeria	524	298	9	5	1	68	47	58	..
Norway	110	144	295	603	1,060	2,174	4,118	5,822	..
Oman	397	950	856	1,540	1,450	2,257	5,704	10,301	..
Panama	37	31	22	20	22	88	486	818	..
Papua New Guinea	28	34	43	16	18	128	394	55	..
Philippines	12	1	5	151	21	195	109	183	..
Poland	..	..	..	262	311	621	1,306	2,185	..
Portugal	33	15	77	527	454	436	506	442	..
Qatar	..	..	..	..	1,355	3,009	8,141	11,230	..
Romania	..	..	..	2	6	22	88	638	..
Russian Federation	..	..	..	3,939	1,099	6,827	21,454	32,640	..
Saudi Arabia	4,090	5,200	11,200	16,600	15,400	14,315	27,069	36,924	..
Senegal	91	47	79	76	55	98	216	..	..

Migrant remittance outflows (US$ million)	1980	1985	1990	1995	2000	2005	2010	2014	2015
Serbia	..	..	..	..	..	..	155	267	..
Slovak Republic	..	..	..	3	8	50	70	225	..
Slovenia	..	..	..	31	29	91	196	215	179.567924
South Africa	1,017	722	1,204	630	685	1,042	1,353	1,094	980.097856
Spain	11	131	254	869	2,491	733	434	363	..
Sri Lanka	..	..	..	16	20	249	526	887	..
Sweden	83	290	654	336	539	537	820	1,427	..
Switzerland	2,343	2,509	8,170	10,120	7,590	9,986	16,878	24,693	..
Tajikistan	..	..	..	..	..	145	231	206	..
Tanzania	..	..	..	1	20	33	123	98	..
Thailand	35	69	199	..	..	..	2,397	3,118	..
Tunisia	22	17	13	36	27	16	13	28	..
Turkey	..	..	..	..	..	96	168	918	..
Uganda	4	..	..	..	353	197	332	289	..
Ukraine	..	..	..	..	10	186	703	1,702	..
United Arab Emirates	..	..	..	..	3,676	5,372	10,566	19,280	..
United Kingdom	..	..	2,033	2,585	2,048	9,643	9,565	11,569	..
United States	1,360	6,330	11,850	22,160	34,400	47,254	50,776	56,311	..
Venezuela, RB	418	217	701	203	331	211	805	193	..
Yemen, Rep.	..	..	106	61	61	109	338	335	..
Zambia	82	24	18	..	24	94	68	81	..

Source: World Bank staff calculation based on data from IMF Balance of Payments Statistics database and data releases from central banks, national statistical agencies, and World Bank country desks.

Note: All numbers are in current (nominal) US $.
For a discussion of the definition of remittances, see Dilip Ratha, 2003, "Workers' Remittances: An Important and Stable Source of External Development Finance", Global Development Finance 2003, World Bank. Data since 2005 are based on IMF BOP Statistics that use the definitions of IMF BPM6.
GDP data is from WDI
For latest data and analysis on migration and remittances, please visit http://www.worldbank.org/migration

Date: April 2016

of a short-term nature: labour market problems (e.g. the 'graying' of the working population in the North) and the balance of payments are often improved. Sometimes migration will also have an impact on growth due to higher consumption. For a long time, migration was considered to not be able to initiate far-reaching social and economic changes that are needed to promote development in most countries of the South (e.g. Fischer et al., 1997: 128). In recent years, the huge amount of financial remittances as well as social remittances through transnational circular migrations let international migrations appear as an important enabler of development (IOM, 2013: 107–15).

The potential for migrations is of a great magnitude: the majority of existing and future global populations live in countries of the global South. The central issue today is whether enough jobs for these large groups of people are available. The prognosis – considering the high unemployment and underemployment in countries of the South, which have already fuelled the social movements of 2011 in North Africa and Latin America – is not favourable. Against the backdrop of emigration pressures from developing countries, the labour situation has become one of the most pressing problems of development in recent decades. The Human Development Report of 2003 already found that, if trade barriers were reduced, the South-North migration (and South-South migration) would increase. Similar to the Marshall Plan in Europe after World War II, assistance was proposed as an appropriate measure given the economic and social differences between the North and the South. This assistance – it was argued - would help to reduce inequalities and the pressure to emigrate, even though in the short term an increased emigration from countries of the South would be the consequence and access barriers in the North would have difficulties to limit this migration flow. Recent developments that have seen the arrival of large groups of migrants and/or refugees in Europe and in particular in Germany (summer and fall 2015) can be explained by the high financial assistance that some Western countries give to immigrants and the recent wars in countries such as Syria.

MIGRATION AND SOCIAL TRANSFORMATION PROCESSES

One of the most important causes of transnational migrations and social transformations is global inequality which has an ethnic dimension. At the country level, a social hierarchy has become obvious, even if an ethnic hierarchy often accompanies this differentiation, so that some ethnic groups (e.g. Latinos, Africans originating from the African continent) are at the bottom of the social ladder. An ethnic hierarchy can also be found at the global level, with some countries of the South at the bottom of the hierarchy and the countries of the North at the top. This has recently changed with the emergence of a multipolar world order, including Brazil, China, and India as fast-growing economies of the South. This hierarchy, as Immanuel Wallerstein suggested some years ago, also refers to social inequality. In order to explain the phenomenon of transnational migrations that began on a large scale in the 1960s, Wallerstein argued that the countries of the South were more and more integrated into the global economy since the European colonization that restructured social, economic, and political systems of countries of the South according to Western development concepts. The slow integration of these countries into a global system meant that global processes affected more and more regions. This influence has still increased with the improvement of transport facilities and migrations crossing national borders. It has thus become less and less useful to analyze processes of social transformations as changes of internal regional structures. The South has been linked to global processes that have helped to integrate these regions into a global system mainly defined by structures originating in the North (the neoliberal economy, democracy, gender equality, etc.).

TRANSNATIONAL MIGRANTS OFTEN OCCUPY LOW HIERARCHICAL POSITIONS

As former members of their home countries, transnational migrants who come from Southern regions and migrate to Western countries (e.g. Europe and the USA) occupy low positions on a social, cultural, and economic hierarchy. The decision to migrate is linked to unequal international relations. To choose the possibility of a migration is one way to change national and individual positions (Hoffmann-Nowotny, 1988). Normally, migrations are directed to countries with a higher GDP. Migration can thus be regarded as a means of mobility between national contexts. Migrants can improve their social positions with higher salaries. In return, they can develop their countries of origin through remittances, using their income to help family members and/or to initiate development projects in their home countries (e.g. by constructing houses, schools, hospitals, and financing small enterprises). Migrants living in more prosperous countries of the South send two thirds of the remittances received by the poorest countries (UNCTAD, 2012a). In several developing countries (e.g. Mali, Senegal), public aid flows have become much less important than private investments (UNCTAD, 2012b).

REMITTANCES

Between 2000 and 2014, migrant remittances to developing countries have increased from USD 81.3 billion to USD 436 billion (Ratha et al., 2011; World Bank, 2015).[2] Moreover, social transfers are added to these monetary transfers: increasing trade flows, the facilitated transfer of skills, new knowledge, new values, and innovations. In the North, migrants often fill labour shortages, particularly in the health and care sectors. Even the 'entrepreneurial spirit' of migrants may benefit both contexts (IT specialists that circulate between the North and the South) (IOM and UN DESA, 2012).

In international history, migrations have always been important, but at the beginning of the twenty-first century it seems as if they have become one of the predominant factors of the interaction between different societies and are now firmly on the political agenda with huge groups of asylum seekers and possibly recognized refugees coming from the South and the East to the North. All over the world, the end of communist regimes and the new political conflicts (e.g. Syria, Afghanistan) have contributed to an increase in migration flows. These population movements are not only quantitatively important but also qualitatively, because they lead to social conflicts with parts of the local populations who are fearing for their jobs (e.g. Pegida movement in Germany, *Front National* in France).

GLOBAL MIGRATION FLOWS

The differentiation between the countries that send migrants and those that receive migrants changed radically in recent decades. The countries of the South continue to participate in transnational migration flows, even if the poorest countries are rarely included in these transfers of wealth between countries (Guilmoto and Sandron, 2003). The former socialist countries in Eastern Europe have become important parts of the brain drain towards Western European countries. But restrictive access rules to most countries with a higher position in the gross domestic product hierarchy form barriers that force many migrants to circumvent them by illegal immigration.

If we want to understand the dynamic nature of transnational migrations and their impact on social changes in the countries of origin, we must consider the remittances these migrants send to their home countries. They are so high that they exceed the official development assistance of Western countries (e.g. in Senegal and Sri Lanka) and even foreign direct investment (excluding China) (World Bank, 2015: 4). Remittances continue to flow even when difficult economic situations reduce official aid flows. Annual remittances are also larger, or equal to, foreign exchange reserves in a lot of small countries (World Bank, 2015: 4). The countries that received the highest amount of migrant remittances in 2014 were China, India, Mexico, and the Philippines. Remittances as a share of GDP are higher in Central Asian countries and Pacific Islands (49 per cent in Tajikistan and 25 per cent in Tonga) (World Bank, 2015: 4). These countries are thus highly vulnerable to fluctuations in remittance-sending countries among their own diasporas.

A reduction in the number of transnational migrants cannot be expected given the actual increasing international stratification of societies (Friedman and Randeria, 2004). Migration is considered an important factor in international development: 'The importance of international migration cannot be overemphasized. It is a powerful force for social change and cultural interaction and has significant impacts on the development process and functioning of the modern economies. Migratory pressures are bound to increase in the future' (UN DESA, 2012a: 47).

MIGRATION, SOCIAL ACTORS, AND NATIONS

Migration processes cannot only be understood at an individual level, but the national and global levels must also be taken into account (see Hammar et al., 1997). Migrants are social actors who are members of national systems that define their life chances. Often, they do not have the possibility to change this situation in the country of origin. This means that each country can favour transnational migrations in order to allow possible migrants an access to contexts that meet their needs. These countries may thus avoid fundamental changes in their economic systems within an unequal global structure. In this way, migrants can initiate gradual processes of status improvements without contributing to the changes of the hierarchical position of their country in the global system (HDI and/or GDP). However, migration as a possibility to change social positions may also mean a better education for children or studies at a university abroad. These brief remarks already indicate that transnational migrations influence global transformation processes (Pries, 1999; Smith and Guarnizo, 1998).

Migration is directed towards higher positioned national contexts. If a high percentage of migrants in a given geographic context was induced by differences between the aspirations and economic opportunities, a development policy should be taken into consideration. If this is not possible, policy measures (growing aid flows) should be undertaken in order to reduce inequalities between different contexts and thus influence migration processes. Transnational migrants may be confronted with access restrictions that allow them to accept a more or less legal immigrant status for a certain period. Often, male workers and/or female service staff migrate without families in order to perform various tasks that the native population no longer wishes to do. These migrants stay for a limited time in the host country and send a large portion of their income home to their families. Better-educated migrants usually have more opportunities to become well-integrated members of the society of the destination country (Schuerkens, 2000).

The economic conditions in the country of immigration determine whether migrants are accepted or not as low-wage workers or specialists. In Western European countries, migrants were recruited in the 1960s as the economies of these countries needed additional workers. Later on, immigration barriers were erected as the economic situation deteriorated. Since the oil crisis of 1973/1974, possibilities for immigration have been reduced. However, migrants have settled with their families in immigration countries. Most often, they did not return to their countries of origin. These migrations were thus permanent, even if some of the factors that caused these population movements no longer are of the same importance. In Europe, the debate on migration defines Southern countries as regions from which poor migrants try to migrate to rich Western countries (Gourvish and Wilson, 1994). This implies that racism has become an important factor of ideological processes that accompany immigrations to richer countries. The recent huge flows of migrants coming from Syria via Eastern Europe to Germany and from North Africa to Italy reflect this link.

SOCIAL TRANSFORMATIONS IN WESTERN SOCIETIES

Often, migrants live in highly developed regions, such as the capitals of the immigration countries. They work mainly in industry and services. These minorities have difficulties getting skilled jobs and their salaries are lower than those of native populations.

They often have precarious jobs that only require a short training period. They are exposed to discriminations. In the capitals, an ethnic stratification can be found according to their country of origin. With the aging of the population in many Northern countries, immigrants are on the political agenda. But governments continue to have difficulties with the acceptance of even qualified immigrants, given the high unemployment rate among poorly qualified local people. Both intellectuals and UN agencies such as the International Organization for Migration are trying to change public opinion, but with little success (see the multiple recorded attacks in Eastern Germany on asylum-seekers' homes in 2015 and 2016).

MIGRANTS CREATE NEW SOCIAL RELATIONS

The case studies below show aspects and new situations of the life–worlds of migrants in various regions of the world. These groups have created new social relations with their countries. The family at home asks migrants for support because their migration is accompanied by an upward social movement. However, the lifestyles of these social actors are highly ambiguous and stressful. International migration connects them to a social system that is outside the familiar world they know. The case studies in this chapter show various adaptation strategies and possible influences of these migrants in their countries of origin and immigration. It becomes clear that the lifestyles of these migrants are characterized by the problematic connection between the North and the South.

International communications, television, and global travelling have contributed to an increasing number of groups belonging to one common world. Future migrants are relatives or friends of better-off migrants who have migrated to the wealthier northern countries. They also want to migrate because of an unchanged situation in their southern home country.

CASE STUDY

RESEARCH INSIGHTS: TRANSNATIONAL FAMILIES

The study of Patricia Landolt and Wei-Wei Da asks the question how physical distance and mobility lead to a reinvention of family practices and gender roles in transnational families, such as child rearing, care, and education. The authors compare multi-locational family practices of two different groups of immigrants: the immigration and emigration contexts of migrants from El Salvador to the United States and Chinese migrants to Australia. They examine transnational practices and their interpretation by family members, and in particular mothers/fathers and wives/husbands. Migration disrupts the family structure; members now live in different cities and countries, in other economic, social, political, and cultural contexts. This movement changes the established power and status structure within the family. There is evidence that permanent multi-local families are becoming more common and the embedding of a reunited family is more and more questioned by the society of the host country. The analysis of detailed interviews with family members shows these new family practices. The results suggest that there are families that do not care to be located at a single location, so that even if a mother-father-child unit exists in one place (the host country), other members (grandparents, aunts, and cousins) continue to play an important role in family practices (care, money transfers, etc.). Furthermore, the imperatives of gender-specific labour migration of female and male migrants to different countries and sectors are emerging, so that men, women, and young people act in different social networks and in different geographical locations. In the case study of El Salvador, the authors found the following elements: the creation of a larger kinship system, unmarried couples, a high number of children within the central couple's relationship as well as in other relationships among couples, whose children were born at secondary sites. The elderly and children can switch and move back and forth, so that households in El Salvador are increasingly spread.

Flexible features also characterize the families of overseas Chinese: men and women are separated and grandparents in China often educate the children. Women display the same mobility as men, so that immigration helps to break traditional family hierarchies and give women more power. Transnational family practices are individualized, a fact that is connected with a frequent unsuccessful economic integration in the host country.

In the last ten years, these transnational family practices have increased. They are linked to new phenomena such as care workers from the South or East coming to the North and caring for children, the elderly, or dependent persons in host countries. In Germany or Italy, this sector is well developed even if care workers are often irregular migrants when they come from outside the EU or have bad job perspectives due to language barriers if they come from Eastern European countries. Even if family members live separated from each other, they maintain solidarity and create a feeling of unity that is maintained by crossing borders virtually (via the Internet and mobile phones) or – if the migrants have a regular migration status in the host country – through travelling back home to their family. Often, migration is seen as a positive factor that improves the living conditions of the family (e.g. health of family members, education of children). However, increasing transnational motherhoods create new problems with children that are raised by grandmothers or other family members left behind. The absence of the mother and/or the father affects the development of these children. In some Eastern European countries, such as Romania, whole generations are concerned, but our understanding of these situations is still in its infancy.

Source: Landolt, P. and Da, W.-W. (2005) 'The spatially ruptured practices of migrant families: A comparison of immigrants from El Salvador and the People's Republic of China,' *Current Sociology* 53(4): 625–653; and some inputs taken from: Confederation of Family Organisations in the European Union (2012) 'Transnational families and the impact of economic migration on families'. Brussels. Available at http://coface-eu.org/en/upload/03_Policies_WG1/2012%20COFACE%20position%20on%20Transnational%20Families%20en.pdf (accessed 10 October 2016).

THE GLOBAL SYSTEM AND MIGRATION

Authors like Wallerstein (2004) and Sassen (2014) have shown that the global system forms a complex structure. The international labour movement is oriented by the mobility of international capital, although in the opposite direction. One can support the hypothesis that the pace of trade liberalization has been faster than that of international labour movements. According to Sassen (2014), the delocalization of foreign investment from the North to the South has triggered migrations from the countries of the South to the North. Migration processes are related to the ideological and material systems that have been introduced by former colonial powers and to continuous processes of market expansion (Massey et al., 1998). Two of the main explanations for the rather slow rate of international migration are restrictive migration policies and regulations such as visa restrictions, border and interior controls. Language and education differences are further factors that contribute to the fact that people prefer staying with friends and families.

GLOBAL CITIES

The theory of global systems (Wallerstein, 2004) has emphasized that transnational migrations are directed towards global cities. These cities have special characteristics, such as being the headquarters of transnational corporations and the place of huge capital flows. The direction of these migrations shows the importance of these cities, their lifestyles, and the consumer goods found there for growing groups in the South. Economic, social, and political transformations of the postmodern age, the end of the apartheid regime in South Africa, as well as wars, famines, and crises in the countries of the South affect transnational migrations. For many countries of the South, migration is an aspect of the social crisis that accompanies their integration into a global system and their social and economic development. The population growth rate and the green revolution in rural areas have led to migrations of large groups into overcrowded cities, where few job opportunities exist and where conditions are often dramatic.

MIGRATION TRENDS

What are the trends of the transnational migrations for the third and fourth decade of the twenty-first century? Migration processes influence more and more countries so that an increase of the diversity of the countries of origin becomes noticeable in Northern countries (Portes, 1997). The economic, social, and cultural origins of migrants in most regions differ greatly. One can only hope that transnational migrations are followed by a type of development of the countries of the South and the East that will lead to economic growth and jobs. Northern countries control borders in order to avoid unwanted migration flows. However, long-term solutions are needed to reduce the migratory pressure. These measures are closely linked to the debate on development strategies of Southern countries. These strategies include trade policies, development aid, regional integration, and international relations.

DEVELOPMENT DIFFERENCES

In general, development differences between the various categories of countries are too large to allow high labour mobility between the North and the East or the South. Political strategies to limit immigrations play a growing role in international relations. Nevertheless, neither restrictions nor development strategies can stop transnational migrations because of the existence of important structural elements that result from the unequal global system. For the foreseeable future, the international community will be forced to accept migrations. But the globalization of migrations also offers an optimistic perspective – there is some hope that a growing global unity can be constructed on our planet, a unity that will allow us to tackle important social transformation processes.

As long as the increasing disparity between rich and poor countries continues and the policies of developed countries don't tackle economic resources in the South, including labour, migration from the South and the East to the North will continue. Migration processes are discussed in political debates. A better knowledge of international migration flows and the impact of governmental decisions on migration patterns, causes, and impacts will allow a glimpse into the new world order of the twenty-first century.

A uniform South does not exist and the impact of migrations is not the same in all countries of the South or the North. The analysis of the link between development and migration leads us to expect increasing transnational migration flows within the South and between the South or the East and the North. Per capita incomes rise in the South and the East. These development processes induce migration as an option for parts of the populations in the South and the East. In most cases, migration is a small development factor in the global world due to the rather limited number of 3.3 per cent of international migrants worldwide in 2015.

MIGRANTS MAY IMPROVE THEIR QUALITY OF LIFE

Migration cannot only help people to increase their income, but also acquire new skills, improve their social status, reduce child mortality, increase human capital development, and, generally, improve their quality of life. Transfers not only reduce poverty, but also support the population in the regions of origin in case of crises, such as natural disasters, conflicts, or economic decline. The IOM report (2013) writes: 'Findings from Nepal, for example, show that almost 20 per cent of the decline in poverty between 1995 and 2004 can be attributed to the remittances sent back home by labour migrants (European Union, 2013: 173). Remittances also make education accessible to members of the migrants' families who remain in the country of origin. Jobs may be created and entrepreneurship developed (Ratha et al., 2011).'

THE TRAGEDY OF THE 2015 REFUGEE CRISIS

The image of Alan Kurdi, a three-year old boy whose dead body washed up the beach in Turkey in September 2015, jolted the conscience of the world; it brought the refugee crisis home. In 2015, over a million refugees reached Europe to escape from war. Europe received 190,960 refugees and asylum-seekers by sea from the war-affected regions of the Middle East and West Asia (as of 25 May 2016, according to the UN Refugee Agency). Syria, Afghanistan, and Iraq accounted for 75 per cent of all refugees. There were migrants from Pakistan and Nigeria, as well. In 2015, nearly 4,000 refugees were drowned as they embarked on a perilous journey on flimsy, overcrowded boats. According to International Organization for Migration, 3,771 died crossing the Mediterranean in 2015. Worldwide, this figure reached 5,350. At the time of writing in 2016, according to UNHCR, 1,375 are presumed dead or missing.

Why would families take such risk? What accounts for such desperation? Perhaps the risk of being bombed to death in the crossfire of a pointless, mindless, and seemingly endless civil war was higher than being drowned in the Mediterranean Sea. It was a choice between two dangerously lethal options. Many chose what they believed to be the less dangerous alternative. It is a real tragedy when such a cruel and dangerous calculus is imposed on people who prefer to live in relative peace in their own communities. In fact, until the onset of the disastrous civil war in 2013, Syria was a country receiving refugees.

The European refugee crises can be read in many ways. First, it is a direct outcome of a callous war imposed on everyday people by external aggressors with neoimperial motives. One may tend to dismiss this reading by labelling it as a radical, anti-Western refrain. Second, it could be seen as a well-intentioned intervention by the champions of democracy and human rights, who sought to 'free' the Syrians (and before them, the Iraqis) from the oppression of local tyrants. As the war progressed, the difference between the external and the internal blurred. It became too messy to identify friends and foes, and yesterday's enemy became today's friend.

Citizens of the war-affected countries became persons without states; once people with dignity, they become faceless refugees. In the unfolding crisis, there are many levels of victimization, cruelty, and inhumanity. It is first and foremost a crisis of the global inter-state system that creates refugees. To label it as a 'crisis of refugees' is to blame the victims.

In the discussion of governance, one of the most frequently heard phrases is accountability. Let us talk about accountability at the level of global governance. Who is accountable for this crisis?

Europe faces the brunt of the refugee crisis; it has become the beachhead of the West. Viewed from the 28-nation European Union, it is a refugee crisis, especially from the point of view of countries that had little or nothing to do with causing the tragedy. The resentment in some European countries is understandable. The Prime Minister of Slovakia is not wrong when he said that Slovakia did not bomb the refugee-sending countries. While for some countries, helping refugees is only a humanitarian responsibility, others bear a direct responsibility for creating them. Though its actions do not hold it entirely blameless, the whole of Europe does not owe shelter to all the refugees and migrants; yet, all of Europe bears part of a shared responsibility. The United States of America also shirks its responsibility to provide a home to people who they made homeless in the name of regime change.

Why should there not be a case of global liability? Why are the USA and its warring allies not held accountable for creating a catastrophe for which they bear direct responsibility? Shouldn't the USA take the lead in rehabilitating the refugees? At least, they should do their best to restore peace so that a large number of refugees can return home to their communities. USA shops post the warning, 'You broke it you buy it,' as a reasonable guideline on the rules of liability. This, or, 'you broke it and you must fix it, or pay for it' may apply to international politics, as well. The USA (and the United Kingdom) broke Iraq, hence the USA – not Europe – bears the responsibility for reparation. In the case of Libya, it is France and the NATO allies who bear the responsibility, though the USA was surely the instigator, the main campaigner for regime change. In this case, a dual liability is in order. The case of Syria is a case of multi-party liability. The refugee crisis is a perfect example of a man-made disaster. [...] International laws for maintaining peace and order were written largely by the USA and the United Kingdom in the post-World War II period; now these powers, according to Philippe Sands (2005), broke the same laws.

In the end, perspectives from the sociology of development may be drawn to analyze the events. Dividing refugees into two types of – political and economic – is inadequate in the analysis of the European refugee crises. Yes, some are political refugees who were forced to flee their tyrannical rulers, and some are economic refugees looking for bread and shelter. In this case, two other categories should be added: a vast majority of war refugees, and a minority of opportunistic refugees who are not from the region of turmoil but were quick to jump on the bandwagon. The four types of refugees – political, economic, war, and opportunistic – need to be dealt with differently. There cannot be one response that would fit all refugee categories.

The refugees, the economic migrants, and the economically disenfranchised who look for opportunities to move to a better place in the global market are all products of the injustices of a world order for which we, as members of the world society, must take responsibility and action.

Source: Khondker, H.H. (2016: 7–10) in the Newsletter of the Research Committee 09 of the International Sociological Association, Summer. Available at http://www.isa-sociology. org/uploads/files/rc09newsletter_summer_2016.pdf (accessed 17 December 2016).

Reproduced with permission.

CLIMATIC TURN IN MIGRATION STUDIES? (FELGENTREFF AND POTT)

Looking at the rapidly growing stock of literature linking climate change and migration, one could find evidence that there seems to be a 'climatic turn' (Neverla, 2007) concerning the explanation of migration. Climate change and its relevance for migration has undoubtedly developed into a strong argument, be it in migration research or in climate impact studies. Interestingly, already in the 19th century, scholars like Friedrich Ratzel and Ernest George Ravenstein considered 'climate' or 'environment' as relevant factors for triggering human mobility, although generally subordinated to other factors (Piguet, 2013: 149). These assumed drivers of migration have been neglected for most of the last century. However, since Essam El-Hinnawi (1985) published an influential report for the United Nations Environmental Program in which he coined the term 'environmental refugee', the idea that natural environments can force people to move, is back on the agenda. Ever since, we have witnessed a dynamic inter- and transdisciplinary field of research on the relation of climate and migration. In this field, environmental and climate scientists as well as scholars from social sciences and humanities participate. From the very beginning, geographers were engaged in this endeavor, too. This is hardly surprising as it is the main goal of geography to bridge the gap between human and physical sciences; therefore geographers seem predestined to contribute to the debate. Certainly, the geographical contribution is just as diverse as the interdisciplinary field itself. It differs in scope and scale, but also in perspective and epistemological position. [...]

While in the context of 'climate and migration' studies more and more empirical investigations are funded, conducted and published, important methodological problems remain unsolved. There is no consensus on how the assumed nexus should be conceived theoretically and how – in accordance to the conceptual decision – it should be approached in empirical research. Did migration researchers, for instance, miss that climatic and ecological conditions are important determinants of human behavior? Are there specific kinds of locations where coupled natural and human systems are put under additional pressure by climate? Or can migration be sufficiently explained by well-known conditions and factors like uneven economic development, educational aspirations, poverty, social networks or vulnerability of precarious livelihood systems? What role do spatial constructions, socio-technical arrangements, images of climate change or figures and calculations play? Should we not pay more

CASE STUDY

attention to power, interest groups, communication and the social production of nature? Do we witness a new migration regime when it comes to climate or environmentally induced migrants? In which discourses and political frameworks do we encounter such migrants?

Against the backdrop of the differentiated research landscape on 'climate migration', recent developments in social and cultural geography bear the potential to productively tie in with current research problems in the context of climate change and migration. Constructivist approaches (let them be action or practice theory, discourse theory or poststructuralist approaches), observer-related conceptualisations of space, or assemblage thinking, hybridity and actor-network theory have all strongly influenced human geography in the last two decades. In particular, debates in the wake of the *cultural turn* could inspire fruitful, but rarely adopted perspectives. They might help to shed new light on 'climate migration' without necessarily calling for a 'climatic turn' (Neverla, 2007) in migration studies or geography. The sensitivity for social and spatial contexts, the insights into the 'maps of meaning' (Jackson, 1989) and the production of significance, the various findings about knowledge production and the political power of scientific description – they all raise particular questions, stimulate to rethink our conceptual framing and ask for geographical inquiry [...].

Source: Felgentreff, C. and Pott, A. (2016) 'Climatic turn in migration studies? Geographical perspectives on the relationship between climate and migration,' *DIE ERDE* 147 (2): 73–80.

Published by permission of the authors and *DIE ERDE*.

CONCLUDING REMARKS

Which conclusions can be drawn on the issue of transnational migrations and social changes? The three case studies display multiple aspects of the relationship between migration and transformation that I have outlined in this chapter. The result is an image of a global world that is connected by transnational migrants. Today, we can no longer take the existence of different geographical units for granted. We are faced with cultures that are influenced by transnational migrations, tourism, international communication flows, transnational corporations, and international organizations.

The end of the East–West bipolarity led to the emergence of a new political world order. The economic, political, and social changes that accompanied this process have affected migrations. The existing large imbalance between the developed world and the world that still 'needs to develop/be developed,' has led to mass migrations. Migrants' remittances help to promote the development of their origin regions so that migration plays a role in international development policy (see Faist, 2014). Even if migrants are seen as a threat in immigration countries and as an inevitable consequence of poverty in the countries of the South, this phenomenon will persist in the coming decades. International migration affects social hierarchies, and immigrant families who live across national borders belong to different but linked geographical contexts.

THE CHALLENGE OF TRANSNATIONAL MIGRATIONS

Today, transnational migrations in a global world are a challenge for disciplines such as sociology and social anthropology whose empirical research has been restricted more or less by national borders. Most scholars are not accustomed to do fieldwork in more than one region. The short case studies presented here show that multiregional field studies are needed in order to analyze social changes triggered by transnational migrants who define themselves by their dual affiliation. This chapter shows that the classical analysis of migration processes in the immigration context has outlived its usefulness. Today, the development of regions with high emigration and immigration rates ask for a sociology that has to conduct its studies in more than one region in a global world.

When one considers the link between migration and development, experts, think tanks, and multilateral organizations have given economic arguments for the benefits of increased labour mobility. The ageing of populations in the North already leads to increasing demands for young workers in economies that have to overcome labour shortages. Moreover, if not enough actions to deal with climate change are taken, natural disasters are likely to have a huge influence on labour mobility.

GROWING NUMBERS OF MIGRANTS

One can conclude by arguing that the free movement of goods and money should be followed by a free movement of people and by growing numbers of migrants. Some of the structural causes of migrations have been evoked: persisting economic inequalities and an uneven globalization. It is probably up to politicians and international elites to change high international inequality levels that cause migrations so that possible migrants no longer decide to leave friends and families behind and migrate to places where access is often denied or difficult. Nevertheless, if employers recruit foreign workers who would be unemployed in their country, if these men and women send remittances, and if returning migrants use skills they have learned abroad to raise their income at home, migration contributes to development. Remittances that exceeded USD 1 billion a day in 2012 (IOM, 2013: 70) can be used to develop Southern countries. Social and 'political' remittances linked to travelling and returned migrants help change cultural elements of societies (e.g. supporting girls' education and changed female roles in society). New skills introduced by returned migrants may lead to new industries and jobs. Today, people move back and forth between countries and even multiple destinations. Higher levels of circulation thus characterize global migration flows and migrants come from a wider range of countries than ever before (IOM, 2013: 110).

DISCUSSION QUESTIONS

1.   What is the link between development and remittances?

2.   Please discuss theories on migration and development.

3.   What are the convergence and the divergence effects of migrations?

4.   What do you know about the 2015 refugee crisis in Europe?

5.   What are the social consequences of the climatic global turn?

ANNOTATED FURTHER READINGS

Haynes, A., Power, M.J., Devereux, E., Dillane, A. and Carr, J. (2016) *Public and Political Discourses on Migration: International Perspectives.* **London and New York: Rowman & Littlefield International.**
Discourses frame the issue of migration and are of crucial importance as they influence both the general public's perception of migration and the policies of national governments. This book brings together scholars whose work addresses the question of whose interests are served by prevailing discourses and the structures they underpin.

Parkes, R. (2016) *People on the Move: The New Global (Dis)order.* **Paris: EU Institute for Security Studies. Available at http://www.iss.europa.eu/uploads/media/Chaillot_Paper_138.pdf (accessed 11 October 2016).**
This paper analyzes the factors that have generated the migration crisis of 2015. It argues that a new strategy on migration and refugees is necessary in order to provide people with opportunities as close to home as possible.

Kahanec, M. and Zimmermann, K.F. (eds) (2016) *Labor Migration, EU Enlargement, and the Great Recession.* **Berlin and Heidelberg: Springer.**
This volume examines cross-border mobility and its role in an enlarged European Union. It discusses the experience of receiving and sending countries with post-enlargement migration and its role during the current crisis. Furthermore, post-enlargement mobility and its impact on economic shocks and on the European welfare systems are tackled.

Freeman, G. P. and Mirilovic, N. (2016) *Handbook on Migration and Social Policy.*
Cheltenham and Northampton, MA: Edward Elgar Publishing.
In this handbook, the consequences of migration for the social policies of rich
welfare states are analyzed. The chapters discuss the impact of migration on the
financial, social, and political stability of social programs in Europe, North America,
Australasia, the Middle East and South Asia.

Websites

http://blogs.worldbank.org/peoplemove/
A blog on migration, remittances, and development.

http://www.worldbank.org/en/topic/migrationremittancesdiasporaissues
An important part of the World Bank's work on migration and remittances involves efforts
to monitor and forecast remittance and migration flows, and to provide timely analysis on
topics such as remittances, migration, and diaspora issues.

http://www.iom.int/
Established in 1951, the International Organization for Migration is the leading intergovernmental organization in the field of migration and works closely with governmental,
intergovernmental, and non-governmental partners.

http://www.isa-sociology.org/rc31.htm
Research Committee on Sociology of Migration RC31 of the International Sociological
Association.

http://www.migrationpolicy.org/article/transnational-migrants-when-home-means-more-
one-country
The Migration Policy Institute is a think tank in Washington, DC dedicated to the analysis
of the movement of people worldwide.

http://www.oecd.org/migration/international-migration-outlook-1999124x.htm
This publication on migration analyzes recent developments in migration movements
and policies in Organization for Economic Co-operation and Development countries
and selected non-OECD countries. It also includes Country notes and a Statistical
Annex.

http://www.sussex.ac.uk/migration/
One of the first centres on Migration in the United Kingdom, the Sussex Centre for
Migration Research (SCMR) builds on a longstanding reputation for original theoretically
driven empirical research in the field of migration and ethnic relations. Sussex hosts one
of the largest groups of migration scholars in the world.

http://www.un.org/en/development/desa/population/
United Nations Department of Economic and Social Affairs, Population Division, International Migration.

(all websites accessed 11 October 2016)

NOTES

1 See http://www.un.org/sustainabledevelopment/blog/2016/01/244-million-international-migrants-living-abroad-worldwide-new-un-statistics-reveal/ (accessed 17 December 2016).
2 Available at http://www.iom.sk/en/about-migration/migration-in-the-world (accessed 24 October 2016).

6

SOCIO-ECONOMIC IMPACTS OF THE GLOBAL FINANCIAL CRISIS

Summary

This chapter has its origins in a comparative research project involving extensive collection and analysis of primary and secondary materials (scholarly literature, statistical data, and interviews with key actors) on socio-economic outcomes of the global financial crisis in all major world regions during the last years. Offering analytical and comparative insights at the global level, as well as an assessment of the overall social globalization phenomenon, the theoretical overview and the case studies will be useful for scholars, students, NGOs, and policy makers who try to understand the still ongoing outcomes of the financial crises of 2007/2009.

INTRODUCTION

The first part of this chapter consists of an analysis of the notions of crisis and conflict, and their importance for social change. My goal is to contribute to an understanding of the concept of crisis and to possible openings that a theory of social transformations can provide. In addition, I want to show how research on social change can suggest outcomes as well as possible reactions in a time of crises.

A MORE RATIONAL HANDLING OF CRISIS SITUATIONS

This chapter will contribute to an *ex-post* analysis of the global reactions from autumn 2008 to summer 2011, an analysis that will permit a more rational handling of future open-ended crisis situations. It is well known that media, politicians, employers, and bankers were involved in a global network of information (news around the clock and the different time zones) that reproduced feelings on the financial crisis, which had little to do with rational actions. In fact, the crisis had a global character.

However, according to their economic, political, and cultural thinking, authoritarian elites were reluctant to act in a global space (e.g. in the global stock exchange market) on a topic that affected peoples and states in a global world where these elites had originally only supported worldviews linked to the national space.

I will show to what extent the weakness of neoliberalism, the doubtfulness of economic thinking on the *free* market as well as the ambiguous global economic future left banking professionals, media, employers, and politicians with few opportunities to act rationally. The credo of the neoliberal economy was challenged by the financial crisis and individual voices – even from scientific economists – evoked the end of the neoliberal era and the *free* market. As economic theory struggles to provide unique theoretical and empirical results, I'll compare different sociological traditions on the notions of conflict and crisis, namely those of scholars such as H. de Saint-Simon, E. Durkheim (Emirbayer, 2003), E. Morin (1973, 1976), A. Touraine (2000), and G. Balandier (1968), who tried to analyze both concepts in pioneering publications. This understanding of the concept of crisis allows providing a rational explanation of the financial crisis on the basis of observation, analysis, and interpretation in order to present possible sociological and socio-economic outcomes of a critical-historical analysis of the current economy.

THE STUDY OF CRISIS IS JUST BEGINNING

Since the global financial crisis, the sociology of conflicts has developed policies and measures in order to objectively approach and improve the definition of crisis situations and phenomena. These tools show the breakthroughs and maladjustments in the transformation of social systems. In fact, people make history and people contribute to events that are associated with history.

I will show that the effective margins of activities of human beings in crisis situations are rather small, but nevertheless they exist, so that a kind of optimism is permitted. People do not want to suffer history: they are active participants, although mostly a relatively small group decides on historical processes, compared to the majority of the population, which is dominated by media, Internet, and public opinion.

THE BEGINNING OF SOCIOLOGY AS A SCIENCE AND THE CONCEPTION OF CRISES

Already at the beginning of sociology as a science, Henri de Saint-Simon was interested in crises. Saint-Simon considered the late eighteenth century and the early nineteenth century as a period in which the social order was exposed to significant changes. At that time, societies largely altered their structures; this transformation gave rise to differences, breaks, and profound changes. Knowledge about societies – in the opinion of de Saint-Simon – could only be obtained with knowledge about changes and social transformations (Ansart, 1969). Nevertheless, these processes only became obvious after a more or less long-lasting period of conflicts. Saint-Simon coined the notion of transition (e.g. the time period when the society changes) through the concept of crisis. According to him, various elements were in opposition to each other. Breaks could occur and differences between coexisting orders could arise. Thus, the formation of a new society, marked by other structures, was possible. It is precisely this dynamic of conflicts that contributes to the changes in a society according to Saint-Simon, rather than the disorder linked to a crisis.

ÉMILE DURKHEIM

Half a century later, Émile Durkheim began a new theorization of crises. He distinguished real structures and their physical support (e.g. territories and populations), which had relatively stable forms and institutions (e.g. norms and obligations regulating the activities of social actors) and collective representations (e.g. values and ideals, ideas and social media), which were rather autonomous and had a creative potential, so that they could become important drivers of change. This thinking came close to what the famous French sociologist G. Balandier wrote some years ago: crises are inevitable periods of societies that create a portion of their future characteristics in these moments (1968: 74). In fact, in a crisis, the different levels of a society do not correspond to each other and manifest fractures and breaks that form the basis of a future social structure.

According to Durkheim, the concept of *anomie* refers to a cultural crisis, when the differentiation at the origin of norms, values, and rules that organize social ties disappears; when economic anarchy arises and some institutions reach a critical point (Balandier, 1978: 75).

THE BIRTH OF THE SCIENTIFIC TREATMENT OF CRISES

Despite these early scientific studies, analyzing breaks and rapid changes, crises have always been a secondary research topic in sociology. Nevertheless, the breakthrough of using models in systems theory in the late 1970s allowed an analysis of the interaction of various elements and the connections between complex units and external events. In addition, the functioning of elements in uncertain circumstances was evaluated. This research setting has contributed to the renewal of the analysis of crises.

CREATIVE CHANGES

Moreover, focusing on the concept of 'the event' in history implies the analysis of creative changes that are characterized by a lack of stability. Diachronic processes were also included in these studies. The connections between events should then cause convergent or divergent processes. According to French historian Georges Duby (1973), there are two types of events. One kind of event can be found in the memory of human actors: it is clear or unclear, changing or firm. Another type of event is composed of historical documents (letters, official documents, etc.) that form concrete memories.

DIALECTICAL MODELS

For a long time, the models of social dynamics were only dialectical models. But in the 1970s, the American strand of researchers who dealt with social systems (e.g. Bertalanffy) suggested instruments to grasp the social dynamics in formal models. Etzioni and Deutsch (see Parrochia, 2008) developed an understanding of sociology which tried to capture the interactions within the changing equilibrium of a system and its surroundings. The social system was defined as a dynamic and changing system in interaction with other elements (people) who – according to certain rules – interact in subgroups. The entire process takes place with the help of various internal transformations over a certain period of time. One could therefore describe the functioning of the social system and collect information about slow or fast changes that were dependent on the social environment and/or on different endogenous elements and structures.

THE FOCUS ON STRUCTURES

The focus on structures and synchronic processes prevented an understanding of the events, which allowed the change of structures and their replacement. René Thom and his theory of catastrophes (1979) finally made a systematic analysis of crises possible. This scholar argued that continuous models and their discontinuous aspects functioned in social, natural, and historical contexts.

Some time later, in order to study the link between structures and events, the systemic approach of Edgar Morin (1973, 1976) suggested an analysis of complexity. According to him, the difference between organizations and disorganizations can be shown in living systems and in historical societies. As Morin stressed (1976: 154), there may be positive feedback, such as economic growth, which can regulate disorder and crises, when new needs and/or new stresses appear. Nevertheless, these considerations were rather vague, and it was only when system theory remembered the idea of deterministic chaos that fractures and breaks could finally be explained.

According to Claude Rivière (1978), a conflict is a rather normal fact that can trigger contradictions as part of life. Balandier (1951, 1988) has pointed out that social crises leading to a dynamic break are opposed to normal dynamic and adaptive transformations. Every social order is thus in a sense problematic, so that every society is exposed at regular intervals to phenomena that show their own imperfections in the form of confrontations, conflicts, and crises. These latter show the shortcomings of social systems and manifest cultural forms and links that need to be surpassed by new and better forms.

CRISES AS CONTRADICTIONS OF ELEMENTS

Rivière (1978) developed a number of interesting studies that showed the 'extreme' complexity of current social systems and their potential to create and modify life. When crises reveal deep contradictions, the results are unstable systems so that the entire functioning of the system is disturbed. If uncertain situations appear in regular stable systems, people feel that a break occurred and they try to find new and often better solutions. Latent antagonisms create new situations that either maintain the integrity of a system or lead to a break. In most cases, politicians in particular look for solutions – they try to find positive results; they can decide to adopt temporary solutions and neglect others. For instance: 'The end of market ideology' could be heard during the financial crisis. Practical creativity is thus required in order to develop more customized solutions from those that may have worked during earlier crises.

CONFLICTS AS MISMATCHES

According to Rivière (1978), conflicts in modern societies are caused by mismatches between moving forces and institutions, between ideological equality and real inequality, between the longing for success and the lack of opportunities. Several outcomes are possible. Both groups may try to eliminate or weaken the other side; or the opposition may be bypassed by innovative solutions that enable the acceptance of new resources and that modify the demand side. These situations show that crises are closely linked to conflicts. As Touraine has shown (2000), social conflicts highlight political contradictions in economic systems, whereas crises are related to the interaction between institutions and their historical connections. This understanding is different from the historical class struggle of the Marxist ideology. According to Touraine (2000), crises are currently not linked to the opposition of capital and labour. If we look at the great crisis of 1989, the socialist economy was at that time a centralized and bureaucratic system that could only be changed by an economic crisis, which finally meant the ideological breakthrough of the neoliberal economy of Western origin.

CRISES AND CONFLICTS

There is a further divergence of the two notions: the outcomes of crises and conflicts are different. On the one side, crises are resolved by asking for the coherence of social, cultural, and economic systems (Galtung, 1984); they are similar to the decisions of politicians at the apogee of the recent global financial crisis. These men and women tried to cope with the crisis by lending public money to banks (Krier, 2009) so that a few months later, the banks could begin to repay these credits: the continued functioning of the neoliberal economic system was ensured. On the other side, conflicts reveal structural contradictions of the whole system (e.g. the 1989 system break in Eastern Europe), which can only be resolved by a structural change of the system or, as Touraine emphasized, by a 'revolution.' A crisis lets ideas and social beliefs on given topics with their weak and strong sides appear. Today, global crises are thus periodic phenomena based no longer on only endogenous factors but on global forces and structures (see Gross, 2007; Schuerkens, 2009).

THE GLOBAL COMMUNICATION NETWORK AND THE FINANCIAL CRISIS

The problem with the recent financial crisis was that the global communication network was no longer controlled by responsible people, but by an irrational belief in numbers. Journalists gave the mass media ceaseless comments, so that the activities and reactions of bankers on the stock markets were published as news around the clock. The future after the crisis was and is still uncertain, and the reactions of the employees of the financial sector are still difficult to predict, such as in the recent (spring 2016) financial situation in China that has shown high debt levels of local authorities and a devaluation of the Chinese currency, or the financial crisis in emerging markets in early 2014. In order to find a solution, politics and media have realized that they cannot remain passive when bankers act irrationally. The basic rules of the complex neoliberal socio-economic system must therefore be understood, so that a global crash with an uncertain economic future can be prevented.

SOME EMPIRICAL EVIDENCE OF THE RECENT FINANCIAL CRISIS IN VARIOUS REGIONS OF THE WORLD

First of all, the recent global crisis was not only a financial, but also a structural crisis. This process meant the end of a model: that of the powerful and insatiable consumer, that of the saver who is confident in the financial system, and that of the producer who believes resources are inexhaustible. Therefore, one should not confuse a moment of the cycle with a possible end of the crisis. In fact, globalization means that every economy in the world is concerned with international trade. Globalization (transnational flows of goods, people, and cultural elements) has contributed to the global spread of the crisis.

What has been important during the crisis was a certain incompatibility between the globalization of the economic system and the political rules that remain more or less on a national level. In this sense, this crisis cannot be overcome by national responses, but only by claims for global solutions. A socialization of the financial losses due to the nationalization of banks has been one of the chosen measures, but most governments have also adopted the injection of liquidities into banks. Since the crisis has been systemic, it has triggered financial, economic, social, and environmental impacts with a time lag.

A TRANSFORMATION OF GLOBAL CAPITALISM

The systemic crisis of recent years has meant a transformation of global capitalism by shifting its centre of gravity and increasing the importance of new areas, countries, and political forces. There has been a transformation of global trade, international production, and the role of emerging economies. Transnational corporations, often those based in the Triad countries (USA, EU, Japan), represent one-third of world production and two-thirds of global trade (of which one half is dedicated to the closed trade between headquarters and subsidiaries). Although the origin of these enterprises is frequently still in the First World, the importance of the emerging economies of the Second World (e.g. Mexico, Russia, Brazil) continues to grow. This means that the bipolar world of the Cold War has changed in the last years to a multipolar world, which is characterized by the emergence of new economic, political, and military powers. In fact, China and some other emerging economies – due to their large dollar purchases – could now be deemed the treasurers of the United States. The balance of the international financial system is being challenged, and voices have been raised asking for a change in the still important role of the US dollar. However, China is interested in maintaining the current system, because the country has large amounts of US dollars. The recent political and economic power shift took place from the West to the East, with the rise of China and India, as well as some Arab oil countries. China and India currently play an important role in Africa and South America, mainly due to their high financial commitment. This 'second' world is interested in obtaining positions in the international governance structure (UN). Brazil, Russia, India, and China (BRIC countries) have already realized a change with their involvement in the G20, even if they are still poorly represented when local events are debated, such as the Libya intervention in 2011 of the United States, Great Britain, and France. The reaction of the BRIC countries was not to vote the military intervention but only to express their negative feelings. Moreover, in March 2014, Russia was suspended from the elite G8 group of leading economies, which said they could not accept its breach of international law in the Crimean crisis. Most often, former political rivalries among the BRIC states avoid the expression of common political ideas. The BRIC states are thus a common economic forum that reunites powerful countries which form huge parts of the global economy. Most often, the interests of ruling family groups are not different from ideas of political and economic elites in the triad countries.[1]

THE EMERGENCE OF A MULTIPOLAR WORLD

The global context of the past 20 years has provided the paradigms that have established the character of North-South relations. Global capitalism has seen a shift from the North to the South and to the Far East with some new powers in the Middle East in the last decade. According to IMF data, the BRIC countries represented 40 per cent of the world's population and a third of world gross domestic product (GDP) in purchasing power parities in 2013. Other countries such as Mexico, Indonesia, and Venezuela also play an important role. The evolving role of global capitalism explains this dynamic which correlates with processes of infrastructure development, human resources transformations, and a changing economic climate. Socio-political changes have emerged, such as the rise of the middle classes in China and India, demographic transitions, and social investments in infrastructure (e.g. health and education). The result has been a plurality of developing regimes whose endogenous dynamic is different. Some geographical areas have benefited from globalization, while others have been marginalized. Global capitalism contains both convergent processes for emerging economies and divergent processes for countries where poverty traps are widespread (e.g. sub-Saharan Africa). The reasons can be found in historical processes that link global heterogeneity to technology access and changed production methods within different socio-cultural systems.

WORLD REGIONS

Historically, Asian countries are in a process of regional growth because of enterprises that came at the beginning from Japan and were later on founded by the Chinese diaspora. African countries could not spread on the continent a European model of growth with a technology transfer and an opening up of European markets for industrial products from Africa. African elites find it difficult to introduce new comparative advantages in their macroeconomic policies and continue to rely on primary commodities or, in some countries, on petroleum (e.g. Gabon and Nigeria). Factors affecting economic growth have been the following: 1) the infrastructure quality, 2) the quality and the price of the labour force, and 3) the structural relations of local and foreign enterprises to the local administration.

AN INFLUENCE ON SOCIAL SYSTEMS AND SOCIO-POLITICAL STABILITY

The global financial crisis had not only financial implications – it influenced social systems and socio-political stability. Since huge numbers of people lost jobs and money, they had to cope with difficult financial situations. These people relied on credits in order to increase their consumption. Poverty has thus increased in many regions; some countries have experienced food crises, particularly rural regions (e.g. Niger). In addition, the importance of the role of the state has grown. Emerging markets, which have accumulated enormous financial reserves, have started programs to expand public spending and have focused on an expansion of the *free* market, a policy option which has contributed to continued high growth rates (e.g. in China and Brazil). Some countries (e.g. emerging Asia and the Middle East) were less affected by international commercial shocks than countries with high debt levels (the southern part of Latin America and sub-Saharan Africa).

Nevertheless, the financial crisis had an impact on poor populations throughout the world, as most countries of the South had very limited social security systems (for example, for health, unemployment, and old-age pensions), even if some of them have recently decided to change this situation in the near future (China and parts of Latin America).

THE OUTCOMES OF THE CRISES IN DIFFERENT WORLD REGIONS

What have been the outcomes of the crisis in different world regions? Countries like China were able to expand domestic demand and consumption for a huge domestic market. Moreover, China could invest in its infrastructure. The country continued to expand its economic relations with other Asian countries in the region, so that high growth rates could be achieved in the years following the crisis. However, the sharp corrections in stock markets led to a gradual economic downturn in summer 2015 that had consequences for the world economy.

Only recently, Latin America has seen improved economic performance because of rising prices for primary commodities, but the sub-continent could barely develop a regional momentum for cooperation, except for countries that cooperate with Venezuela and Bolivia. Resistance to the crisis was higher in the major countries of the South than in Central America and the Caribbean. Countries like Brazil are composed of a growing middle class and have the ability to produce goods for final consumption, so that organic growth was ensured by an increase in consumption. In the region, however, hardly any social and income disparities could be reduced even if there have been some tax measures (e.g. an increase of social transfers (Brazil) and income taxes).

The Middle East could better cope with the impact of the crisis because of its enormous financial reserves from the oil boom in the past. But domestic demand was not high, regional cooperation has been limited, and the bourgeoisie has been weak, so that the Arab Spring in 2011 drew protests against long-time corrupt political elites (Tunisia, Libya, Egypt, and Morocco).

Sub-Saharan Africa has been the region that was most affected by the crisis, so that on the continent some of the Millennium Development Goals (MDGs) for 2015 could not be achieved (marginal progress in the reduction of poverty, low gender equality in many countries, low reduction in maternal mortality, etc.). Nevertheless, since the beginning of the millennium – also due to investments from China and India – internal dynamics have contributed to a growing domestic demand of the middle classes and thus an increase in economic growth. The diversification of economic partners in Africa (e.g. China, India, Brazil) and a focus on South-South economic connections have contributed to an improvement in the socio-economic situation in countries that have received financial support. In some regions (e.g. Senegal, Mali) major transfers of remittances from migrants continue to support development efforts. Even if these migrants are trying to cope with difficult situations in their countries of destination, they continue to send their savings in order to support their family members in the respective origin countries.

The economies of the United Kingdom and the United States were particularly affected by the crisis of 2007–2009, by rising unemployment and a decline in GDP in 2009. Canada experienced similar processes; Australia and New Zealand did hardly better than the USA or the United Kingdom. Other countries that are known for their integration in the global economic competition, experienced reductions in their GDP and a rapid increase in unemployment (e.g. Ireland). The European Union (EU) has been at the centre of the crisis with an increase of 0.9 per cent of GDP from 2006 to 2010 (compared to 1.9 per cent in 2015) and an unemployment rate of nearly 10.3 per cent in the Eurozone and 8.9 per cent in the EU-28 in February 2016.[2] A large number of countries show high private debt rates and high rates of real estate speculation. These processes can explain the close links of these economies with the USA as the country where the crisis had begun and in which a similar type of development exists. Specific examples are Spain and Ireland. Here the real estate sector collapsed. Germany, which had recorded a substantial decrease in GDP in 2009, had a fairly high growth rate in the years 2011–2015, so that this 'model' has been interesting for other countries in the EU.

The Baltic States, which had opened up their economies to international trade, saw their GDP rate decline by about 14 per cent in 2009. Meanwhile, their gross domestic product has bounced back with a relatively high growth rate.[3] The states of the former Soviet Union achieved very different results. Depending on their relations with Asian or Western European countries, their development differed. Countries whose economies have been dependent on Asia appear to have better results than those that have cooperated more with the EU. Another recent example is Greece, whose government has for several years received high financial support from the EU and the International Monetary Fund (IMF) in return of strict austerity measures. Subsequently, the Greek population protested against the harsh austerity measures put in place by a government that wanted to implant financial reforms. In 2012, the Greek government began to implement saving measures to reduce the current account deficit: taxes on fuel, tobacco, and alcohol were raised and the retirement age was extended by two years. Thus the global economic downturn created a high level of debt and deficits in many regions of the world.

IN 2011: A NEW FINANCIAL CRISIS

Nevertheless, further questions have been asked. In 2011, a new financial crisis had emerged that influenced the euro region as well as the USA and thus the world economy. But politicians were better prepared and knew that political activities did not change quickly when bankers made risky operations on stock exchanges. However, in the EU region (e.g. France, Greece, Spain, and Portugal), high public debt rates have forced governments to adopt unpopular austerity measures mainly in social sectors (health, education, old-age pensions, etc.) as a consequence of large state assistances to banks in the financial crisis. The result has been a rising poverty of middle classes and poorer groups.

China and India, as the two locomotives of Asia, have limited the global economic downturn not only in Asia but also in the global economy. Political and economic plans to invest in the infrastructure and the internal market were a success, as Chaponnière has shown in his case study below. However, many poor countries of the global South, especially in some sub-Saharan regions of Africa, which are characterized by poor macroeconomic policies with a negative impact on poorer sections of the population (austerity measures) have been unable to cope with the crisis because they have no or only weakly developed social security systems (e.g. health, unemployment, and old-age pensions). Massive protests of these populations have led to political changes of the ruling party or to the independence of the region such as in Sudan (e.g. the conflicts in Thailand (2013–14), Central Africa (2014–15), Mali (2012–13), and the independence of South Sudan (2011–2013)).

GLOBAL HIERARCHY OF STATES

Asian countries and China were able to improve frontline positions in the global worldwide hierarchy of states. China has begun to invest in the countries of Western Europe and to support economic sectors with serious difficulties. Lebaron highlights an interesting fact: the more a country was associated with the neoliberal economic policy, the more its economy had difficulties in the crisis, particularly in terms of growth of GDP and the unemployment rate (2010b: 110). For 2011/2012 this meant that these countries began to enforce their austerity measures to reduce the high government debt, which was created by money that had been issued to banks and enterprises during the management and control of the financial crisis (a practice that was applied in large parts of the EU and the USA).

This also means that there was a crisis of globalization, as the former Triad countries (Europe, USA, and Japan) are no longer the dominant world powers. The importance of Chinese enterprises in accordance with the Fortunes classification (Lebaron, 2010b: 111) is growing, but an alternative to the political discourse of Western countries does not yet exist, as the events in North Africa have shown in the first months of 2011. Nevertheless, China has begun to voice criticism of the USA, the dollar, and the US debt crisis, although this discourse is presented as a cautious assessment. The large dollar reserves China holds mean that the country is not interested in another global financial crash of this important economic partner.

CASE STUDY

THE CRISIS IN ASIA

J. R. Chaponnière shows in his study that in the first decade of the second millennium, Asia was the most dynamic region of the world, with China as the Asian workshop. By mid-2008, the Asian countries held three quarters of the world currency reserves. In exchange for financing their deficit, the United States opened its market to Asian exports; this allowed China to create jobs for hundreds of millions of low-skilled workers. Asian countries responded to the crisis by launching stimulus packages, in the case of China this was extremely ambitious and prioritized investment. Despite these packages, the crisis led to a deterioration of the overall employment rate, so that large groups had to leave the formal sector in order to work in the informal sector. However, in 2011, most Asian countries had reached pre-crisis levels of employment. In the Republic of Korea, workers' wages were cut and temporary work increased. The Philippines saw a shift from the formal to the informal sector due to reduced domestic demand. In other countries of the region, where migrants contribute to support the economic development, the decline in remittances and job losses among migrants resulted in an indirect local impact of the global crisis (e.g. Bangladesh). Nevertheless, the consequences of the crisis in the Asian region were, as expected, less severe than elsewhere in the world. According to World Bank data[4], emerging Asia's growth slowed down to 6.5 per cent in 2009 while Latin American economies contracted (-2.8 per cent) and sub-Saharan African economies slowed down to 0,8 per cent. In China, migrants were the biggest losers of the crisis, as they were sent back to their home region after the closures of enterprises. Their number rose to 225 million in 2009. These migrants are second-class citizens, as they are not entitled to the same social benefits as city dwellers. Chaponnière concludes that the Asian emerging markets are not decoupled from Western economies. What has changed is that the growth in the West is more dependent on Asian wealth than vice versa. As China chose to respond to the global crisis by more investment financed by the State budget and credit expansion, the country deepened its budget imbalance, since the gap between its investments to the GDP ratio (48 per cent) and consumption to the GDP ratio (38 per cent) has no equivalent. Private consumption has never been less than 60 per cent of GDP in Japan or emerging Asian economies, where the rate of investment has never been over 40 per cent of GDP.[5] The investment surge led to a fast and worrying increase of the overall debt ratio (household, enterprises, provinces, and State). Since 2013, as the new Chinese government has advocated a 'new normality' and a rebalancing of the economy, growth is slowing and the production structure evolves. On the demand side, Chinese transition to a consumption-led economy has yet to be materialized as the investment ratio has only slightly diminished; however on the production side, the transition accelerates as new industries (renewable energy, information, and communication) develop rapidly while traditional sectors (such as iron and steel) decline. In the meantime, China – which holds 25 per cent of world savings – has become a large overseas investor. These transformations modify the relations of China with her neighbours through trade and finance channels. Lower exports to China,

(Continued)

CASE STUDY

(Continued)

their main trading partner, also reduce Asian economic growth, while a surge of Chinese direct investment and loans (through the Asian Bank for International Infrastructures or special funds linked to the OneBelt OneRoad ambitious program) deepen their integration.

Source: Chaponnière, J.R. (2012) 'The socioeconomic consequences of the global crisis on Asia,' in U. Schuerkens (ed.) *Socioeconomic Outcomes of the Global Financial Crisis: Theoretical Discussion and Empirical Case Studies.* London and New York: Routledge pp. 191-221 and remarks to the readers of *Futuribles International* (7/2016).

THE OUTCOMES OF THE CRISIS FOR PUBLIC ACTORS, ENTERPRISES, AND THE BANKS

In all world regions, the outcomes of the crisis have led to a changed meaning of public actors because national strategies were implanted to help enterprises and banks in financial difficulties. The outcome of these crises is not the end of history or the end of neoliberalism, but a change in the role of public and private actors in the economic field. States could support enterprises and tried to introduce new rules for the functioning of banks and transnational corporations in order to avoid similar crises in the future and to achieve an improvement of the economic situation. The crisis could no longer be treated in accordance with the discourse of the *free* market that global economic players had defended in the 1980s and 1990s. The privatization of parts of the social security systems (e.g. health, old-age pensions) – systems that were introduced in Western countries in the first half of the twentieth century – has continued in the EU countries; other regions such as Latin America and Asia have instead expanded social security systems for the benefit of their populations (e.g. health, unemployment). Middle classes and poorer groups were particularly affected by the crisis in these regions due to the lack of welfare systems covering unemployment and old-age pensions.

THE DISCOURSE ON THE WORLD ECONOMY

The most important lesson for this new era of globalization is that China has become a world economy and its role in the US debt crisis has made the country a major global player. In fact, Chinese savings have ensured the stability of the US dollar and US consumption and have thus contributed to the perpetuation of the global neoliberal economy (Lebaron, 2010b: 128) that was favoured by important parts of economic and political elites in the North and the South. These elites accept university discourses which influence economic thoughts. Many of these university intellectuals defend the neoliberal dogma as a credo and a natural process. American and British universities are those that give global and national economic elites in business, government departments, and international organizations a scientific legitimacy in the form of promotions or MBAs, and thus create a scientific discourse that emphasizes neoliberal ideas. The 'Nobel-Prize' for Economics awarded by the Swedish Central Bank has been mainly awarded to US economists (Friedman, Mundell, Merton, Phelps, etc.). The dominant scientific thinking in economy thus acquires a worldwide legitimation so that the neoliberal credo continues to defend its economic strategies. There are connections between theoretical and financial thinking, economic departments in universities and the international financial community. This means a symbolic supremacy of US economic thinking and the ability to rationalize ideas about the modern economy (see Lebaron, 2010b: 138). In fact, the discourse on the American economy and the financial world is the usual discourse of these global elites, which constitutes a form of global economic dominance. However, the crisis was also a challenge for these ideas, although less than the previously anti-imperialist ideology. Economists have emerged who argue for a change of the neoliberal economy; students question the credo of the *free* market; large population groups worldwide challenge economic thinking and in particular austerity measures imposed by the IMF and national states (e.g. Greece, Portugal, and Spain).

MODERATE CRITICAL POSITIONS

The economic development of the crisis is linked to the success of the moderate critical positions of Joseph Stiglitz (2006) and Dani Rodrik (1999), who argue that the globalization of financial markets has not permitted a harmonious development of the world economy, but has triggered dysfunctional situations and instability. The increasing importance of the emerging economies challenges the Western model that the neoliberal economy has tried to implant after the fall of the Iron Curtain at the end of the 1980s. The consequence has been that key political actors have seen a renewal of their political influence on the economy which was no longer considered to disrupt the function of the market order as under Reagan and Thatcher. At a global level, the creation of the G20 has determined the dominant political actors in the global economic system in times of crisis. Professional politicians that were rather marginalized for the past two decades have re-conquered a new form of authority and power on global and national economies. Fiscal stimulation in terms of social medicine has received an official character. Senior managers and public servants in central banks, financial institutions, and ministries try again to define public issues and implement structural reforms. In this realm, trade unions have led a discussion on economic policy since 2008, which was sometimes linked to global or local mobilizations. Nevertheless, these actions are still very disparate so that mergers are rare. They concern, for example, the delocalization of enterprises from North to South, salary increases, the defence of purchasing power, the fight against work-related stress, and protest against budget cuts. However, the crisis of the labour market and high unemployment make the trade unions with their traditional policy unattractive for political movements, so that the absence of alternative economic programs amongst them has contributed to their feeble influence.

CONTRADICTIONS OF THE CURRENT FORM OF CAPITALISM

The capitalism that has been created by the crisis has contradictory aspects. On the one hand, the high indebtedness of the state that resulted from the intervention in the economy in 2008-2009 has challenged political actions of State authorities so that they are again subjected to the pressure of the central banks. The cyclical return of financial gains in banks and at stock exchanges, largely disconnected from industrial dynamics that maintain a high degree of uncertainty, has once more been used to justify high salaries in the financial sector. Only slowly, if at all, the efforts of trade unions, political actors, and central banks are moving forward to regulate the private banking sector. These facts have created a structural tension that rarely forms the focus of public discourses.

SOCIAL MOVEMENTS

Meanwhile, populations in the European Union have begun to protest, as the examples of Greece, Portugal, and Spain show. Low wages, cut unemployment benefits and welfare for the poor have become some of the new instruments implemented in these countries in recent decades. These measures were often supplemented by tax cuts for wealthier populations and a deregulation of financial markets. However, this model caused wage stagnation – except for the elites. An insufficient demand is one of the consequences, although the average citizen is encouraged by banks to borrow more money in order to afford their living standards. Yet, this model, which is based on ever-increasing debts, is exposed to regular financial shocks.

AUSTERITY MEASURES

As one of the remedies for an economy affected by high levels of debt is to raise interest rates, the consequence is an increasing insolvency for private individuals, so that a deep crisis as those of the years 2008 to 2009 could follow again. The first signs were noted in summer 2011 with the crash of stock exchanges. High public debt rates in many regions did not allow more supporting measures; in some states, a recovery was observed (Germany); in others, the limits of economic and political debts were reached so that austerity measures were introduced. As the example of Greece has shown, the IMF and the European Union have demanded that the successive governments introduce huge cuts in social programs, which were considered the only way to overcome the crisis. Due to structural economic conditions, unemployment in some countries remained at a high level. In contrast, Asian economic growth has led to an increase in the consumption of material goods (China and India) by the growing middle classes. Large Asian middle classes try to participate in the consumer society of the West. The result is a sustained economic growth in the region that has restructured the power balance in the world. In Latin American and Asian countries, this process means a change in the structural relationships between richer and poorer groups with all the known consequences (e.g. high crime rates and widespread uncertainty) and the creation of a large middle class that is interested in high consumption rates.

To summarize, we can say that there were and still are large differences in response to the financial and systemic crisis in the various regions of the globe. These differences can be explained by the historical integration into the global economic system and respective internal dynamics. In fact, the crisis has affected all regions of the world; no region could be ruled out with the argument of a poor integration into global capitalism, as some voices at the beginning of the financial crisis, for example, for sub-Saharan Africa and parts of Latin America, stressed.

THE CRISIS OF GLOBALIZATION

The crisis was more a crisis of globalization than a crisis of the prevailing economic model. The regional power structure of the world economy has been questioned with the rise of the BRIC countries and stabilized by their integration into the G20. The management discourse has been introduced in all fields of human life: from schools to jobs to private life. The crisis revealed another influence: universities introduced the striving for success and efficiency everywhere, from health care to the social field. The capitalist ethic therefore affects more and more social systems because of the implementation of this ideological management discourse that rationalizes success and failure through individual characteristics.

The Stiglitz-Sen-Fitoussi Commission – nominated by the former French President Sarkozy in 2008 – illustrated this demand to improve the appreciation of wealth and performance by avoiding the exclusive use of statistical measures (Lebaron, 2009). Economists who are known to be critical voices participated in this Commission. Nevertheless, they defended a neo-classical approach strongly supported by the majority of the international community. They also suggested including a growing and better use of incomes and real household consumption in national statistics. These specialists insisted on including social services, such as health or education that contribute to the well-being of households, but are often forgotten in national statistics. Furthermore, the Commission asked to include inheritance in national statistics – a value that is, however, difficult to assess. The experts emphasized the difficulty of measuring and comparing well-being and the economic capacity of a household. GDP can also increase, according to Stiglitz, when most households do not have more income, as was the case for the United States and France after the financial crisis.

THE RELATIONSHIP OF INEQUALITY AND POVERTY

It is interesting that the crisis revealed a process that is barely measured by official statistics: the relationship of inequality and poverty. In fact, in official statistics information on these issues is only collected with a relatively large time delay, so that the socio-economic consequences of the crisis were largely hidden from official discourse in the last years, even in a country like France. Higher unemployment, precarious working conditions, and higher levels of poverty have now been introduced in a number of countries, even in states where social protection systems exist, such as in southern European countries (Greece, Spain, and Portugal). The case studies below show that people react differently depending on their local socio-economic and cultural situations and opportunities. These studies testify what surveys showed on attitudes and opinions since the crisis began in 2007: the number of jobs in the informal sector has increased in all regions of the world; the number of working poor, unemployment, and underemployment have increased, even if these numbers go back in some countries (e.g. Germany) where economic growth can be observed, so that enterprises have hired more employees or have reduced working hours.

RAISING PRECARIOUS EMPLOYMENT FORMS

The financial crisis did not only affect the Triad countries, but also Latin American and Caribbean countries, as well as parts of Eastern Europe (the Commonwealth of Independent States). In this latter region, the number of self-employed persons and those receiving family assistance, who are not or barely covered by the social security system, increased. According to the International Labour Office (2011: 7), in recent years, precarious employment has increased from 1.48 to 1.59 billion people, which means that 50 per cent of the world's working population is affected.

But these developments are dependent on the particular region of the world: China and India strengthen their middle classes of employees and self-employed people with rising incomes. Local underemployment has increased in rural areas, so that people have migrated to urban centres. In France, the crisis has led to growing criticism of the shareholder system: workers and employees declared in public opinion polls that they favour the use of force in certain circumstances, for example if workers and employees are not willing to accept the rights that the economic hierarchy in a company defends (Lebaron, 2010b: 209) so that they see violence against the directors as the only way out. Smaller French business owners saw the French Sarkozy-Fillon government (2007-2012) as helpful for large enterprises and the companies that make up the CAC 40 stock index. These small and medium entrepreneurs have great difficulties obtaining loans, so that they fear the economic future of their country (72 per cent in 2010) and their own future (Lebaron, 2010b: 209).

STRESS AND ANXIETY

At a global level, opinion polls show that the global crisis has increased mental stress and anxiety in the labour force.[6] Although the impact of the crisis on their professional lives was not obvious in the public space, surveys have shown psychological consequences such as suicides and insomnia as the lot of numerous workers and employees. There is also a strengthening of social movements: one can mention the events in North Africa in 2011–2012 and the protest movements in Spain, Portugal, Greece, and Turkey of the last five years. In all these regions, political and economic discourses of the political elites are being challenged. Along with the global community, the people of North Africa have begun to protest against corrupt and authoritarian political elites, so that democratic political upheavals were the result. The political world community, together with the United Nations (UN), has supported these movements for political freedoms, even if the results have led to more or less uncertain provisional situations, such as in Libya and Egypt. These movements began after the global financial crisis of 2007–2009 in 2010, when the signs of a temporary recovery had begun to emerge in some regions (e.g. in Germany). They demonstrate that, through the use of mass media and Internet, social tensions may quickly degenerate into social movements that involve states and regions.

The global financial crisis of 2007–2009 has been different from previous ones insofar as this crisis has triggered strong doubts about the foundations of the global economic order. The targets of our social organizations have been challenged: well-being and equality, the link between society and the economy as well as between the South and the North. It seems as if we are living a transition period, which could eventually mean a change of the socio-economic order. Capitalism in its current form does not avoid social injustices but legitimizes them with a discourse that is no longer supported by groups that are increasingly excluded. In the near future, there might be new speculative crises triggering new social tensions anywhere in the world. The new socio-economic order after the crisis is not yet clearly defined. It may be that a kind of 'post-capitalism' will be created when other crises arrive. This future will be arising from the joint efforts of critical intellectuals, politicians, and civil society. Some of the tasks may include political measures concerning global governance, global and national inequalities, and the global ecological crisis. The perspective to create a different world is therefore given, a world in which not only financial dynamics affect global socio-economic circumstances but where social aspects are increasingly important.

POTENTIAL SOCIO-ECONOMIC CONSEQUENCES OF THE RECENT GLOBAL FINANCIAL CRISES

The results and implications of the recent global financial crisis have been varied, so that the crisis had different outcomes depending on geographical and social factors. It is difficult to generalize from these results. It seems as if there were similar results in some regions, but in others, the results were divergent and not convergent. Although it is tempting to generalize from the European and North American cases, the outcomes in various Asian countries that have experienced the socio-economic crisis as a challenge to their role in the global context are quite different. African and South American countries seem to create similar consequences for some social groups. Nevertheless, the crisis meant a realignment of the world in terms of politics, economy, and power, which has already been discussed in the first part of this chapter. Moreover, there are some common themes that will be tackled increasingly in the next years at an international level, such as environmental issues, changing relations between the genders by moving away from a focus on men who support the household budget, or the role of remittances of migrants from host countries on socio-economic developments in their countries of origin and the geographical South.

A few years after the beginning of the crisis, jobs and growth in different urban centres of global capitalism remain low and precarious employment is increasing. This represents a challenge for the legitimacy of the market mechanism and has triggered violent protests in Southern and Eastern Europe, parts of Asia, and North Africa. Moreover, financial markets around the globe slow down at the slightest sign of debt trouble in Europe or decreasing economic growth rates in China. Emerging markets show signs of overheating in the form of inflation of the prices of goods and/or assets, such as in China and India. Due to austerity measures in some countries in Europe, growth there is expected to remain at a low level for the foreseeable future. The European project (not least the Euro currency) appears to be fragile in a way that was unimaginable before. The Brexit referendum has been a milestone in this trend with political elites that try to solve internal political problems by focusing on European and global aspects that are barely understood by populations that continue to argue on a national scale. Public debt in many countries entails the risk of a decline in living standards of broad masses. Politicians speak of an 'era of thrift.' In the USA, the unemployment figures have recovered. However, this development appears to have been financed by borrowing so that the global imbalances increase (e.g. China and Japan as the principal creditors of the United States).

SOME COMMON CHARACTERISTICS OF THE SOCIO-ECONOMIC IMPACT OF THE CRISIS

One can deduce from the very different socio-economic impacts of the global financial crisis several factors that are more or less present everywhere. As a rule, the groups most affected are those who were already in a situation of uncertainty, i.e. children, women, and the poor. An increase in poverty and unemployment, lack of education for children, food shortages, problems due to high prices, and an increase in child mortality can be reported (see Arguello, 2010; Cohen; 2010; Elson, 2010; Montaño and Milosavljevic, 2010; de Gaulejac, 2011).

GENDER

It is necessary to begin to focus here in particular on employment and gender inequality. With regard to gender inequality, the progress of recent decades seems to have come to a standstill and a growing gender inequality can be observed (e.g. in the fields of education, employment, and the reproductive sphere). As in the northern countries of Europe, gender relations are put more under stress so that increasing intra-family tensions have become the norm. The mix of political and economic elites in the USA – as the election excesses have shown – let reappear stereotypes in the country that women fought against some 30–40 years ago.

GENDER AND WORK IN CHILE

Tamara Heran's approach deals with Chile, a cradle of neoliberalism and a development model that was based on the export of raw materials and that was the first country in Latin America strongly affected by the financial crisis of 2007-2009. The Chilean model has been a growth and development model that led to the membership of Chile in the OECD in 2010. But during the financial crisis, the country showed significant weaknesses: especially children and women had problems. Heran's approach has focused on the transformation of gender roles in the financial crisis, which led to changes in economic activities. Her study shows that the mining industry, which was severely affected by the crisis due to falling copper prices and the disappearance of a male working space, resulted in an exodus of male workers to other economic sectors which were less affected by the global crisis. The miners found jobs in agribusiness, jobs that were traditionally reserved for female workers. Heran's fieldwork was carried out in the province of Limarí where both activities can be found.

One of the peculiarities of this study is that Heran's approach focuses on the flexibility of the labour force and the working system. The liberalization of employment, among other things, meant declining employment protection, layoffs, temporary work, fixed-term contracts, as well as the stagnation of wages, and the creation of jobs with neither job security nor health insurance. In addition, Heran emphasizes the increase in poverty and unemployment as the immediate consequences of the economic crisis in Chile as well as in other South American countries.

The pension system was particularly affected by the crisis. The Chilean pension funds suffered losses which reached up to 26 and even 40 per cent of the capital invested. Poor people and the middle classes lost their pensions and savings.

(Continued)

CASE STUDY

(Continued)

They returned to a state of poverty they had fled years ago. Between 2008 and 2009, unemployment rose from 7.8 to 9.7 per cent. It was even two percentage points higher for women. There were many layoffs so that informal and sporadic activities have become alternatives. When jobs were cut in the mines, the miners began to work as seasonal agricultural workers and sometimes replaced women working in this field. Wages were also affected and began to approach the Chilean minimum wage.

For activities such as cleaning, packaging, and sorting of the fruit for export, female skills were traditionally needed. But these attributes changed in the crisis. Both genders have – according to this new discourse – the same skills allowing them to perform these tasks. Thus, the immediate consequence of the crisis meant lower wages and more competition for agricultural jobs. The crisis changed the local socio-cultural lifestyles and the working sphere of men and women according to transformed gender relations. The crisis created new labour cultures, which meant a transformation of gender relations and the working field. Heran's approach shows that people have learned to reorganize their lives in this new global economy.

Source: Heran, T. (2012) 'From Male to Female: Conversion and Gender Relations in Times of Crisis: A Study of Seasonal Workers of Agribusiness in Chile,' in U. Schuerkens (ed.) *Socioeconomic Outcomes of the Global Financial Crisis: Theoretical Discussion and Empirical Case Studies.* London and New York: Routledge and recent updates. pp. 65–85.

EDUCATION

In education, studies have shown that families in Southern countries, if they are struck by unemployment, rapidly decide not to send girls to school (see Elson, 2010; Seguino, 2010). Education for young men is preferred because they will become heads of households with family responsibilities requiring stable employment.

WORK

In terms of work, both the formal and the informal sector have been reconfigured. A rise in unemployment and the loss of jobs in the formal sector have forced people to seek work in the informal sector in order to ensure their survival. Even the very modest economic growth in the first phase after the crisis until the early summer of 2011 has been associated with the lack of job creation. The massive job–stimulus package in the USA in autumn 2011 faced with a growing likelihood of recurrence of a global economic downturn represented a desperate response to the limited options available for economic activity in times of computer technology. This has had consequences for gender equality. Depending on the activity sectors, women or men have been mostly affected. Some studies mention that women are disadvantaged in those sectors in which both genders are employed (see Elson, 2010; Seguino, 2010). Elson (2010) points out that the norm of the male breadwinner is still widely accepted, so that men have the 'right' to continue their professional activities, while women stay unemployed. This idea is characteristic of a patriarchal system that defends the employment opportunities of men against women. This has meant that women in emerging countries, who worked in the export industry, have lost their jobs and had to cope with the reintroduction of poverty and unemployment in the 'post–crisis' situation. In particular, single mothers have experienced situations of extreme poverty and marginality (see Arguello, 2010) in both the South and the North.

In fact, with the decrease of formal job offers, precarious working conditions, temporary jobs, jobs within the household, or poorly paid illegal jobs have seen an increase because they have been considered an alternative to the abyss of unemployment. Women who could combine these jobs with housework and childcare have often favoured them. Thus, a new gender competition has emerged over the delimitation of these areas (Montaño and Milosavljevic, 2010). Such processes can be found globally as formal jobs are becoming more precarious and uncertain, as suggested by Sassen (2014) in her well-researched recent book.

REDUCED WELFARE MEASURES IN MANY COUNTRIES

The ongoing financial crisis has also meant that deep austerity measures have been on the agenda in European countries and the USA in response to the demands of the IMF and the European Commission. Correspondingly, the lack of democracy in terms of political alternatives to the imposition of austerity policies has become more apparent as there is an uneven burden sharing of the fallout of the crisis in terms of unemployment, reduced services in health and education, and a general insecurity spreading from the working class to the middle classes. In addition, a growing impoverishment of parts of the middle classes can be found in Northern countries due to the decline of social services and the growth of precarious jobs.

As has been demonstrated by Piketty (2009, 2014) and Sen (2011), in recent years, political elites have mainly served the interests of a small portion of shareholders and financial capitalists, rather than the interests of those who make up the real productive economy. Krugman (2011) has estimated that these fortunate few provide money for the election campaign so that they have access to politicians and can influence their decisions. In fact, the recent debt crisis is mystified by the creation of financial instruments that are only understood by a few specialists. Scandals involving Swiss banks and the Panama papers reveal the extent of these forms of financial criminalization that politics has only recently begun to combat.

In Europe, the handling of the financial crisis meant that countries such as Greece, Spain, and Portugal had to accept assistance packages from the EU, which protected the international financial system. These States had to implement austerity policies that have been controversial among impoverished populations. The loss of national self-determination in terms of fiscal and monetary instruments has led to a subordination of state administrations to economic decisions from Brussels. J. Barroso, the former President of the European Commission called for a unity of left and right wing politicians as an answer to the crisis. The former president of the European Central Bank J.C. Trichet suggested in 2011 that the European Union should be given a right of veto over certain aspects of national economic policies, even though its chief economist, J. Stark, left the bank for 'personal reasons', which led to a further decline in equity markets (Carrel, 2011).

In Spain, Italy, Portugal, and Greece, the populations protested against political elites (left- and right-wing), who wanted to pursue the neoliberal project. A widening popular resistance has come to understand 'necessary structural reforms' as direct threats to their way of life and expectations of what were legitimate entitlements, both for themselves and their families. The Euro crisis and the US crisis in summer 2011, which had triggered another financial crash in stock markets, show that these situations are connected. The globalization process of the last three decades has given rise to privileged groups who have stock options, compared to a middle class that tries to maintain its standards of living with the accumulation of debts. Layoffs and wage cuts mean that an even wider range of social groups begins to protest (e.g. in Israel, Chile, Spain, and Greece). The riots of summer 2011 in London can also be seen as symptomatic of globalized austerity measures which are accompanied by social unrest and a deeper legitimacy crisis of the existing order. The financial crisis of the year 2011 let privileged groups review their social responsibility. For example, in France a group of 10 per cent of the population with an annual income of more than 37,000 euros only paid 20 to 25 per cent taxes due to tax concessions of the right-wing government of former President Nicolas Sarkozy; under the Socialist President Hollande, these groups have been more heavily taxed.[7] One per cent of the population with the highest income (from an amount of 88,200 Euros to more than 732,300 Euros) had to pay a 10 per cent income tax in 2007 according to the statistics of the French statistical office INSEE. A new debate regarding additional taxes on those with high incomes began in France, Germany, and the USA. The former socialist mayor of Paris, Delanoë, and businessmen like Pierre Bergé have supported this idea; the socialist government under President Hollande is therefore implementing this project to tax higher income groups. This also means that politicians no longer only refer to the idea of the enterprise and the *free* market. Economic, political, and social interactions now require crossing the borders of nation-states.

CONCLUSION

Given the important social movements that followed the financial crisis, it is hardly possible to govern 'as always'. Slowly, new possibilities of social change crystallize in some places to a still unimagined extent. It will be a political challenge to translate these opportunities into reality and draw lessons from the current socio-economic problems in order to contribute decisively to a re-democratization of political and economic life on a global scale, so that a turning point might occur in this first century of the new millennium.

CASE STUDY

A SHORT ANALYSIS OF THE RECENT BRAZILIAN CRISIS – 2015/2016

A. Ivo and R. Laniado give a short account of the internal and external events that occurred in the past decade in Brazil and that enabled the country to face the 2008 crisis in a favourable way. However, soon after 2010, the country was exposed to both economic and political difficulties that resulted in a profound political instability.

The successful performance of Brazil during the 2008 crisis was due to a strategy of combined social policies, such as income transfer, a real increase of the national minimum wage (over 70 per cent), and the formalization of the labour market (30 per cent from 2003 to 2014). This strategy contributed to the reduction of income inequalities; it increased the social mobility of poorer groups, and had a positive impact on 25 per cent of the population. Furthermore, during the crisis, the government pursued a counter-cyclical policy of tax reduction, an increase of public spending, and an extended policy of popular credit facilities that stimulated consumption and boosted the internal market. However, since 2011, a few international factors and domestic decisions on economic policies caused a negative impact on the Gross Domestic Product (GDP): a decrease from 2.7 per cent in 2011 to -3.8 per cent in 2015.

The negative international factors that affected the Brazilian economy since 2010 have been the rapid decrease in the value of commodities (minerals and grains) on the international markets and the reduction of Chinese demand for Brazilian commodities. From 2011 on, the price of iron decreased from US$180 a ton to US$55; the price for soya beans from US$40 per 60 kg sack to US$18; and crude oil went down to US$50 a barrel.

However, domestic economic policy also contributed to a reduction of economic activities. Policies concerning the industrial sector have been sporadic and uncoordinated. Nevertheless, since 2011–2012, subsidies and tax reductions were introduced to boost the industrial production, aiming at reducing costs and maintaining employment. But these fiscal incentives were introduced without any conditionality; as a consequence, they became a capital gain and did not prevent the dismissal of workers.

The car industry is a good example of these uncoordinated policies. In April 2015, despite fiscal incentives, popular credit facilities to buy cars, and over-taxation on car imports in order to favour the domestic production, sales fell by 21 per cent

(Continued)

(Continued)

compared to the same month of 2014. In addition, between January and April 2015, 12,000 workers were dismissed. The crisis in the car industry caused a strong negative impact on several supply chains.

The government also intervened in the economy by controlling the prices of gas and electricity, and by introducing changes in the contracts of electricity companies, causing a considerable crisis of this sector. In addition, the interest rate related to government bonds (public borrowing), the Special System of Clearance and Custody, known as Selic tax and controlled by the Central Bank of Brazil, increased considerably: from 8.75 per cent at the beginning of 2011 to 14.25 per cent in the first semester of 2016. This high rate has made credits more expensive for individuals and companies, has increased the costs of the payment of public debt, and has reduced the capacity for investments, both in infrastructure and in social programs.

Unemployment increased to nearly 11 per cent in the first three months of 2016, as compared to a 6.9 per cent rate for the year 2015, according to the National Bureau of Geography and Statistics (IBGE). Unemployment is higher in industry, civil construction, and the state administrative sector. Jobs in the formal and informal labour market decreased by 1.17 million and the average income of workers decreased by 3.2 per cent. In addition, the high inflation rate has had pervasive effects on the purchasing power of wage earners.

In order to maintain the primary budget surplus of 1.2 per cent of the GDP, Rousseff's government adopted in 2015 unpopular measures concerning labour: the reduction of the unemployment insurance benefit and a stricter regulation of the outsourced labour market. Both policies meant a breaking of agreements made with workers and supporters during the presidential electoral campaign of October 2014.

The reduction in tax revenue due to the economic crisis and uncoordinated incentive policies, the high amount of interest payments for internal debt, and the need to keep the established budgetary goals under control formed a complicated setting, intertwined with several political conflicts. National politics have been polarized between Rousseff's supporters and the opposition and many allegations of corruption were revealed in the last two years. These factors contributed to deepen the economic crisis and erode confidence in the government and its political institutions, mainly supported by urban middle classes.

Despite these economic difficulties, there were no determinant motivations for Rousseff's impeachment. In fact, this act was a multifaceted political one, with strong emphasis on the efforts of the opposition parties that wished to stop the corruption investigation carried on by the Ministry for Public Affairs and the Federal Police Department. In contrast, the support of former President Rousseff for the investigation intensified the clashes between the government and the opposition that finally succeeded in dismissing the President.

Sources: Ivo, A.B.L. and de Volta, C. (2016) 'A nova agenda do ajuste contra a democracia social.' Paper presented in the Workshop *Nuevas (y Antiguas) Estructuraciones de las Políticas Sociales en AL.* Claco and Universidad de la República, Facultad de Ciencias Sociales, Montevideo, Uruguay, 4–5 May 2016.

Ivo, A.B.L. and Laniado, R.N. (2012) 'The Brazilian approach to crisis: Growth recovery, basic social income, and a wide social pact,' in U. Schuerkens (ed.) *Socioeconomic Outcomes of the Global Financial Crisis: Theoretical Discussion and Empirical Case Studies.* London and New York: Routledge. pp. 154–72.

CASE STUDY

DISCUSSION QUESTIONS

1. What do you know about the theories of crises in sociology?

2. What are the differences between crises and conflicts?

3. Can you please give some information on the outcome of the 2007/2009 financial crises for different societies in the world?

4. How can you describe the emergence of the multipolar world?

5. How do you explain the crisis of globalization?

ANNOTATED FURTHER READINGS

United Nations Conference on Trade and Development (UNCTAD) (2016) *Rethinking Development Strategies after the Financial Crisis. 2, Country Studies and International Comparisons.* **New York: United Nations.**
The authors of this publication think that developing countries can and should learn more from each other, as well as from their own past experiences. Four countries are here selected based upon the role that they play in the developing world and the current discourses on development: Brazil, Chile, China, and India. These countries account for a large proportion of the world population and their corresponding regional GDP. Chile is a small country, but among the most developed in Latin America.

Dallago, B., Guri, G. and McGowan, J. (2016) *A Global Perspective on the European Economic Crisis.* **London and New York: Routledge.**
This book explores the connection between internal EU actions and institutions and the external factors that influence the ongoing response to the European crisis. It considers the complex macroeconomic and challenging political landscape of

Europe and outlines what Europeans should do in order to avoid harmful internal consequences. This volume confronts the causes of the crisis' persistence, its economic and political consequences, and the impact of more recent events and policy decisions.

Tombs, S. (2015) *Social Protection After the Crisis: Regulation Without Enforcement.* **Bristol: Policy Press.**
Austerity policies include pressures to 'free up' private capital to produce wealth, employment, and tax revenues. This book considers the economic, political, and social consequences of the economic crisis, the nature of social protection, and the dynamics of the current crisis of regulation. Based on empirical research and with a focus on environmental, food, and workplace safety, the book considers how we reached the current crisis of anti-regulation and how we might overcome it.

Websites

http://topics.nytimes.com/top/reference/timestopics/subjects/e/european_sovereign_debt_crisis/index.html
New York Times commentaries on the European debt crisis.

http://www.ft.com/indepth/euro-in-crisis
Financial Times commentaries on the euro crisis.

http://www.crisisgroup.org/
The International Crisis Group is an independent, non-profit, non-governmental organization committed to preventing and resolving conflicts.

http://www.africancrisisgroup.org/
Consulting firm and strategic studies organization (in French).

http://www.worldbank.org/financialcrisis/
Articles on the World Bank website regarding the financial crisis.

http://www.imf.org/external/np/exr/key/finstab.htm
International Monetary Fund website on the topic of the financial crisis.

http://www.pewresearch.org/
Pew Research Center is a nonpartisan think tank that informs the public about the issues, attitudes and trends shaping America and the world.

(all websites accessed 12 October 2016)

NOTES

1   Available at http://www.foreignpolicyjournal.com/2015/08/21/the-truth-about-brics/ (accessed 24 October 2016).
2   Available at http://ec.europa.eu/eurostat/statistics-explained/index.php/Unemployment_statistics (accessed 24 October 2016).
3   Available at http://www.gtai.de/GTAI/Navigation/DE/Trade/maerkte,did=443398.html (accessed 24 October 2016).
4   See http://data.worldbank.org/indicator/NY.GDP.PCAP.KD.ZG?view=chart (accessed 19 December 2016).
5   See http://data.worldbank.org/indicator/NE.CON.TETC.ZS?view=chart (accessed 19 December 2016).
6   Available at http://www.people-press.org/2011/05/04/section-4-the-recession-economic-stress-and-optimism/ (accessed 24 October 2016).
7   Available at http://impotsurlerevenu.org/la-fiscalite-francaise/728-qui-paie-l-impot-en-france-.php (accessed 24 October 2016).

COMMUNICATION, MEDIA, TECHNOLOGY, AND GLOBAL SOCIAL CHANGE

Summary

The acceleration of social change, linked to technological innovations and new research results, is now a global phenomenon. Technology influences the direction and the forms of global change. Capitalism and competition contribute to the development of new technologies and their global spread. Change in technology alters the use of time and effort and thus human societies all over the globe.

INTRODUCTION

Technology permits us to influence the social and physical environment and to solve problems. As Moore (1972: 5) wrote: '[Technology is] the application of knowledge to the achievement of particular goals or to the solution of particular problems.' It includes physical objects (e.g. a smartphone); a way of doing something (e.g. communicating by written language); and, an organization of practices (e.g. housing loans) (Massey, 2012: 139). According to Rudi Volti (2001: 6, 11), technology is 'a system based on the application of knowledge, manifested in physical objects and organizational forms, for the attainment of specific goals [...]. [It is] not just material artefacts [but includes] human skills, organizational patterns, and attitudes.'

Technology is created, supplied, adapted, used, and affects the life of people. They use these resources, possess skills, and understand this cultural element. If one regards computers and the Internet, one recognizes that this technology has meant new manners of interactions that are adapted to the interests of its users.

HOW DO TECHNOLOGIES CHANGE SOCIAL LIFE?

Each technology depends on its historical and socio-economic context. But there are some commonalities insofar as changes in technology alter the use of time and effort. If one thinks of computer word processing, it eliminated the retyping of entire documents that had to be error free. Or think of the washing machine which helped reduce household chores or the airplane that reduced the time of travelling and changed our concept of distance. Inside a cultural, political, and economic system, technology makes people change their behaviour and their relationships to one another. Thus technology is an ongoing process that can be slow or rapid. Technologies influence the speed and the course of social change based, as they are, on human agency rather than merely on technological possibilities. Powerful corporations investing in research may change university education and political practices. In so doing, they have contributed to the social changes of the last decades.

Technologies may be based on a clear need that motivates people to look for improved ways of living. These technologies are slowly adopted. At first a few people adopt new devices and most others observe the process. A rapid increase of followers happens at the second stage. The process is terminated by a slower rate of adoption of the last actors.

CHANGES IN INFORMATION TECHNOLOGY IN THE TWENTIETH CENTURY

The changes that occurred in information technology in the twentieth century have been astonishing. While at the beginning of the century, paper-based bureaucracies dominated the functioning of organizations, digital bureaucracies dominated by the end of the century, even if paper continued to play a certain role. Production processes, education, administration, entertainment, and travelling were transformed because of their increasing dependence on IT. Today, for the populations in the global North, life-worlds are characterized by a wide range of IT-based systems, such as call-centres or smartphones that did not exist in the 1980s. The convergence of telecommunications with computers enabled many aspects of the current life-world, such as mobile phones, tablet computers, credit or debit cards, etc. By the end of the twentieth century, IT was integrated in modern life, so that one began to speak of an information age based on new forms of work and a new global economy, as opposed to the industrial age of the century before.

IT has to be seen as a particular dimension of modernity. One can argue that the focus shifted from 'science' to 'technology' during the twentieth century (see Lyon, 2007). The global age is characterized by IT linked to the global mobility of information, persons, goods, images, services, wastes, and entertainment.

FLUID SOCIAL RELATIONS

Another important aspect is the shift to instant communication and thus fluid social relations. In the workplace, at home, or in the entertainment sector, social and economic life-worlds are exposed to change. But how does information technology alter social life? How are labour processes, organizations, police, and the state implicated in these changes?

IT is a technology that is essential for many production and consumption processes. IT is a major economic factor and important facilitator of current globalization processes. The topic began to become a field of the social sciences in the 1980s when IT was regarded as bringing about major social transformations (Webster and Robins, 1986; Mosco, 1998). A second phase could be called IT studies; they were concerned with the workplace organization in government administrations and enterprises as well as 'virtual communities.' Another phase followed that made contributions to political economy and analyzed questions of gender and race in IT developments (Wajcman, 1991).

An early sociological treatment came from Daniel Bell (1974) and his 'post-industrial society'. He argued that the industrial society was replaced by a society based on technical knowledge. He finally spoke of 'information society', a term that remains in use in the early twenty-first century. More recently, Manuel Castells (2000) published a large comparative study on the 'Information Age'. Castells has been interested in network society, in global cities, and in new social movements whose existence depends on information technology. During the last years, Internet studies have emerged as studies in their own right (e.g. Jones, 1999). Moreover, the debates over the negative sides of globalization have begun, such as where sweatshops are located, how global consumerism is extended to all parts of the world, how power is maintained by anti-terror techniques and intelligence services, etc.

IT-BASED KNOWLEDGE

A fact is that in knowledge-based societies, this knowledge-based work is dependent on IT so that IT knowledge makes a difference in employment, services, and the domestic sphere. One can say that information technology has become as basic to social life as industrial organization was in the twentieth century. Nevertheless, technology is one of several factors that trigger social change and is dependent on the social environment out of which it arises. Moreover, a given technology may be implemented in several different ways so that the outcomes depend on the socio-economic context in which it is introduced and implemented.

THE NETWORK SOCIETY

According to Castells, network society is the social structure of the current global age that is organized around relationships of production and consumption. This form of capitalism is global and flexible; it recasts time and space relations all over the globe. Castells suggests that the information technology revolution, the economic crises of capitalism and the state, and social movements appeared together. The interactions that resulted from these interdependent processes engendered network society as a dominant social structure. Castells believes:

> The distinguishing feature of the network society [...] is its dialectical interaction between modes of production (goods and services are created in specific social relationships) and those of development (especially technological innovation). (Castells, 1996, quoted in Allan, 2013)

Thus it is a new power system that goes beyond the control of the nation-state. According to Castells, we are living a technological revolution centered on microelectronics, communication technologies, and related sciences (such as genetic engineering or nanotechnology).

Moreover, the international division of labour is changing insofar as it becomes increasingly reliant on information-based production and competition. This current economy is global and networked, different from the historical economic geography. '[T]ools for networking, distant communication, storing/processing of information, coordinated individualization of work, and [the] simultaneous concentration and decentralization of decision-making' (Foran et al., 2007: 183) are playing a decisive role. For the first time in history, this new form of capitalism is now found on the entire globe.

DURKHEIM'S AND WEBER'S APPROACH APPLIED TO ICTS

Sociological thinking about information and communication technologies has its foundation in Durkheim's and Weber's sociological approaches, as Ling and Schroeder (2014) argued. However, these important sociological thinkers did not discuss Information and Communications Technology (ICT) in their work – because it did not exist in this way at their time of living – but they provided concepts at the micro-, meso-, and macro-social levels that permit understanding of the use of ICTs. They address the question of the implications of mediated relationships that go further than the simple focus on individuals and technology. According to Ling and Schroeder, their thinking provides a realistic understanding of ICTs and social change (2014: 789).

> Weber provides a way for understanding how, for example, technologies like the Internet and mobile communication have become widespread and indeed embedded in everyday life in a very short period of time. (Ling and Schroeder, 2014: 792)

Weber's notion of increasing rationalization can be applied to interpersonal communications which use media channels. The rise of large infrastructures that support many communication tools is linked to the increasing impersonal side of this technology.

On the consumer side, there was a growth of mobile phones, the Internet, and social networking sites. Connecting one device to another has provided the ability to have face-to-face interactions from different places for some time. There are currently multiple channels of interaction with others (Skype, chats, SMS, tweets, etc.). At the same time, there are more technologically mediated experiences of sociability and access to information and entertainment. This also means that these ICT activities become routine as they shape our daily lives.

Instead, Durkheim was interested in social cohesion. ICTs

> cultivate sociation of the intimate sphere and [...] provide a space for this neo-mechanical solidarity, which could be characterized as co-presence fostered by mediated interaction and shared digital objects. [...] We use ICTs to reach out to others who we trust and upon whom we rely. (Ling and Schroeder, 2014: 797)

The use of the telephone supports solidarity and thus permits shared interaction with close friends and family. We use mediated interactions when we participate in meetings or in other routines of our daily life-worlds. Our current rationalized world let us develop this sort of refuge as a contrast to harsh comments of our professional groups. Social cohesion is, according to Ling and Schroeder, built 'on our wish to be together with our closest sphere' (2014: 798). Another scale is reached with larger groups of social networking sites and Internet interaction. However, the mobile phone is an instrument that permits links to the closest sphere. This also means that our closest contacts are always available, even if it is in a mediated form. As Ling and Schroeder (2014: 799) argued: ' [...] nowadays, there is an ever-increasing connectedness via multiple modalities. [...] They (our closest sphere) are always just a text message, a Facebook entry, an IM chat, Second life login or tweet away.' This expectation to be available to one another via mediated forms of communication has become a widely shared social fact.

Weber and Durkheim explain 'common everyday practices in terms of how ICTs are pervasive routines which have become part of the management of mediated content and relationships' (Ling and Schroeder, 2014: 801). ICTs play a powerful role in society, not only in social interactions and personal life but also in mass entertainment and politics. Thinkers such as Castells and Habermas argue that ICTs change societies in a hopefully emancipatory way. One of the changes can be found in the growing importance of consumer opinions on websites that influence competitive market decisions.

AGING AND TECHNOLOGY

Technological developments in the fields of health and medicine have contributed to increases in life expectancy and the aging of populations. Population aging has become a worldwide tendency as birth rates decline and life expectancy increases not only in the global North. As aging and mobility limitations make more demands on homes and neighbourhoods, technology can redress these imbalances. Assistive devices can compensate for mobility problems that are often experienced in old age. They lengthen the period of independent life and reduce the dependence on caregivers. Personal computing and the Internet can facilitate social interactions and social integration. The elderly have thus much information at their fingertips, which allow new ways of social and political participation. Online networks may also reduce burdens associated with caregiving and give social support.

But there are negative consequences, too. Population aging has led to an increased competition for jobs between generations and has contributed to a decline of the status of older persons. The high costs of medical technology in the last life years have sometimes triggered demands to ration scarce, expensive health care according to the age of the person concerned. Another structural aspect is that users cannot always follow changes in communication and information technology.

The above-mentioned examples show ways in which technology affects the lives of the elderly and influences the aging process. But the aging process can also influence technology insofar as there are technologies specifically created for the elderly. The aging of the baby boomers and the 'graying' of the labour force have implications for commercial markets. Health problems and functional limitations of elder cohorts expands the market for assistive and other enabling technologies.

Studies have shown that the elderly have been slower to adopt and to understand forms of technology than younger people. The question is if this cohort behaviour will persist or change in the future and will contribute to the persistence of age differences and differences among the elderly limited by factors such as costs and individual intellectual capacity. Education and income have an influence on the adoption and the use of new technologies. As younger cohorts are currently familiar with IT, age differences in IT use may diminish in the coming years. Inequalities in access may continue even if 'smart' home technology is increasing, but perhaps it will not be affordable for parts of the elderly in the global North. Costs of transportation may continue to be more important for parts of the elderly even if self-driving automobiles have been created that facilitate elder persons to reach a destination via GPS systems. For actors with limited income, technological change may be inaccessible, creating therefore a 'technological divide' as a further form of inequality not only in the global North but even more in the global South.

INFORMATION TECHNOLOGIES AND AGRICULTURE: EVIDENCE FROM SEVERAL CASE STUDIES

CASE STUDY

A Nigerian case is cited as a success story of the adaptation of IT-technology by farmers (Fadairo et al., 2015). In fact, the Nigerian state has implemented an electronic wallet through its growth-enhancing scheme in order to overcome a high level of corruption and several failures in the existing subsidies system.

(Continued)

(Continued)

Defined as an efficient and transparent electronic device that implements the use of vouchers for the purchase and distribution of agricultural inputs, the e-wallet allows bypassing intermediaries and links small farmers receiving subsidies directly to agro-dealers. The voucher is used to redeem fertilizers, seeds, and other agricultural inputs from agro-dealers at half of the cost. Two case studies (Adebo, 2014) of the states of Kwara and Oyo in Nigeria showed that although organizational order limitations persist (a low level of awareness by farmers, fertilizer supply failure, low density coverage of agro-dealerships, and a poor phone network), the e-wallet project has reduced corruption in the supply chain and increased the farmers' output.

Perspectives different from the Nigerian case could recently be found in the Ivory Coast. In a country that covers only 42 per cent of its rice needs, the establishment of an information system by SMS for the commercialization of rice seed under the leadership of the FAO seems[1] to be a good initiative in order to achieve self-sufficiency. Faced with the seed growers' difficulty in finding profitable markets to sell their seeds and the inability of buyers (farmers, traders, and distributors) to gain timely access to certified seed varieties adapted to the farmers' needs (despite the existence of quality seeds), the development and implementation of an information system adapted to the context of the sector was supposed to avoid some of the constraints. The seed information system can in fact enable the collection and distribution of data through the automatic transmission of text messages (SMS). This system aimed primarily to provide buyers, on the one side, with updated information on the availability and quality of certified seed, and on the other side, to give access to information to seed producers about the varieties and volumes requested by buyers. Unfortunately, the project was not renewed after its pilot phase. Three main limitations can explain the failure of this project. The first point concerns technical limitations: no database updates were available to farmers. Moreover, there were funding problems, including high costs of seed certification by producers and organizational difficulties including a lack of coordination of project stakeholders.

Source: The case study from the Ivory Coast was collected for a PhD thesis in progress by Abdul-Aziz Dembélé at the EHESS, Paris, 2016 under the supervision of Ulrike Schuerkens.

WOMEN, INFORMATION TECHNOLOGY, AND ASIA

ITs have the potential to change women's social status and socio–economic opportunities in various ways. Sociologists are divided on the outcomes of women's use of Information and Communication Technologies (ICTs): some argue that ICTs

provide women with effective opportunities to participate in mainstream economic activities in Asian societies, others that ICT are yet another tool of
masculinized social, economic, and political power that is merely perpetuating
gender differentiation. (Johnson, 2007)

Sociologists of this region link gender to ICTs in order to gather information on
this social practice. Female Internet users continue to increase in Asia but the digital
gender-divide remains. In some countries, women are half as likely as men to be
online. In India, 21 per cent of women use the Internet compared to 41 per cent of
men. Many women are still not convinced that the Internet would be useful to them
or don't understand how to look for information. Around 20 per cent are excluded
from the Internet because of its high prices.[2] In Thailand and India, government
programs are organized to instruct women in using the Internet, showing them how
they can use the Internet for their daily lives. Once they are given the possibility to
use the Internet, women are empowered and have the ability to choose from a wide
range of activities or eventually jobs. Women may use the Internet to be informed
on health issues, and how to care for babies. In rural regions, smartphones are used
for weather forecasts and agricultural questions. Nevertheless, the Internet and its
technology may also lead to a loss or ignorance of local knowledge.

If one discusses the relationship between gender and technology, recent research
shows that it changes over time. It seems as if it is the social and economic context of a particular technology that appears to be significant. In India, technology
is viewed as woman-friendly and 'the computer-related professions are viewed as

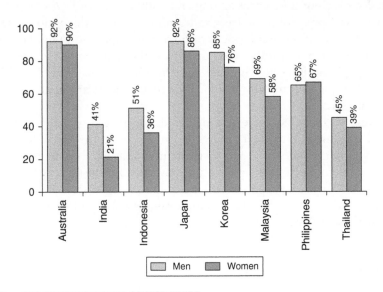

FIGURE 7.1   ASIA PACIFIC'S DIGITAL GENDER DIVIDE

Source: http://googleasiapacific.blogspot.fr/2014/10/women-will-closing-asias-digital-gender.html
(accessed 13 October 2016).

suitable for women' (Gupta, 2015: 668). In fact, working in this sector helps Indian women to accumulate 'symbolic capital' so that they can improve their status in society. Because of a high market demand, the number of women working in this sector is growing.

OVERCOMING THE DIGITAL DIVIDE IN DEVELOPING COUNTRIES

The digital divide refers to information inequalities among individuals and groups in a given society. This problem is not only confined to the global South; it also exists in the global North where marginalized groups have little access to computers and the Internet. Norris has categorized the digital divide in the following way:

> The *global divide* refers to the divergence of Internet access between advanced industrialized countries and developing countries. The *social divide* concerns the gap between information rich and poor in each nation. (…) the democratic divide signifies the difference between those who, and who do not, use the panoply of digital resources to engage, mobilize, and participate in public life. (2001: 4)

Ohemeng and Ofusu-Adarkwa (2014: 301) and Keniston (2004: 13-19) have enriched this concept by including linguistic and cultural facts that separate those who speak English from those who do not. According to the OECD, '[t]he digital divide reflects various differences among and within countries' (2001: 5). However, the international point of view has also been criticized as this problem serves the economic interests of powerful groups through the propagation of policies to overcome the digital divide. Another discourse maintains that 'the rest will follow' once sufficient telephone lines are supplied and the Internet made available (J. Miller, 2005). But the question remains if this knowledge is necessary in all situations and in all communities.

According to the UN, there is a digital divide in the global South between urban and rural areas. This internal divide can also be studied in different dimensions, such as gender, age, race, and social status. Some scholars maintain that ICT can solve problems such as inequality and poverty. The existence of public spaces and networks can then permit exchanges among people, shared knowledge and experiences, and sites where open sources can be consulted (see Ohemeng and Ofusu-Adarkwa, 2014: 304).

INFLUENCE ON CULTURAL FACTORS

ICT can also have an influence on cultural factors. A study of laptop uses of young Ethiopian girls has shown that '[l]aptops had medium to strong effects on value and attitude change, particularly in rural areas. Children with laptops endorsed modern values more strongly' (Hansen et al., 2014: 1229). And the authors continue: 'They also become more egalitarian with respect to gender' (2014: 1245).

Regarding the economy, ICT promotes economic equality, growth, and innovation through increasing education and job possibilities. In Kenya, 'ICTs were responsible for roughly one-quarter of Kenya's GDP growth during the first decade of the twenty-first century' (Ohemeng and Ofosu-Adarkwa, 2014: 305-6). ICT may also increase e-democracy insofar as it can facilitate information and communication processes. Citizens may participate in the decision-making process of politicians through electronic channels, as evidenced by President Obama's elections and the new social movements in North Africa in 2011 that led to the end of several long-lasting autocratic regimes (Tunisia, Egypt).

Ohemeng and Ofosu-Adarkwa (2014) describe an ICT pilot program in Ghana that was established with the help of India. It led to more than 90 Community Information Centers (CIC) 'equipped with Internet access, printers, fax machines, photocopiers, telephones, televisions, and radios' (2014: 309). These centers should give school children electronic access to their communities after school and facilitate private and business communication. Private tele-centers are most often found in urban neighbourhoods where residents lack access to telecom services; wireless local loop technology is used to establish tele-centers in rural areas. However, the CICs are affected by the poor infrastructure of the country. Internet connectivity may be too slow for any work to be done and power shortages may occur. However, programs to introduce IT in secondary and post-secondary schools and training centres have been realized in Ghana. Moreover, Mobile Library Vans equipped with computers and modems have extended services to these rural regions. The National Library Board and regional libraries have been connected to the Internet. However, the government is conscious that there is still a digital divide, e.g. caused by a high illiteracy rate that includes the inability to understand and use ICT despite formal education and infrastructure development. Nevertheless, it remains a fact that 'the information revolution is threatened by the digital divide, or the gap between the haves and the have nots, not only in the developing world, but in the developed one as well' (Ohemeng and Ofosu-Adarkwa, 2014: 317).

TECHNOLOGY, MEDIA, AND GLOBAL CHANGE

By the mid-1990s, the Internet became a familiar media, included in the everyday life of many people. The Internet has accelerated communication processes not only across the globe but also in regional groups where networking across borders was facilitated. While political actions and demonstrations became easier to sustain, activists began to target transnational levels (della Porta and Tarrow, 2005). 'Alternative globalization' movements started to use websites to ensure visibility of their protests and demands. Emancipatory communication practices followed thanks to camcorders, laptops, and cheap Internet connections. Media websites, independent video productions, online radio stations, and 'telestreet' (broadcasting to a neighbourhood, see Berardi et al., 2003) emerged. The 'media activist' with his particular skills and his critical usage of technology has become a distinctive figure who has been at the service of these movements.

The Internet has changed way supporters operate. Online and offline communication spaces have become popular regardless of institutions. Hacktivism tactics have emerged, such as net strikes and Distributed Denial of Service attacks even if they were confined to groups of net activists. In 2003, the agenda of the World Social Forum focused on media and technology so that media activists could meet, exchange skills, and initiate joint projects. However, there is a process of hyperprofessionalization of this issue at work so that parts of these activists disengaged from civil society organizations and widened the gap between established thematic groups and grassroots groups (Hintz and Milan, 2009a, 2009b). Moreover, the many ways of filtering and censoring the Internet have attracted the attention of some specialized groups and citizens (Deibert et al., 2008, 2010).

NEW SOCIAL NETWORKING SERVICES

The diffusion of micro-blogging and social networking services is changing our understanding of participation and mobilization. These processes have an impact on protest dynamics as Juris argues. Social media use 'has led to new patterns of protest that shape movement dynamics, beyond the realm of technological practice' (Juris, 2012: 297). And Bennett and Segerberg (2012: 739) observe that shared media content across networks changes the action dynamic of movements. Stefania Milan coined the concept of 'cloud protesting' that indicates a specific way of connecting individuals in order to organize collective actions. She argues:

> As an online imagined space, the cloud stores the know-how, narratives, and meanings associated with collective action, including the building blocks of collective identity. It makes them available to individual activists, who can 'shop' for existing meanings but also contribute to creating and sharing new ones. The cloud is enabled by and accessible via digital technologies, social media services, and mobile devices in particular. It has the ability to reduce the costs of mobilization by offering resources that can be accessed and enjoyed independently by individual activists in a cherry-picking fashion. In this way, individual participants can tailor their participation [...] by means of posts, tweets, links, and videos, but also with 'retweets' and 'likes'. (Milan, 2013: 40)

Individual stories are thus placed in a broader context. One can argue 'that the internet, and the direct participation of the average citizen enabled by web 2.0, has changed many realms of contemporary life, including journalism practice, cultures, and norms [...]' (Milan, 2013: 41). Traditional news media, for instance, increasingly incorporate citizens in order to encourage a conversation over an article. On one side, people may criticize, express their viewpoint, mobilize protest, scrutinize governments or parties, and deepen their participation. However, on the other side, cyberspace is increasingly controlled. For example, during the Arab Spring, social media were used to control protesters (see Wilson and Dunn, 2011). In Egypt, the 'government attempted to curtail Internet access in order to inhibit people's ability to organize through social media' (Milan, 2013: 41).

ALTERNATIVE MEDIA SCENE

The alternative media scene has contributed to a promotion of social change as social relations are transformed and become more and more individualized but connected. This media utilization empowers resistance movements. A better understanding of current social movements that live online is thus possible. They are often opposed to institutions and existing norms (see the group Anonymous, which support *WikiLeaks*). As the forms of protest concern values and norms, these movements can be analyzed by cultural and ideological explanations and not by structural ones in opposition e.g. to the neoliberal economic order.

MICROCREDIT AND TECHNOLOGY

CASE STUDY

Technology can help individuals, organizations, and states to improve their situations. Currently, many sectors – e.g. agriculture, health, trade, finance, governance, leisure time, etc. – are experiencing profound transformations because of new uses of technology. Southern countries are not at the centre of technology but have benefited from the technology of the North, so that most innovations haven't originated in the South.

In developing countries, particularly in rural areas, technology contributes to the fight against poverty. During Azize Manzo's field surveys in Niger (several weeks from 2011 to 2014), he collected information from several microfinance organizations that had used decentralized financial systems and new technologies in their financial services including microcredits, savings, and the transfer of money. The omnipresence of communication technology, such as the Internet and the mobile phone network, have led microfinance organizations to adapt and take ownership of other services in order to improve their activities.

In Niger, microfinance organizations, including ASUSU, Capital Finance, Taanadi, KAANI use mobile phone networks for their microcredit services and money transfers. In remote villages with no Western Union or other bank offices, customers can receive money via their mobile phone[3] through an SMS

(Continued)

(Continued)

notification; they present themselves to the microfinance organization with the message and its full details (amount, secret code, and reference checks) to recover the announced amount of money. Customers can also directly send money if they have their own account with a given phone operator; otherwise, the microfinance organization is in charge of this task.

In villages that have no microfinance office, big traders and small traders, such as teachers, have the mobile banking monopoly for the services of transfers and receipts of money. In the locality of Sandire (Niger), Azize Manzo's interviews with the focus groups highlight:

> We happen to repay the microcredit with a mobile phone by sending an SMS to the credit organization. This functions in this way: We give money to Moussa, a grain trader, who has an 'Mkoudi' account, who will then transfer an equivalent amount, subject to up to 60 FCFA (0.091 euro) for transportation costs. Immediately after the transaction using the customer's mobile phone, the staff member checks the good reception of the SMS and thus gives money. (Interview 20 September 2011, Sandire, Niger)

TABLE 7.1   MICROFINANCE DATA FROM THE WEST AFRICAN ECONOMIC AND MONETARY UNION IN 2012

Countries	Number of decentralized financial systems	Service points	Customers	Deposits in million Francs CFA	Credits in million Francs CFA	Outstanding credits in million Francs CFA	Percentage of portfolio quality
Benin	56	694	2,088,878	60,023.33	85,264.44	5,677.78	6.66%
Burkina Faso	76	532	1,384,673	121,358.43	80,118.06	2,409.46	3.01%
Ivory Coast	72	472	1,661,058	115,542.49	54,192.01	2,980.56	5.50%
Guinea-Bissau	18	110	23,618	414.64	75.20	43.86	58.32%
Mali	125	1,070	1,724,490	60,618.56	67,778.41	5,449.41	8.04%
Niger	52	212	280,872	15,627.43	18,102.23	2,628.93	14.52%
Senegal	238	900	2,586,040	186,750.96	233,244.13	9,669.60	4.15%
Togo	92	846	1,908,608	121,462.04	108,083.03	6,978.08	6.46%
Total WAEMU	729	4,836	11,658,237	681,797.88	646,857.51	35,837.68	5.54%

Source: Central Bank of West African States, December 2012. Available at http://www.bceao.int/IMG/pdf/indicateurs_au_31_decembre_2012.pdf (accessed 6 December 2016).

This virtual money transaction via the mobile telephone network allows credit facilitators to avoid making long trips (sometimes it takes up to one day to reach a village) and to save their time in order to ensure the daily needs of the services and to scout for other customers. This appropriation of Internet technology for microcredits and money transfers impacts on the management of space and time by allowing people to collaborate and work together over several thousands of kilometres and according to impressive deadlines.

Source: Manzo, Azize (2016) 'La Microfinance dans une économie locale dominée par l'informel: Le cas du Niger.' PhD in socio-economy of development. Paris: EHESS.

RESISTANCE TO TECHNOLOGY

Technological change is often linked to the modification of established social roles and values. Power relations are restructured, wealth and income may be redistributed, and human relationships are altered (Volti, 2001: 18). Resistance to change can be observed among peasants who fail to understand different farming methods that ask for a change in the adoption of new seeds, the designation of their harvest for sale, the utilization of fertilizer, herbicides, and insecticides that the new seeds need to survive. Poor peasants may be reluctant because of worldviews that are incompatible with the rational methods of the market and instead prefer fairness, family obligations, and community well-being. They are sceptical or hostile to those who try to change their agricultural life. For them, long established measures are important and the past is highly valued so that changes in the way things function are refused. Their belief system is embedded in local religion and the authority of elders. They may remember the time when Western farming methods were introduced that led to ecological disasters, famine, and poverty.

THE GLOBAL SPREAD OF TECHNOLOGY

The acceleration of social change, linked to technological innovations and new research results, is now a global phenomenon. Technology influences the direction and the forms of global change. Capitalism and competition contribute to the development of new technologies and their global spread. Technology transfer is a special case of the diffusion of innovations. Today, there are many jobs that use, sell, and transfer information based on technology in the fields of music, literature, and other creative and scientific products.

There is a debate over technology transfer. On one side, the open market and minimal obstacles to global trade and the flows of capital contribute to a search for raw materials, low-cost labour, assembly sites, and markets. Multinational enterprises and governments of the North can be found in this category. Neoliberal economic practices are defended by what is called the Washington Consensus. On the other side are advocates of poorer nations and some quickly-growing non-Western countries, as well as NGOs that are committed to solve problems in poor countries. These groups question the private ownership of many resources (e.g. water) and the commercialization of scientific products that ensure human comfort and health. Some of the advocates try to restrict what foreign enterprises can do in their state so that state planning may be used to influence the development of economic activities and improve the life of the poor. In fact, people in poor countries cannot afford to buy expensive goods, including pharmaceuticals so that these advocates argue that many of these things should not be patented. Bolivia, Brazil, and some other countries argue that 'their vegetation was "stolen" and is now being sold back to them as genetically modified seeds and pharmaceuticals' (Massey, 2012: 172). International corporations argue instead that research and development expenditure is included in the high cost of these commodities.

In fact, the West (Europe, Japan, and the US) controls huge parts of the technology sector and thus its growth and its influence on the South. Chinese (Hyundai) and South Korean (Samsung) plants have, however, increased their influence in recent years with new technologies and innovations based on their own R&D teams or on inputs from other brands, such as Apple in the case of Samsung. Technology transfer is at the centre of the debate over social change in the South. In order to improve peoples' lives, government agencies, corporations, and non-profit organizations in the global North have encouraged the global South to use new technologies. However, this was too often done without understanding what local people needed and what the impact on their current situation would be. Nevertheless, technology plays a major positive role in realizing better life situations (shelter, food, water, and education) in poorer countries. The technologies introduced have to be understood so that they become a good fit and people can make adjustments in a world open to digital communication and commercial culture. Technology tends to focus on cleaner water and healthier, better-fed, and better-educated populations who exercise productive work with an access to the entire world. UN organizations (e.g. UNICEF) and numerous NGOs work according to this viewpoint.

CONCLUSION

Technology signifies applying scientific knowledge to solve specific problems. Technological advances such as automobiles, airplanes, radio, television, cellular phones, and computers have brought major changes to world societies. In fact, twentieth century technology has fundamentally changed the way people meet, interact, learn, work, play, and travel.

DEVELOPMENT, NEW TECHNOLOGIES, AND SOCIAL TRANSFORMATIONS IN AGRICULTURE: A STUDY OF THE LIMARÍ VALLEY, CHILE

This case study is based on socio-anthropological research and analyzes social transformations arising from the implementation of new technologies in the agricultural and rural world. This study examines the social, economic, and cultural changes in a rural area based on an ethnographic survey conducted in the Limarí Valley – a fruit exporting region, especially of grapes – and the use of a methodology involving participant observation, non-structured interviews, and questionnaires with actors in the current agricultural setting.

Rural development strategies implemented in Chile since 1970 have promoted the incorporation of new technologies in farming and agricultural production. Following the system of large landed estates and several failed attempts of agrarian reform, the modernization of agriculture has involved boosting exports through increased agricultural production. The expansion of huge agricultural plantations managed by national and transnational corporations has been possible thanks to the introduction of new cultivation and irrigation technologies such as drip irrigation, dam construction to ensure the water supply, pesticide use, and the renewal of equipment and farming tools. In addition, large processing, packaging, and cold storage plants were built in rural areas.

The introduction of these new technologies has triggered profound changes in the forms of production and patterns of agricultural work, but these technologies have also led to significant changes in society, for instance in social and gender relations. New types of work have emerged, such as seasonal agricultural labourers and subcontractors of agricultural work. Moreover, women were introduced as workers in this activity, changing the roles and identities of household members.

Source: Heran, T. (2014) 'Le monde invisible du travail de l'agro-industrie d'exportation au Chili. Étude de la Vallée du Limarí.' PhD thesis in socio-economy of development. Paris: EHESS.

DISCUSSION QUESTIONS

1. How do technologies change social life?

2. How do you understand the notion 'network society'?

3. What do you know on 'graying' societies and their link to technology?

4. What are the benefits of IT to agricultural societies?

5. What do you know about IT and recent social movements?

ANNOTATED FURTHER READINGS

Castells, M. (2009) *Communication Power*. **Oxford: Oxford University Press.**
The author focuses on communication as power and argues around international politics, mass communication, media convergence, networks, and social movements. With an impressive overview, Manuel Castells creates new perspectives and alternates between the local and the global.

Deibert, R., Palfrey, T. Rohozinski, R. and Zittrain, J. (eds) (2010) *Access Controlled: The Shaping of Power, Rights, and Rule in Cyberspace*. **Cambridge, MA: MIT Press.**
The book includes chapters that analyze Internet control in both Western and Eastern Europe and a section of shorter regional reports and country profiles drawn from material gathered around the world.

Ling, R. (2012) *Taken for Grantedness: The Embedding of Mobile Communication into Society*. **Cambridge, MA: MIT Press.**
The author shows how the mobile phone can be regarded as a social mediation technology. Ling analyzes how technical systems become embedded in society and how they support social interaction within the sphere of friends and family.

Milan, S. (2013) *Social Movements and their Technologies: Wiring Social Change*. **Basingstoke: Palgrave Macmillan.**
The author explores the interactions between social movements and their technologies. She provides an overview of the relationship between social movements and technology, and investigates what made the main protest events of the past 15 years possible.

Websites

http://appropriatetec.appstate.edu/
The sustainable technology program at Appalachian State University, USA.

http://www.nytimes.com/column/bits
A blog filled with news, insight and analysis on Silicon Valley and beyond.

http://www.ases.org/
American Solar Energy Society.

http://www.europarl.europa.eu/EPRS/EPRS_IDAN_527417_ten_trends_to_change_your_life.pdf
Ten Technologies Which Could Change our Lives: A report by the European parliament.

http://www.fao.org/themes/en/
Food and Agriculture Organization of the United Nations.

http://www.nytimes.com/pages/technology/index.html
Features and columnists from the newspaper are supplemented with breaking news from CNet, Reuters, and AP.

http://www.pachamama.org/appropriate-technology
A movement that uses energy efficient and environmentally sustainable technology to achieve the desired benefits of modern technology.

http://www.telegraph.co.uk/education/universityeducation/student-life/11256382/How-technology-has-changed-student-life.html
A report on student life and technology.

http://www.who.int/hiv/amds/en/
World Health Organization: Access to AIDS medicines and diagnostics.

http://www.wipo.int/portal/en/index.html
WIPO is the global forum for intellectual property services, policy, information and cooperation.

https://www.ncat.org/offices/
Helping people by championing small-scale, local, and sustainable solutions to reduce poverty, promote healthy communities, and protect natural resources.

(all websites accessed 13 October 2016)

NOTES

1   Available at http://www.fao.org/ag/portal/agp/agp-news/detail-fr/fr/c/196574/ (accessed 24 October 2016).
2   Available at http://googleasiapacific.blogspot.fr/2014/10/women-will-closing-asias-digital-gender.html (accessed 24 October 2016).
3   The customers of the phone providers Airtel and Orange have to join a local office or an itinerant staff member when they want to use the services of Mkoudi Airtel or Orange Money.

GLOBAL SOCIAL CHANGE AND THE ENVIRONMENT

Summary

Currently, the necessary ecological transformation of modern societies is widely discussed. One should ask the question why we don't succeed in interrupting the predominant non-ecological development trend. The ecological transformation of societies will certainly be one of the main challenges of the coming years. It is therefore important to reflect on the chances of an ecological restructuring of modernity in order to see which conflicts and dynamics are important.

THE ECOLOGICAL TRANSFORMATION OF MODERN SOCIETIES

Many publications of national and international organizations currently contain discussions on the necessary ecological transformation of modern industrial societies. The UNESCO *World Social Science Report* of 2013 with the title *Changing Global Environments* underlines this in particular. It argues in the preface: 'The gap between what we know about the interconnectedness and fragility of our planetary system and what we are actually doing about it is alarming. And it is deepening' (ISSC-UNESCO, 2013: 3). In this sense, the report is in line with a reform movement that tries to bring forward the socio-ecological transformation of modern industrial societies. This change is, however, slow and contradictory.

The question is why despite all activities (state programs and international conferences), we don't succeed in interrupting the predominant non-ecological development trend. Not only problems of poverty and inequality, but also problems of climate change, the continuing loss of species, overfishing, deforestation, and the scarcity of drinking water are not addressed adequately. One can see in day-to-day activities of politicians and in personal activities that sustainability targets don't matter. Why is the balance sheet so contradictory? Why do we rarely translate principles of sustainable development in a concrete way in politics, the activities of organizations, and daily life?

ECOLOGICAL MODERNIZATION

The ecological transformation of societies will certainly be one of the main challenges of the coming years. It is therefore important to reflect on the chances of an ecological restructuring of modernity in order to see which conflicts and dynamics are important. Huber (1991, 2011) and Jänicke (2008) introduced the notion of ecological modernization at the end of the 1980s into the ecological and political debate in Germany. The institutionalization of the environment movement had a positive influence on this notion (Brand et al., 1997). Mol and Spaargaren from the Netherlands introduced this approach into the international socio-ecological debate in the 1990s (Mol, 1997, 2010; Mol and Spaargaren, 2006).

For the political scientist Jänicke, the notion of ecological modernization is an approach of innovation based on technologies that respect environment policy (2008: 58). Ecological modernization is also linked to a modernization of democracy due to the inclusion of actors of civil society. The other important scholar in this field, the social scientist and economist Huber, considers ecological modernization according to an evolutionary systemic understanding of societal modernization (Huber, 2011: 279ff.). For him, the notion is multi-dimensional with cultural, political, economic, social, and technological aspects that are closely linked and that are influencing the development of society and nature. Ecological modernization is meant to be a sustainable construction of the link of society and nature characterized by labour and technology, as well as production and consumption. Technological innovations that are eco-efficient are thus important.

For the social scientists Mol and Spaargaren, the approach of ecological modernization offers a framework for the analysis and understanding of the institutionalized reform processes of the ecological restructuration of industrial societies (Mol, 1995: 3–4). This approach is linked to Giddens' sociological debate on the 'radicalized modernity' (Giddens, 1990), that is, a post-traditional society. Social relations are no longer linked to interactions at a given place due to abstract systems of experts and symbolic mechanisms (such as money). Processes of individualization and globalization as well as the reflexive character of social actions are favoured. Individual and institutionalized activities are based on new information and scientific perspectives that question the knowledge basis of an activity. The notion of institutionalized reflexivity gives Mol the foundation of his theory of ecological modernization that is based on a model of reflexive institutionalized learning (Mol, 1996). Mol focuses on the industrial dimension of modernity, one of the four dimensions of modernity which, according to Giddens, are at the heart of the ecological crisis. According to Mol, an institutional differentiation of an ecological rationality is the precondition of ecological reform processes faced with constraints of the dominant economic rationality (Mol, 1995: 28ff.). He writes: 'This means that economic processes of production and consumption are increasingly analyzed and judged, as well as designed and organized from both an economic and ecological point of view' (Mol, 2010: 67).

What is important to understand is the fact that central institutions of modernity such as science, technology, the state, and the capitalist economy are not questioned. Instead, with the assistance of science and technology, a new balance of economy and ecology is sought. The theory of ecological modernization considers that this is possible in both the global North and South and that these processes are already realized in some regions. This theory is explaining a global political reform program of ecological modernization and is not only a descriptive-analytical theory. For the last ten to fifteen years, global-local processes have been analyzed in empirical case studies on Africa and Asia so that theory could already include geographical settings other than Western Europe (Mol et al., 2009).

This approach of ecological modernization underlines the importance of competition and market dynamics for ecological reforms.

> Producers, customers, consumers, credit institutions, insurance companies, utility sector and business associations, to name but a few, increasingly turn into social carriers of ecological restructuring, innovation and reform (in addition to, and not so much instead of, state agencies and new social movements). (Mol, 2010: 68)

Ecological technology thus permits developing new markets for 'proper products' and improving the ecological image of the enterprises producing them.

ENVIRONMENTAL MOVEMENTS

The role of environmental movements has changed in recent years because of the ecological modernization of state and economy. These movements are no longer characterized by anti-institutionalized actors but they have become critical partners in the transformation processes of industrialized societies that legitimate reform processes and mobilize societal support for questions of environment (Mol, 2010: 68).

GLOBAL GOVERNANCE AND THE ENVIRONMENT

From a development perspective, environmental degradation presents an enormous challenge. It has led to multiple international conferences and treaties that have created rules to respect. The 1972 UN Stockholm Conference on the Human

Environment decided that environment was an important area of concern for national and international governance. Therefore, the UN Environment Program (UNEP) was created in 1972. The Rio Earth Summit of 1992 confirmed the importance of sustainable development on the international agenda. 176 countries attended this United Nations Conference on Environment and Development (UNCED). World leaders signed five agreements on topics such as climate change, deforestation, and the prevention of species extinction. The summit outlined different approaches for the North and the South. Southern countries put an emphasis on a revision of the international terms of trade so that they could leave their indebtedness behind. Northern governments focused instead on the dissemination of green technologies to the developing world with the goal to meet environmental challenges. Moreover, the North acknowledged its responsibility for the environment as these countries industrialized first. However, ecologists consider the summit as a disappointment because of the fact that economic growth and ecological modernization continue to be the main points of the political agenda. Some activists argue that economic growth is not compatible with an ecological modernization.

A further large event, tackling environmental questions was the 2002 World Summit for Sustainable Development in Johannesburg. The summit agreed to promote energy-efficient technologies and the removal of lead in petrol. Moreover, it argued that the global share of renewable energy had to be increased. Some countries have underlined that hydroelectric schemes and nuclear power should be included under this heading.

The Kyoto Protocol, signed in 1997, has attracted much international attention. This treaty aims to curb air pollution to slow down global warming. It came into force in 2005 when 141 countries had ratified the treaty. They promised to cut their greenhouse gas emissions by 5.2 per cent by 2012. However, India and the USA had signalled that they would not sign any treaty that committed them to reduce CO_2 emissions.

A second commitment period was agreed on in 2012, known as the Doha Amendment in which 74 states (November 2016) have binding obligations. This second commitment covered the period 2013-2020 but affected only 14 per cent of global emissions as at the beginning only EU members, other European states, and Australia had commitments. Some more countries have recently made voluntary pledges for climate action up to 2020. However, 175 countries signed a new climate agreement in New York on 22 April 2016 after the 21st Conference of the Parties in December 2015 in Paris. This new climate agreement covers 93 per cent of global emissions and seems to be a promising step into the future.

If one has to take a conclusion on these international activities, the results have often been disappointing. Plants and animals extinctions have continued at the same pace as in the pre-Rio period. In 2002, the global rate of rainforest destruction was 1 per cent as it was in 1992. When one regards the Millennium Development

Goals such as the decrease of the number of human beings who have no sustainable access to drinking water and sanitation, one finds that world leaders put instead a focus on health, education, and poverty. However, this does not seem the right way, as dirty water is responsible for poor health conditions. In fact, one billion people lack safe drinking water on earth (Hopper, 2012: 216). Nevertheless, these summits act on sensitive issues and contribute to attract media attention. They provide the opportunity for NGOs and environmental campaigners to exert pressure upon governments and to disseminate topics such as sustainable development throughout the international community.

SUSTAINABLE DEVELOPMENT

Sustainable development describes a vision of global societal change that intends to realize the needs of all human beings – currently and in the future – and to assure a good life for all people (see Di Guilio, 2004: 145). This term was first published in the Brundtland Report[1] and then introduced since the UNCED conference in Rio in 1992 in numerous UN-documents (e.g. Rio declaration; Agenda 21). It constitutes an answer to the problems that became more and more important since the 1970s: increasing global ecological problems and the deepening of social inequality. While these problems are still discussed in rather different forms, the notion of sustainable development is aiming to find an integrated solution. How does this happen?

In order to link these topics, the Brundtland report has used two steps. The first has been to transform the understanding of ecological sustainability that has connected the resource in question to a notion of sustainability which covers the satisfaction of primary human needs including those of coming generations. The second step is to consider economic growth as no longer a limit but instead a precondition of sustainable development. In this way, the Brundtland report has conceived the negative ecological consequences of the industrial growth model to be the consequence of the existing technology system and the social organization of industrial growth and not to be a consequence of growth itself (Hauff, 1987: 46). On the other hand, poverty and the growth of populations are considered to be the causes of the local destruction of environments in the South. Economic growth is then, according to this discourse, a solution for both problems when growth is made sustainable. The solution of global problems of environment and development is thus not to be found in a renunciation of growth but instead in sustainable growth.

AGENDA 21

The conference in Rio used an argumentative change for this framework. The agenda adopted at this occasion (for the twenty-first century) did no longer consider poverty as the decisive cause of ecological problems but instead blamed the specific production and consumption model of the North. This model has to be transformed – so the discourse – into a sustainable model that makes use of new sustainable technologies and a science that focuses on a rationalized management of resources. Moreover, Agenda 21 emphasizes instruments that favour the environment, liberalization, and the opening up of markets. The discourse of the Brundtland report that favoured primary needs is thus changed into a discourse of ecological modernization of economic growth. A sustainable development in the South would therefore include the transfer of the ecological and modernized model of growth from the North into the South.

PARTICIPATIVE CHARACTER OF DEVELOPMENT

Another element is added to this notion of sustainable development: The focus is on the participative character of development and the tentative nature of new sustainable models of production and consumption. For Agenda 21, asking for an inclusion of all societal actors in the planned transformation process is an important aspect. In the framework of sustainable processes on a local and national level, participative forms of governance and a cooperative win-win solution of action strategies are highly important.

This form of sustainable discourse has been introduced in many policy fields. Local processes of Agenda 21 have initiated many sustainable projects. Engaged consumers and enterprises have tried new approaches of a sustainable economy. These approaches have become important tendencies, such as bio-consumption. On an international level, multiple conferences have been organized that have tried to introduce international environmental rules in fields such as climate, forest, fishery, protections of rivers, etc.

CRITICS OF SUSTAINABLE DEVELOPMENT

This dominant strategy of sustainable development has been exposed to significant critics in the North and the South. One can find two discourses (Sachs, 2002): contra-discourses that follow another understanding of nature and contra-discourses that follow another understanding of development. One can resolve the international debate on sustainable development into two axes:

a) One axis of different nature and technics images with techno-centrism (a technical and industrial model of progress) and eco-centrism (that includes industrial development into ecological circuits);

b) Another axis with different models of development and economy according to two poles: an industrial growth model that tackles the world market and a community model that tackles subsistence.

ECO-CENTRISM

Eco-centrism considers human societies not as the centre but only as one element of a life community of natural elements, animals, plants, eco-systems, landscapes, and the entire planet that have the same right to develop as human beings (see Dryzek, 1997: 155ff.). Eco-centrist positions are known as deep ecology, eco-feminism, and bio-regional models of human life.

DEEP ECOLOGY

Deep ecology is concerned with fundamental changes.

> The idea is to cultivate a deep consciousness of organic unity, of the holistic nature of the ecological webs that in which every individual is enmeshed. [...] Biocentric equality means that no species, including the human species, is regarded as more valuable or in any sense higher than other species. (Dryzek, 1997: 156)

Eco-feminism has been developed since the 1970s in women's groups in the peace and environment movements in the North and the South. These approaches are linked by common elements in research on nature exploitation and female discrimination, and follow the target to link ecological politics to the empowerment of women. Vinz (2005: 7) distinguishes two directions: cultural and social eco-feminism. The cultural model underlines a special proximity of women to nature based on bodily (menstruation and birth) and spiritual reasons, and expresses particular female values (feelings, empathy, and bodyness) against the instrumental use of nature from men. The female approach is in this sense a guarantee for a respectful treatment of nature and for a life in peace (Mies and Shiva, 1995).

BIO-REGIONALISTS

Bio-regionalists ask for a practical utopian critic of industrialization that favours subsistence agriculture and a return to ruralization (see Sale, 1985). They propagate small, decentralized forms of settlement that are oriented on the subsistence model and an ecological equilibrium with the surrounding nature. However, the actual urban life-frames can hardly permit realization of these options. These eco-centric positions are therefore mainly expressed in radical protests on communication lines, or agricultural and energetic conflicts. Greenpeace, Friends of the Earth, the Sea Shepherd Conservation Society, and Earth First! are established environmental organizations but also radical animal protectors and adversaries of gene technology. They are united by the defence of nature, animals, landscapes, and human beings.

Biologists and ecologists, in their role as scientists and as activists, share the assumption that human society is only one part of the natural world. The utilization of nature is linked to the dynamics of ecosystems and reacts in return on them. This topic is discussed in categories of energy and material flows and according to the sustainability of the earth and her ecological load-bearing capacity. As an economy can only grow until the physical limits of the system are attained (Daly, 1996), the position of heavy sustainability suggests harmonising the 'sphere of human beings' with the 'sphere of nature' (Manstetten and Faber, 1999). This intention requires the acceptance of certain societal measures. This discourse is coupled with different reformist, top-down- and bottom-up-strategies. The approach of Meadows was based on a neo-Malthusian discourse that focused on survival (Dryzek, 1997: 23ff.) and included control strategies to limit population growth and economic growth. Both, according to this discourse, have already transgressed the 'limits of growth' (Meadows et al., 2004).

ANTI-DISCOURSES

Anti-discourses, based on development and growth, focus on a fundamental critic of the notion of development and the capitalist notion of growth. In the South, this discourse is based on an anti-imperialist thinking of small communities and indigenous populations that are marginalized by economic globalization. In the North, this criticism is based on the discourse of post-growth and self-sufficient growth. Development is then seen as a neo-colonial strategy that has created an industrial sustainability discourse in order to marginalize life-worlds based on the subsistence of small farmers and indigenous populations. According to these critics, the model of development of sustainability constitutes a model of neo-colonial development and the destruction of local life-worlds and economic systems under a new ecological framework (Escobar, 1995b; Sachs, 2002). According to this viewpoint, Western rationality devalues local knowledge systems or exploits them economically in a biological-medical way. The winners of this hegemonic system are then enterprises and national governments that make profits from green and innovative technologies, and the modernized ecological growth of the economy, but also international consumers. Losers are two billion people that depend on land, forests, and water as a means of survival.

EMANCIPATED PERSPECTIVES

From these findings, critics conclude that the former notion of progress and development has to be questioned. Local and regional peasant protest movements are seen as supporters of these emancipated perspectives. They struggle for a decentralized self-determination of resources, life-worlds, and landscapes. This is not only a strug-gle over land and resources but also one about the recognition of cultural diversity. The myth of the primitive ecological wisdom of indigenous peoples that lived for many generations in a 'harmony with nature' links these local communities to radical ecological discourses (Milton, 1996).

POST-GROWTH AND SELF-SUFFICIENT DISCOURSES

Post-growth and self-sufficient discourses can be found in the North and constitute a critical part of the hegemonic sustainability discourse. Both are linked to the argu-ment of ecological justice and to a new notion of 'good life' (Sachs, 2002). Due to the social and ecological consequences of the global development model based on economic growth, this approach asks for a decrease of global industrial dependence, exploitative systems in the South, and a limitation of consumption in the North to a 'right degree'. This new model of wealth is oriented towards a 'cosmopolitan localism' (Sachs, 2002: 157). For several years, economists have discussed these alternative development models as a 'post-growth society' (Latouche, 2009) or a 'post-growth economy' (Paech, 2012). The central argument is that it is not possible to separate green economic growth from ecological damages and that a surplus of mate-rial goods at a particular level does not increase the subjective well-being but leads to more charges and more dependence. Therefore, a fortification of regional economies and an improved balance between subsistence and external supply is planned that should lead to a life that is determined less by ostensible consumption (Latouche, 2009).

As we can see, this program of ecological modernization as a solution to global sustainability problems is challenged from different positions. Yet the participative character of sustainability processes after Rio has diminished some conflicts. This development means an increase of new forms of citizen participation and coopera-tive networks at the local and regional level to improve sustainable development with the help of dialogues and cooperation.

THE ENVIRONMENTAL JUSTICE MOVEMENT[2]

In 1982, the North American movement for civil rights was founded after various cases of pollution had proven that poor districts with predominantly African-American, Hispanic, or native populations were the most affected by environmental problems. This movement has called for 'environmental justice' and has gradually implemented environmental policy in the United States (Lejeune, 2015). This idea then evolved from the discussion of preservation and nature conservation to the claim for social justice (Martinez-Alier, 2014: 385).

During the 1990s, South American NGOs introduced the concept of ecological debt into the debate. *Acción Ecológica* (1999) defines it as 'the debt accumulated by northern industrial countries towards third world countries on account of resource plundering and use of environmental space to deposit wastes'.[3] According to Martinez-Alier (2014), ecological debt is based on two main reasons: 'unequal ecological exchange' and the fact that industrial countries use a proportion of natural resources and ecosystem services far greater than their proportion of the world population.

ENVIRONMENTAL DEBT

One of the problems of justice concerns this environmental debt (Gaudillière and Flipo, 2009) that is emphasized internationally by the topic of greenhouse gas emissions. Even if climate justice is not part of international climate negotiations, this idea has been discussed by churches and think tanks, such as that of Mary Robinson (see note 4). Above all, since the beginning of the third millennium, it is a request of many local and international movements of civil society. In 2009, at the World Climate Conference in Copenhagen, the 'Principles of Climate Justice' were defined by these civil society movements:

> Leaving fossil fuels in the ground; reasserting peoples' and community control over production; re-localizing food production; massively reducing over-consumption, particularly in the global North; respecting indigenous and forest people's rights; and recognizing the ecological and climate debt owed to the people's in the global South by the societies of the global North necessitating the making of reparations. (Chatterton et al., 2012: 5)

CLIMATE JUSTICE

An overview of social movements shows that the argument for climate justice is primarily used to protest against the unequal impacts of climate change, both geographically and socially (Chatterton et al., 2012: 2). However, if many actors base their claims on the responsibility of industrialized countries for climate change, some put forward a more political approach around debts and the challenges of the capitalist mode of production (Friends of the Earth, Attac, Via Campesina, the anti-globalization movement, etc.) while others have a more developmental approach, more 'solidarity', and less 'political' factors (environmental NGOs and international solidarity NGOs such as Oxfam, CARE, Greenpeace, Amnesty International, GERES, etc.).

Climate justice is thus distributive justice and fairness concerning their necessary burden-sharing that is addressed in article 3 of the UNFCCC which says:

'The Parties should protect the climate system for the benefit of present and future generations of humankind, on the basis of equity and in accordance with their common but differentiated responsibilities and respective capabilities.'[5] But its implementation is not realized without any difficulties as shown in the international climate negotiations, such as the Paris Climate Conference (COP 21).

By highlighting the inequalities between countries in their ability to respond to the consequences of climate change, to withstand shocks and to adapt, climate justice also questions the notion of development. The climate issue highlights the fact that rich countries have developed to such an extent by taking advantage of natural resources that poor countries cannot do the same today. Can 'sustainable development' remedy these inequalities? Can we think sustainable development without climate change? Today, the media coverage of scientific data and the urgency to act are such that the issue of climate change and sustainable development matters. While sustainable development is a concept that reunites on the same level economic, social, and environmental factors, it remains little operational (see Zaccai, 2011: 52).

Development that does not meet the requirements of climate justice and is based on an increased consumption of resources for which the competition between countries and individuals increases, causes conflicts, so that issues of environment are acquiring a strategic dimension. The global environmental justice movement cannot thus be reduced to the fight for equality of the economic and environmental decisions. For the English philosopher J. Garvey (2008), the fight against climate change is not just economic and political, but also has a moral justice dimension.

CONCLUSION

To conclude, one can argue that it seems as if sustainable development has been replaced by 'green' development and industrial innovation insofar as these are better accepted in discussions in the North, the South, and emerging countries. Growth has been declared indispensable in the different international financial and economic crises of the last years. The notion of green economy is

> [a] concept that embodies the promise of a new development paradigm, whose application has the potential to ensure the preservation of the earth's ecosystem along new economic growth pathways while contributing at the same time to poverty reduction. (UN DESA, 2011c: v)

Sustainable development must currently be understood within the context of globalization and environmental decline. In a time of globalization, states have difficulties to implement coherent and effective national sustainable development

projects. As developing countries are most vulnerable, they have even more difficulties to implement sustainable development. Today, it continues to be difficult
to observe the impacts of sustainable development. This may signify that we need
a new approach of sustainable development that respects national environmental
strategies. As we live in a period of accelerated environmental decline which had
already been predicted by international scientists some 40 years ago (Meadows,
1972), the dominant approach of sustainable development that includes social,
environmental, and economic goals needs to be rethought. The UNRISD Flagship
Report 2016 gives interesting insights to this development and the necessity of
policy innovations to realize this transformative change.

DISCUSSION QUESTIONS

1. How do you understand the ecological transformation of modern societies?

2. Please give an overview on global governance and the environment for the
    last decades.

3. What does sustainable development mean in the Sustainable Development
    Goals (SDGs)?

4. What do you know about the Environmental Justice Movement?

5. How do you explain the Papal Encyclical on humanity's relationship with the
    environment?

ANNOTATED FURTHER READINGS

Crate, S. A. and Nuttall, M. (eds) (2016) *Anthropology and Climate Change:
From Actions to Transformations* **(Second edition). New York: Routledge.**
This second edition lays out what anthropologists know about climate change
today, introduces new theoretical and practical perspectives, gives insights gleaned
from sociology, and displays international efforts to study and curb climate change.

Newsham, A. and Bhagwat, S. (2016) *Conservation and Development.* **Abingdon
and New York: Routledge.**
By the utilization of conceptual resources from political ecology, social-ecological
systems thinking, and science and technology studies, this book sets the relationship
of conservation and development against the background of the political and
economic processes implicated in environmental degradation and poverty alike.

Vogler, J. (2016) *Climate Change in World Politics.* **Basingstoke: Palgrave Macmillan.**
This book examines the international politics of climate change, with a focus on the United Nations Framework Convention (UNFCCC). It considers how the international system treats the problem of climate change, analysing the ways in which this has been defined by the international community and the interests and alignments of state governments.

Websites

http://www.unep.org/
Site of the United Nations Environment Program.

http://www.unep.org/annualreport/2014/en/index.html
The Annual UNEP report.

http://www.mrfcj.org
Mary Robinson Foundation for Climate Justice.

http://www.rac-f.org
Réseau action climat (French).

http://350.org
Global Climate Movement.

http://www.ipcc.ch
The website for the Intergovernmental Panel on Climate Change and a link to the Assessments Reports.

http://www.foe.org
Site of the Friends of the Earth, a leading environmental NGO.

http://www.worldwatch.org
Environmental research organization.

(all websites accessed 14 October 2016)

NOTES

1   *Our Common Future.* Available at http://www.un-documents.net/k-001303.htm (accessed 21 December 2016).

2   Marie-Noëlle Reboulet prepared this part on the justice movement while writing a master thesis with the title *Energy and Climate Change: the GERES, a NGO between Ground and Advocacy* prepared under the direction of Ulrike Schuerkens at the EHESS, Paris in 2015.

3   Available at http://www.ejolt.org/2013/05/ecological-debt/ (accessed 24 April 2016).

4   http://www.mrfcj.org/news/statement-mary-robinson-papal-encyclical.html (accessed 14 October 2016).

5   Available at https://unfccc.int/resource/docs/convkp/conveng.pdf (accessed 24 October 2016).

9

CONFLICT, COMPETITION, COOPERATION, AND GLOBAL CHANGE

Summary

In our current global world characterized by the neoliberal credo, the notion of competition is becoming even more important as scholars begin to do research on the success or the failure of economic policies in various world regions characterized by different cultural life-worlds (Schuerkens, 2004 and 2008). The results of these studies of recent transformations of local socio-economic practices may have wider implications for development cooperation. Conflicts may thus be strongly based on aspects linked to particular cultures, a fact that would validate Huntington's thesis that the central political actors of the twenty-first century will be civilizations rather than nation-states.

INTRODUCTION

In this chapter, I present the scientific meaning of the notions of conflict, competition, and cooperation and their possible influence on global change. These three notions are important for the analysis of social change in societies of the geographic, or better, the economic North and South. The notion of conflict was of interest mainly in the 1980s and was used by scholars such as Dahrendorf, Coser, Rex, and Collins. In recent years, with the end of the Cold War and the consequent decline of states in Eastern Europe, there has been a renewed interest in the topic. Scholars have asked why social transformations in these countries have resulted in difficult social situations and why social conflicts, often based on ethnic identities, have been widespread. The notion of cooperation is another important term of this research field because of the fact that the whole development project is based on processes of cooperation, linking Northern and Southern countries in common endeavours. This chapter surveys the history of development cooperation since the 1950s when large groups of countries have been included in an ever-growing world-system. Since the end of the global competition characteristic of the era of the Cold War, processes of competition play a lesser role in global change insofar as democratic institutions in the South are often weakly developed and elites tend to confront each other on ethnic grounds, which often occasions violent conflicts. Insofar as globalization is linked to economic competition, the question is which cultural characteristics competition are asked for in different world regions. The three notions are important at the macro, meso, and micro levels depending on socio-historical situations. In this chapter, principally because of constraints on length, we focus on the macro level. In the last 50 years, the international political situation has influenced local groups, nation-states, and transnational relations in different ways. The changing importance and meaning of the three notions in this research field can redraw this situation. To summarize, focusing on societies from several regions of the world, this chapter addresses the challenge of these notions, the types of explanations proposed, and outlines some of the main recent empirical findings.

THE NOTION OF COOPERATION[1]

After the declaration of US President Truman in 1947, aid emerged as an international task that had to include the non-European world in the twentieth (European) century by increasing the standards of living of all societies. The relation of subordination of colonized people to colonizers changed insofar as former colonies were gradually integrated into a world system, organized as an economic hierarchy. In fact, the United States were interested in gaining access to the markets in the colonial empires of European colonial powers (see Rist, 1996: 126). The 'development project', as McMichael (2012) defined it, lent legitimation to political actions aimed at developing 'underdeveloped' nations. The increase of economic production was considered the element that could transform the situation of developing countries. The Bandung Conference (1955), where Asian and African nations met, declared that cooperation was necessary in order to integrate 'underdeveloped' nations into the global economy. In 1962, the Secretary-General of the United Nations, U Thant, wrote a report in which he asserted that development was considered an economic change accompanied by social transformations. The influential economist W. W. Rostow (1960) thought that cooperation with the West would mean economic growth and the possibility of democratic development in the South. Rostow's idea was that a universal 'modernity' would replace 'traditions'. The French economist F. Perroux (1961) analyzed the 'colonial situation' (Balandier, 1985) that he condemned, and asked for transformations of the unequal social, political, and economic structures after countries achieved formal independence.

THEORY OF MODERNIZATION AND DEPENDENCY THEORIES

During this period, the theory of modernization was shown to be applicable, insofar as the political strategies of cooperation implemented by the countries of the North privileged internal growth in and international assistance to the South. Latin-American intellectuals counter-attacked with the idea that international cooperation would not improve the situation in the South but that external dependence had increased instead. The arguments of these intellectuals were progressively adopted by political opponents to the USA and by groups in the South that tried to criticize modernization theories. Yet the adoption of the dependency theory was not followed by concrete political measures.

For Rostow, internal inequality was considered positive because, as he saw it, competition would lead to development. In contrast, Latin-American scholars underlined that inequality was problematic and required state intervention. The former declared that an increasing integration of 'young nations' in the global market would automatically result in development; the latter declared that separation from the unequal world economy would be necessary to improve the situation of these countries. Studies of the ECLA (Economic Commission for Latin America) (Frank, 1967) had shown that free exchange brought advantages to the North and disadvantages to the South, which would result in the 'core-periphery' scheme of the global world. These scholars asked for regional economic integration, industrialization that would substitute for imports, and the intervention of the state in order to avoid inequality. The Third World movements that appeared during this period tried to correct the disparities of the colonial division of labour (primary goods exchanged for manufactured products).

The result of this discussion was that 'development' and 'underdevelopment' were considered to be linked globally (Azoulay, 2002). Cooperation was situated in the *longue durée* that insisted on structural conditions of internal (local elites) and external (world economy) domination. Numerous scholars from the South and the North contributed to this discussion by analyzing different factors (for example, Cardoso and Faletto, 1979; Frank, 1967) and presenting evidence of unequal relations, characterized more by conflict than by cooperation.

NEW INTERNATIONAL ECONOMIC WORLD ORDER

In 1973, the movement around the New International Economic World Order asked for a redistribution of the advantages of economic growth. The idea was to improve the integration of the countries of the South into the global system. But financial crises, the beginning of the debt regime, and structural adjustments changed the focus of this movement. The new regulation system had less consideration for the protection of labourers than it did for the protection of financial credits. The imposition of austerity measures by indebted governments worsened social inequalities even more. During these years, the importance of the 'basic needs' approach began to emerge, even if its theoretical foundations (a common 'human nature') were rather limited.

THE 1980S

Finally, theoretical approaches began to lose their importance in the face of actions taken by international cooperation actors, such as the World Bank, the International Monetary Fund, and other organizations of the United Nations. The 'laws' of the market were increasingly opposed to humanitarian actions of UN agencies and NGOs. Political actions placed the Westernization of the world by economic, political, and social leaders in question. Indigenous groups were defended to a greater extent. The fall of the Iron Curtain resulted in the disappearance in Eastern Bloc countries of a model of development that had been favoured by parts of the South. In 1987, the World Commission on Environment and Development (WCED) published a report entitled *Our Common Future*. The document came to be known as the *Brundtland Report* after the Commission's chairwoman, Gro Harlem Brundtland. It focused on the necessity of supporting environmental measures and international development. The Earth Summit organized by the United Nations Conference on Environment and Development in Rio de Janeiro in 1992 popularized the idea of an irreversible sustainable development. 172 governments participated in the conference; 108 at the level of heads of States or governments.

THE 1990S

Since the final years of the twentieth century, the UNDP (United Nations Development Program) has favoured a development approach that added a human dimension to economic growth. Cooperation in a global world had become a condition for development. International organizations, together with national political and economic elites, increasingly favoured international cooperation while numerous counter-movements appeared that criticized the globalization process, such as Attac (*Association pour la taxation des transactions pour l'aide aux citoyens*) or the Zapatista movement in Mexico.

FEMINIST CRITIQUES OF DEVELOPMENT

It is interesting to analyze feminist critiques of development that are concerned with the negative impact of mainstream development on the lives of women. In some cases, development projects, introduced to improve welfare of certain groups, have led to a decline in women's well-being. Since the 1970s, the women's movement and women's activism have contributed to research programs in both the North and the South. In the 1970s, women were brought 'into' development; this focus was named the women-in-development (WID) approach. The WID approach influenced the policies of the World Bank without challenging existing gender ideologies that conceive all reproductive work (= childrearing) as women's work. Some ten years later, the focus was extended with the influence of feminist theorizing about research on women-and-development (WAD). More recently, feminist researchers in the North have underlined the need to contextualize the discourse on development in order to show its effects on women. These studies are complementary to those of indigenous feminists. Moreover, current feminist research on development covers issues such as the debates about the environment and about sustainable development. Feminists have underlined the fallacy of using numerical measures of economic growth to assess the attainment of goals. In this connection, one of the main problems is the public-private dichotomy, which maintains that women can gain equality by participating more in the formal economy, without assigning any economic value to women's reproductive work. Unequal gender relations became a central concern of development in the 1990s. Some feminists have insisted that development policies have to be 'engendered' and women have to be empowered so that development will be beneficial to them. Neo-classical development theories that consider indigenous attitudes and institutions as barriers to development tend to place women's understandings of life outside their concepts of development. Feminist scholarship has contributed to an examination of the ways women's labour is used in factories and in export-processing zones. These scholars have documented how women in developing countries receive lower wages than men for comparable work (Chow, 2003).

Using a gender perspective means asking what kinds of development can promote the interests of women in the South. This may be the necessary link between human development and economic development in a world characterized by the neoliberal globalization credo.

NATIONAL SOCIAL POLICIES

Amartya Sen, the 1998 Nobel laureate in economics, added a further dimension to recent discussions on cooperation: he underlined that globalization needs to be backed by national social policies, a sort of social safety net like the one which was created in Western European states at the beginning of the twentieth century. Wide protest movements in the 2000s (e.g. Greece, Portugal, Spain, France) suggest that not only developing countries are concerned with these effects of globalization when economies open widely to international capital inflows so that people find it difficult to survive in highly competitive environments. According to Sen, programs that empower people have to focus on micro-credits, literacy, and land reforms. In his book *Development as Freedom*, Sen (1999) underlines the conception that freedoms include political freedom, economic facilities, social opportunities, and security. He reiterates the advantages of capabilities ('substantive human freedoms') over narrower measures of human development. In Sen's opinion, the idea of human capital fails to capture the contributions of human capabilities to well-being and their influences on social change. New concepts are thus incorporated in the development discourse: empowerment and participation.

In summary, up until the 1970s, development theory and practice were dominated by the idea of economic growth and economic indicators. This understanding reflected a lack of knowledge about the low level of investment in human and social capital, and the weakness of markets. The further assumption that growth would trickle down from the rich to the poor, reflected ignorance about rather different social structures. Distributional issues began to emerge in the 1970s in the South American centre-periphery approach with a focus on topics such as poverty and inequality. The dependency theories school highlighted the constraints imposed on development processes in the periphery by an unequal international economic system. In the 1980s, world systems theorists interpreted interdependence in dynamic terms in order to prepare the ground for studies of the impact of globalization on poor people and poor countries in the 1990s. North-South cooperation thus remains complex, with a slowly changing focus.

We can conclude this part on cooperation by underlining the fact that, despite cooperation measures for over 50 years, the elementary needs of more than one billion of people are not satisfied. Furthermore, the possibility of satisfying them in the future is questionable. Thus, we confront a double global crisis: a crisis in the distribution of income and a crisis in growth. The only convergent phenomena in the economies of the South and the North seem to be the growth of social inequality and of poverty during the last two decades (see Sassen, 2014). In the South, development is necessary because of the fact that the most important needs of huge population groups are not satisfied. In the North, an improved life quality of the whole population should be privileged, not only a quantitative growth. Perhaps it is necessary to reverse priorities: the economy might be transformed in order to become an instrument. Consistent with this choice would be that economic and financial criteria would no longer be societal priorities. Projects for a sustainable human development would then tackle problems such as the spread of wealth and improving quality of life.

THE NOTION OF CONFLICT

In the 1960s, a growing scientific literature was convinced that conflict, defined as opposing social classes, allowed social change to emerge. In the 1990s and at the beginning of the twenty-first century, some scholars have begun to stress that the absence of social change has led to conflict situations that can be found in several African countries, such as the Ivory Coast, Sierra Leone, and Liberia, but also in the Balkans.

CONFLICT THEORIES OF THE 1960S

A common feature of all conflict theories of this period is the assumption that change is explained by contradictions or elements that generate tensions in all societal systems. The reasons for these conflicts are linked to elements of the social structure that, on the one hand, determine or sanction norms and, on the other hand, control and award resources such as income, wealth, prestige, influence, etc. Theoretical approaches insist on processes of societal life that lead to instability and conflicts within the different sectors of a society. Change is considered to be taking place due to a dialectical relationship of important structural elements of a society (values, ideologies, power relations, distribution of resources, etc.) and elements that are in competition with these arrangements. The result is societal change. Power relations of a society in economic, political, and cultural systems are tackled, but normative elements, such as rules or attitudes, are not considered.

Marx, one of the earliest theoreticians of conflict, studied the capitalist 'revolution', which he described as a historical phenomenon that contributed to providing the 'proletariat' with opportunities to realize human liberty and self-determination in order to control historical processes. This idea had two important consequences: first, according to Marx, relations of production determine the distribution of professional and financial possibilities, the influence on enterprises, and the interest structure of a society. The second conclusion is that an improvement of material conditions will be linked to the institutionalization of democratic forms of interaction.

Marx saw two causes for societal conflicts: structural contradictions and antagonistic class relations. The structural contradictions were seen in the negative consequences of the social division of labour and the link between productive forces and relations of production. Marx and Engels considered the division of labour the main factor that caused contradictions between individual and societal interests. These contradictions, according to Marx, should increase, because of structural contradictions between 'base' (*Basis*) and 'superstructure' (*Überbau*). The changes in the base (the productive forces) would imply further changes in the societal superstructure (laws, political institutions, educational programs, family structures, etc.).

The history of human interaction was, according to Marx, determined by the conflict of two social groups: one that controlled the means of production and another that did not possess this power. A potential for conflict leading to a spontaneous change was thus created by the 'natural' difference of interests between both groups. This conflict not only changes system relations, but also leads to a breakdown of the given social structure and the development of new kinds of relations based on new means of production.

VARIETIES OF NON-MARXIST CONFLICT THEORIES[2]

The theories of conflict conceived by Ralf Dahrendorf (1964), Lewis A. Coser (1967a), David Lockwood (1964), Raymond Aron (1963), John Rex (1981), and Randall Collins (1975) maintained many elements of the Marxist approach to the explanation of social change, but dropped the utopian idealism of Marx. By contrast, earlier theoreticians of conflict, such as Gumplowicz (1885/1926) and Ratzenhofer (1907), did not explain social change as deriving from social structure; rather they looked at change as the outcome of conflict between different social systems. We can still find this position today, expressed in claims that:

- 'Underdevelopment' is the consequence of the relation between different parts of the world ('First World', 'Second World', and 'Third World'; 'core countries' and 'periphery').

- Less developed and more developed societies are distinguished by looking for characteristics such as individual traits of modernity.

- Social change of less developed societies is understood as the result of their own history and that of Northern countries.

DAHRENDORF

Dahrendorf (1967), who discussed the Marxist theory of class structure and social change extensively, accepted the model of a dichotomous class structure and the Marxist position that class theory explains social change. He developed a theory of conflict where group interests confront each other and where change results from the conflict of antagonistic interests that are characteristic of a given power structure. Dahrendorf thought that the exercise of any form of authority implied a latent conflict of interests within the affected groups: those who have power and those who must put up with the power of the powerful. He considered the opposition of interests to be the main cause of social change while conflicts among interest groups represented the medium that led to the change of a given power structure. Societal norms and rules that are fortified by law are, according to Dahrendorf, the main reason for the opposition of interests.

COSER

Coser (1967a) was interested in the conflict approach insofar as he considered that social change was the result of tensions resulting from competition for scarce resources, such as power, wealth, and prestige. There is a constant tension amongst those who have an interest in maintaining the status quo and those who seek an increase in their share of power, income, ownership, and prestige. This tension does not always mean conflict, because efforts to maintain or to change a given structure of distribution result from a comparison with others. Coser (1967b: 17-35) considered that the degree of legitimacy of an unequal distribution of rights and opportunities plays a decisive part and may create conflicts between members of groups occupying different hierarchical positions in a society. A social conflict between underprivileged and over-privileged groups is created only when the first has developed a consciousness that its members are negatively privileged, in short, that their shares in societal resources are inadequate. Conflict always occurs during the interaction of two or more actors. There is a 'transaction' in order to create a changed social structure. Social change is induced because conflict always leads to the establishment or reestablishment of a system of social relations.

In contrast to Dahrendorf, Coser succeeded in using a conflict approach to explain not only power and its consequences for social change, but also how social interests, needs, and the power structure of a society are inter-dependent as they are modified and strengthened. Coser could thus develop a typology of social conflicts that included international and internal conflicts between and within groups, as well as varying degrees of violence. In addition, he included conflicts that take place directly (for example a strike) or indirectly (for example through competition); moreover, he considered conflicts that include real participants or their substitutes.

WEBER VS. MARX

The history of industrial society is characterized by a multiplicity of forms of conflict (among them conflicts between employers and employees) that have changed from violent direct conflicts to organized conflicts via labour unions. While the Marxist theory of societal change predicted a widening of industrial conflicts in the political sphere, theoreticians influenced by Weber's notion of power[3] believed that modern Western industrial society would be able to regulate economic conflicts politically, by fixing laws for employer-employee relations, for example, and by elaborating schemes for assuring a minimal wage and social security. Other conflict theoreticians explained the weaker effects of class conflict by the weak link between differences of interest and real conflict behaviour. They pointed out the pluralism of interests according to social positions and social life-worlds (Dahrendorf, 1969) or the stabilizing effects of some conflicts (Coser, 1967a). In their efforts to explain conflicts, however, functionalists underlined the far-reaching disappearance of divergent interests between classes, a fact that was empirically proved by the existence of a multiplicity of social classes and groups, the delimitations of which presented empirical–methodological challenges.

ARON

In a classical article, Aron (1950) examined conflicts of interest that arise in pluralistic societies, but he criticized the Marxist notion of a classless society. He wrote: 'In one way a classless society resolves the conflicts found in fully mature capitalist societies, but the solution involves the reduction of society to obedience rather than general liberation' (1950: 134).

The relations between different groups that are in competition for their share of income and which can be distinguished from one another by their power and by the political and economic means that they can often utilize become conflictive. The two principal sources of conflict in a modern society are, according to Aron, on the one hand, unequal conditions in the means a given group in competition for income has at its disposal, and, on the other hand, the problem of an economic recession that may affect industrialized societies. Change takes place when interest groups are formed and when they enter into open competition.

While it is possible to analyze types of conflicts, as well as their causes and consequences at the level of social groups or societies, it is also possible to tackle the sociological analysis of conflicts at an international level. Aron's book *Peace and War* (1963) is a good example of the importance of the vocabulary of conflict theory for the analysis of relations between states, when power, violence, types of war, and peace are discussed. Aron saw two alternative interpretations of war as a means to regulate relations between states that insist on their national interest. Whether there is peace through law (for example by inter-state treaties and international committees) or peace through government (for example through the construction of a world empire or simpler, through zones of influence) depends on

1.   the extent of power that participant nations can have at their disposal,

2.   the interest that the participants display, and

3.   the role that these elements have while producing or changing these constellations.

Together with further indications of the integrative functions of conflicts (Coser, 1967a) and conflictive characteristics of norms (Dahrendorf, 1964; Lockwood, 1964), these remarks allow us to note a decisive characteristic of social life: the consensual nature of conflict and war, and the antagonistic nature of order and peace. Aron's full meaning is shown in his proposal (1963) of a third alternative to war, namely peace through power equilibrium. This situation can be explained, on the one hand, by the consensus of power blocs on minimal rules of behaviour and on limits to spheres of influence and, on the other hand, by an equilibrium in the possession of weapons of deterrence (for example the Cold War).

Treaties on rules of behaviour may control conflicts and conflicts may have positive consequences for the further existence of a society; but the history of most societies provides many examples that relations between members of societies, based on norms, may be founded on force and rule, and may develop a great potential that can lead to conflict and change.

RESEARCH INSIGHTS: CLIMATE CHANGE AND SOCIAL CONFLICT IN AFRICA

CASE STUDY

C. S. Hendrix and I. Salehyan published in 2012 a study using a database of over 6,000 instances of social conflict over 20 years – The Social Conflict in Africa Database. They examined the effect of deviations from normal rainfall patterns on different types of conflict. Their results show that rainfall variability significantly influences both large-scale and smaller-scale instances of political

(Continued)

(Continued)

conflict. According to them, rainfall correlates with civil war and insurgency, while particularly wet or dry years are associated positively with all types of political conflict. Violent events are more responsive to abundant than scarce rainfall. They conclude their study by demonstrating a significant relationship between environmental shocks and unrest.

Source: Hendrix, C.S. and Salehyan, I. (2012) 'Climate change, rainfall, and social conflict in Africa', *Journal of Peace Research* 49 (1): 35–50.

To conclude this section on the notion of conflict, we are able to show that theoreticians of conflict locate the origin of social contradictions, conflicts, and social change in the redistribution of power. This may be economic, political, or status power, or the 'cultural' power to define goals and norms. Conflicts between those who control access to scarce and valuable resources of a society and those who wish to have a greater share in these resources induce significant changes. While social structures may be explained by behaviours that result from different types of available societal resources, social change results from movements within these possibilities or from preceding conflicts (Collins, 1975: 61, 89). To simplify, one could describe non-Marxist theoreticians of conflict as proponents of a cyclical conflict theory, because they consider conflict and rule of law as universal. By contrast, Marx and his followers present a dynamic and evolutionary conflict theory. They consider conflicts necessary for social change. The first theory speaks of gradual change as a consequence of conflicts and the second theory sees conflicts as the triggers for sudden changes. However, both recognize that the flexibility of a given societal system can induce gradual and/or violent change.

When we return to current political situations, it is an essential task of international political and social development measures to try to maintain and fortify state structures in order to prevent the collapse and the degeneration of states that may cause political conflicts. Without development, ethnic conflicts may not end. Therefore, many states are dependent on external aid measures that permit them to democratize, decentralize, and demilitarize societies successfully. A desire for self-determination, a lack of opportunities for political and economic participation, undermining a particular cultural identity, etc., may cause conflicts that are expressed in power struggles of competing elites for the control of the state and of its material resources. In such situations, the cultivation of ethnic and religious identities helps to create images of enemies. Political entrepreneurs (two recent examples are those in the Democratic Republic of the Congo and the Ivory Coast) do not hesitate to mobilize a politicized ethnicity as an instrument for their conquest of power.[4]

THEORIES ON WAR AND CHANGE

Classical theories of war and change have produced a statistically based theory known as the 'Phoenix Factor' (Strakes, 2006: 1677). This theory states that a country that is defeated in a war will catch up and eventually overtake the victor as its post-war development accelerates. In the framework of this theory, it is the country's domestic economic performance that is important for its recovery and not the provision of foreign aid. In fact, this theory may apply to major industrial nations, but not to the majority of developing countries faced with different structural problems inside and outside their region. Conflicts may even be perpetuated here when there is a lack of effective means of dispute resolution. Political leaders may, furthermore, be responsible for policies that intend to maintain their power or that intend to benefit society as a whole. Certain privileged groups, as some theoretical approaches have emphasized, can hinder growth after a conflict. The deficiency in growth will perpetuate tensions and the result will be further domestic conflicts. Political and military repression implemented to maintain the power of the reigning elite will contribute to fuel resistance movements. It is obvious that these conflicts waste valuable resources and hinder investments that may benefit the whole society. Illustrative cases are concentrated in sub-Saharan Africa in particular. The above-mentioned findings demonstrate that civil wars, which have become more prevalent than international conflicts, cannot be ignored by prosperous nations. They are largely concentrated in low-income countries. Yet these conflicts can impact the world as a whole, not only neighbouring countries, as the Iraqi and Syrian conflicts demonstrate. The attempt to impose democratic accountability and constitutional government has been destructive in these cases. Reconstruction aid must certainly be linked to reforms and institution-building efforts, but political pragmatism has to be supported by research-based programs in order to assure successful post-conflict environments.

EMPIRICAL EVIDENCE OF CONFLICTS IN THE POST-WORLD WAR II ERA

Conflicts have seldom become a topic of empirical transformation and development studies,[5] yet some rather general remarks can be formulated. The world of the end of the nineteenth century was a world of nation-states in competition. The global world of the twenty-first century is a world characterized by political unity where territorial frontiers no longer form violent borderlines. After World War II, the new global order was based on the cooperation of states in the United Nations. Violence no longer occurred at the frontiers between the principal Western states, but existed between the 'free world' and States with communist regimes. The Cold War led to a bipolar system of military conflicts, even in developing countries, favouring one or the other. The period beginning in the 1990s marks an era when major conflicts between larger states disappeared and when minor, but often highly violent, conflicts of smaller states and societies have become more frequent.

The beginning and the end of the period of the Cold War were marked by two principal military and political crises: that of the period from 1945 to 1947 and that of the period from 1989 to 1991, when the global order emerged from the breakdown of the Cold War order. The former national-international order was characterized by international, or rather, interstate conflicts. Revolutions and civil conflicts were based on this international structure. Conflicts of this period displayed the antagonism between the two sides of the Cold War. After the end of the Cold War, new forms of disintegration appeared, linked to the failure of communist states. Conflicts arose in the former Soviet and the former Yugoslavian multinational states, where elites fought for political control of new states and territories. In Somalia and in some other African states, local forms of rule disintegrated. Recent conflicts are thus geographically localized. In unstable forms of some states there are now conflicts that question the global order, rather than the Cold War order, as was the case in the past. Currently, interstate conflicts are more or less limited to 'villain' states, as was the case of the Iraq of Sadam Hussein. Most of the states in the world no longer accept violent situations with other states, although some may indirectly support conflicts against populations in their own territories or in those of their neighbours (for example the Republic of the Congo (Vlassenroot, 2003) or Turkey in 2015–16). Often, these later states are no longer able to impose taxes and/or raise armies. New forms of policing, a function that the USA, the United Nations, and the European Union began to carry out in the 1990s, may characterize the future. The political aim has been to guarantee respect for law and order. Yet, it seems to be certain, as Shaw underlines, that future social transformations and global development will continue to be characterized by conflicts (Shaw, 2003: 75).

CASE STUDY

RESEARCH INSIGHTS: WOMEN'S AGENCY IN WAR AND POST-CONFLICT SRI LANKA

The case study of Darini Rajasingham-Senanayake focuses on women's agency in post-conflict Sri Lanka. The author asks if and how a return of peace may affect women's empowerment. As armed combatants, principal income generators or heads of household in the absence of men, women have carved new roles and new spaces of agency. The question was if they would be pushed back into traditional women roles as mothers and housewives with a return to peace and thus would return to the pre-war gender status quo. Based on ethnographic fieldwork, the author finds that 'the structure of the "new war" in

Sri Lanka may not permit a return to a pre-war gender status quo' (2004: 141). For women who have lost the head of household in the conflict or in the violence, there is no possibility to return to the former status quo of the nuclear family, headed by the father. For these widows, the changes after almost two decades of armed conflict were too complex and of a fundamental kind.

Source: Rajasingham-Senanayake, D. (2004) 'Between reality and representation: Women's agency in war and post-conflict Sri Lanka', *Cultural Dynamics* 16 (2/3): 141–68.

RESEARCH INSIGHTS: CIVIL WAR AND LIFE CHANCES

Civil war has a negative impact on life chances such as economic well-being, food production, health, and education. These life chances are important for social and economic development. Moreover, civil war affects the most basic life chances such as mortality. In the last years, national development was not only seen as a function of economic development but had to include both economic development and infrastructures, such as agricultural and educational development. These infrastructures improve the life of the average person so that these populations are well fed and well educated. However, human capabilities are degraded by civil wars that precipitate a process of economic decline. The production of food is impeded and mortality rates of children are higher than in non-war countries. Recovery may require decades of development efforts. Rebuilding societies means to rebuild infrastructures (physical and social) and reinvest in economies. Military expenditures have to be requested; development financed and included in the global economic context. The development of peace and increasing human capabilities may permit the building of peaceful societies.

Carlton-Ford, S. and Boop, D. (2010) 'Civil war and life chances: A multinational study', *International Sociology* 25 (1): 75-97.

THE NOTION OF COMPETITION IN TRANSFORMATION STUDIES

With the growing globalization of the last decades, the breakdown of the communist system and the spread of the neoliberal economic credo, the notion of competition began to be discussed in the sociology of global change. The discussion centred on whether the economic ideology linked to the notion could be an impetus for development in countries socially and culturally very different from the Western core countries. As there was no real alternative to the Western economic ideal of competition, economists and sociologists began to ask whether the notion of economic competition could be integrated into social, cultural, and economic systems in Asia, Latin America, and Africa. The answer depended on the social structure of societies in the different world regions.

CULTURAL LIFE-WORLDS

In this context, it is necessary to define the notion of culture, which will make it possible to show the importance of cultural elements in economic endeavours. Culture can be conceived as a system of common experiences on the basis of which one can understand one's own group and confront other groups. Culture is thus a network of meaning structures that help social actors to orient their ideas toward a common worldview. These values facilitate and orient human actions in concrete situations. It is obvious that some cultures are better suited to active participation in global phenomena than others. In the tradition of Max Weber, a Confucian performance ideal, for instance, is more adapted to economic competition than egalitarian African conceptions. The German historian Hans-Ulrich Wehler stated some years ago that the prevalence of socio-economic and political constellations in social history should be replaced by the prevalence of cultural life-worlds that govern the construction of social reality (1998: 9). This reflection on the cultural construction of life-worlds in a global society seems to be a precondition for the analysis of discourses on economic globalization in non-European societies. In this sense, it is not the image of globalization that is in the foreground, but the construction and development of worldviews deriving from cultural contexts. These worldviews determine the results of cultural dialogues and the outcomes of socio-economic globalization processes in different world regions.

It can no longer be denied that today all cultures are exposed to a new historical process of change, and that elites and masses are challenged to confront the outcomes of global processes with creative answers, protest, selective adaptations, etc. The era of the uncritical acceptance of Western elements has been abandoned by non-Western cultures for a greater self-consciousness. Nevertheless, global players pressure local and regional cultures to adopt Western definitions of adaptation and efficiency. The world market – defined by competitive capitalism, the importance of private property, and the virtue of individual aspirations for gain – has become the dominant world system, a system that was introduced by colonial processes in non-Western societies during the last several centuries. World cultures are shaped by their adaptability to global economic processes. To be declared as an acceptable culture may accommodate capital investment and capital use (see Tetzlaff, 2000: 41).

Experience has shown that societies that possess structural equivalences to Western societal models have been preferred by transnational enterprises, and societies where solidarity and equality are high social values have been avoided. In its *World Culture Report* (1998: 283), UNESCO shows that in Asian countries values such as independence and responsibility receive high social scores whereas in African countries values such as obedience and religious beliefs are favoured. According to global players, competition for socio-cultural systems that permit the highest profits has become established. Societies that are capable of learning changes required by capitalist logic receive higher scores than societies that resist these changes.

This approach that intends to unite economic interests, cultural preferences, and political institutions in one logical system permits an analysis of why some societies are more able to confront world market conditions than others. The notion of competition is not easily accepted by societies that value traditions and mythical conceptions and which favour, for example, strong reciprocal exchanges based on kinship.

THE NOTION OF COMPETITION IN SOUTHERN COUNTRIES

Globalization has been considered by influential elites in Asia as merely an economic endeavour that could be separated from its parallel societal structures, such as democratization or Asian values, family values, respect of ancestors and community, hard work and thrift (see Schubert, 2000: 141). The integration of Asia into a global economic world, with its required international competition, is generally not challenged. The discussion focuses more on the right way to undertake this transformation than on the goal as such. Asian values have been considered responsible for rapid economic growth in the region. Western critics emphasize that these values favour small enterprises, but that they are not capable of expanding their growth because of the centralized family organization. There is a need to encourage the growth of the formal sector, as informality in the region is concentrated in smaller firms, operating away from the international sector of the economy. Strategies are needed to discourage informal employment by assistance for SMEs (Small and Medium-Sized Enterprises), a change in the tax and regulatory environment, and investment in formal sector productivity. The need for a cultural adaptation to the economic conditions of globalization has been realized in countries such as Singapore, Malaysia, and South Korea. At the same time, the region is beginning to consider democracy as the necessary political regime for a market economy, even if some countries such as China or Vietnam continue to resist this understanding and corruption at all levels is high. After the crisis of the 1990s, the problem of social inequality has received growing attention in some countries in order to permit the creation of fairer social conditions.

CHINA

In China, several understandings of globalization co-exist (Keping, 2000): there are scholars who insist that the visible side of globalization is represented by economic integration and the invisible side by the integration of democratic and global values. Others consider globalization as the final form of capitalism in its current structure. In general, Chinese political elites think that opportunities for globalization have to be combined with challenges to Chinese society that became obvious in the crises of the 1990s. Many intellectuals argue, however, that globalization should be accepted in Asia without a Westernization of society (cf. Keping, 2000; Schubert, 2000; Lin, 2001).

AFRICA

In Africa, the situation is quite different: elites in most African societies have not favoured economic competition (Damon and Igué, 2003). Africa is situated at the margin of economic globalization with few transnational enterprises in a limited number of oil producing countries, such as Nigeria, Gabon, and the Republic of the Congo. Private capital flows are low except for South Africa. Most of the countries are highly indebted and have low productivity rates. The level of human capital is low so that an economic take-off is difficult to realize even in the service sector because a qualified workforce is needed. Intellectual elites leave the countries for Europe or North America. Economic elites place their savings in Northern countries. Structural economic factors can hardly be changed, with agriculture the primary employer of the continent and industrialization that cannot create enough jobs for the unemployed youth of the continent. Social and cultural values, such as the family or strategies of survival, traditional values, jealousy of another's success, vertical networks of redistribution between elites and masses, hinder the advance of economic competition. All these elements contribute to a marginalization of Africa that can only be bypassed in a few economic niches (see Aderinwale, 2000; Kappel, 2000).

SOUTH AMERICA

South America shares some of the characteristics of the African continent. Economic growth does not form the primary target of society, and individual success has not become the main aim of social actors (Naím and Tuchin, 1999). During the twentieth century, the market mechanism had no chance to expand because of the many small interior markets. State intervention was the means for ensuring, and the consequence of, the growing importance of the state. South American societies are characterized by a stability that has been guaranteed by an extreme heterogeneity of economic sectors, societal groups, and states and which has become a negative factor restraining economic growth, learning, and competition. Traditional economic and power structures continue to exist. With a power base in the latifundia, elites have been interested in consumption and the maintenance of their privileges and fortunes. They have been closely linked to church, military, and conservative forces in the United States and other Western countries. Throughout there has been no interest in the social integration of poor black and underprivileged white people. There is thus an inadequate supply of skills (in quantity and quality) that explains the limited role of the Latin American development model. Skills of current and future workers need to be improved through traditional education and technical and vocational training. The region is caught in the middle-income trap in which shifting wealth is making it difficult to identify and acquire the necessary skills. The elites have not favoured capitalist production and economic competition. Integrative tendencies have remained weak, despite a more or less common history. Recent crises in several states have shown that new values and attitudes of workers and managers have become necessary. But change will be slow in a barely favourable societal environment. In contrast to Asia, a reappraisal of traditional values and norms that could support societal transformations seems hardly possible. An outstanding example is the authoritarian and paternalistic attitudes and expectations and the neglect of a technical culture in Cuba (Esser, 2000). In many countries, remittances sent home by transnational migrants are substitutes for economic progress. Since 1970, more than 10 million women and men from Latin America have settled in the United States. This means a growing cultural and economic interdependence between Latin America and the North. Asia's participation in transnational migrations is even higher (1,000,000 emigrants in 2000) while Africa's emigrants were 500,000 in 2000 (Guilmoto and Sandron, 2003: 62–83; Schuerkens, 2005).

COMPETITION AND THE WEALTH OF NATIONS

The causes of inequalities between nations have been discussed for more than two centuries. In 1748, Montesquieu published *De l'Esprit des Lois* where he suggested that temperate climates were more favourable to economic development than tropical climates. Some 30 years later, Adam Smith in his *Wealth of Nations* proposed that the skills of a group are the main factors influencing national wealth differences. More recently, Diamond (1998) re-introduced arguments on the significance of climatic and geographic factors. There is a further theoretical explanation that suggests that national differences in intelligence may play a crucial role in economic development. Even if this approach does not seem to be 'politically correct', there is some evidence for this argument. Lynn and Vanhanen (2002) published a book with the promising title *IQ and the Wealth of Nations*. It is widely assumed that the peoples of all nations have the same average level of intelligence, even if psychologists know that there are large differences in average levels of intelligence between different countries. The main argument against these results seems to be that intelligence is measured according to skills which are highly valued in Western countries, so that the result is culturally biased, and that emotional and social capacities highly valued in, for example, African cultures do not interest these scholars. Nevertheless, there is evidence that intelligence is a determinant of earnings among individuals, a fact that has already been established for early adulthood and that continues to be valid in later life phases. Since the 1950s, these findings were extrapolated in different studies to groups and then to nations (Lynn and Vanhanen, 2002). The recent study of Lynn and Vanhanen used data from the World Bank and the UNDP. The authors could confirm the hypothesis that national per capita incomes and rates of economic growth are positively correlated with national IQs. The following quote gives the authors' main argument:

> Nations whose populations have high IQs tend to have efficient economies at all levels from top and middle management through skilled and semi-skilled workers. These nations are able to produce competitively goods and services for which there is a strong international demand and for which there is therefore a high value, and that cannot be produced by nations whose populations have low IQs. (Lynn and Vanhanen, 2008: n.p.)

The conclusions are based on a sample of 60 nations that the authors regard as representative of the totality of nations because all categories of nations were included (South, North, East, and West). If one accepts the premise of the study about the definition of the IQ and its worldwide acceptance based on Western success criteria, the evidence given by this study may have significant political and social implications.

CONCLUSION

This analysis of the use of the concepts of cooperation, conflict, and competition in the study of social transformations and the sociology of global change has shown that cooperation is one of the fundamental notions of our field and remains an important element in the explanation of developmental processes in our contemporary globalized world. The notion of competition is of interest because the global economy introduces competitive economic behaviour in all regions of the world even if the upper social classes are those most affected. The notion of conflict was important during the period of the Cold War. In recent years, it has begun to interest scholars studying social transformations, because the poor outcomes of transformation processes in Southern countries often mean a growing escalation of conflicts, such as ethnic conflicts, civil wars, or violence in other forms of social relations, as for example gender roles. If one compares the meanings of the three notions, one sees that cooperation and conflict are notions that are very helpful for Marxist approaches or world system approaches, while competition and cooperation are notions favoured by scholars influenced by the Weberian tradition and modernization studies.

In our current globalized world characterized by the neoliberal credo, the notion of competition is becoming even more important as scholars begin to research the success or the failure of economic policies in various world regions characterized by different cultural life-worlds. The results of these studies of recent transformations of local socio-economic practices may have wider implications for development cooperation. Conflicts may thus be strongly based on aspects linked to particular cultures, a fact that would validate Huntington's thesis that the central political actors of the twenty-first century will be civilizations rather than nation-states.

As shown in this chapter, analysis in our field is often at the macro level, but the meso and micro levels interest scholars as well.[6] Most of the time, individual actors are constrained to participate in macro settings characterized by these notions, even if there may be factors that exclude privileged and/or underprivileged actors (for example, elites who go abroad during societal conflicts or the poor who participate in an informal economy, who are hardly influenced by social competition).

DISCUSSION QUESTIONS

1. What are the meanings of conflict, competition, and cooperation and how are these notions related to one another?

2. What do you know about women and development?

3. What do you know about social policies (health, unemployment, and old-age pensions) worldwide?

4. How do wars influence transformation processes? Please give empirical examples.

5. What are the characteristics of economic competition schemes e.g. in Africa?

ANNOTATED FURTHER READINGS

Bellamy, A., Williams, P. and Griffin, S. (2010) *Understanding Peacekeeping* **(Second edition). Cambridge: Polity.**
This book provides a comprehensive introduction to the theory, practice, and politics of contemporary peace operations. Drawing on more than 25 historical and contemporary case studies, this book evaluates the contemporary field in which peacekeepers operate, what role peace operations play in global politics, the growing impact of non-state actors, and the major current challenges of peacekeeping.

Junne, G. and Verkoren, W. (2005) *Postconflict Development: Meeting New* **Challenges. London: Lynne Rienner.**
With the multiplicity of civil wars since the end of the Cold War, many developing countries exist in 'post-conflict' societies, which pose important development challenges for national and international actors. This book addresses these challenges in sectors such as security, justice, economic policy, education, the media, agriculture, health, and the environment in countries around the globe. The authors suggest the creation of new social and economic structures that can serve as the foundations for a lasting peace.

McGrew, A. and Poku, N.K. (eds) (2007) *Globalization, Development and Human Security.* Cambridge: Polity.
The contributors to this volume intend to re-unite the study of development with the study of international relations or global politics. Although globalization has transformed the context of development, it has yet to significantly transform the prospects for real development or human security amongst the world's most vulnerable communities for the better. The growing securitization of development makes this book a timely study of a topic that is on the global political agenda.

Websites

http://www.usip.org
United States Institute of Peace website.

http://www.un.org/humansecurity/sites/www.un.org.humansecurity/files/chs_final_report_-_english.pdf
UN Commission on Human Security: *Human Security Now.*

http://www.un.org/en/peacekeeping/resources/reports.shtml
Access to the Report of the Panel on United Nations Peace Operations (A/55/305) (2000) and other reports.

(all websites accessed 19 October 2016)

NOTES

1   The widely acclaimed book of Philip McMichael *Development and Social Change. A Global Perspective* (2012) was particularly helpful in preparing this part of the chapter on cooperation. The author gives a historical and theoretically inspired overview of the topic of cooperation since the 1940s. For other approaches see the reader edited by J. Timmons Roberts and Amy Hite, *From Modernization to Globalization. Perspectives on Development and Social Change* (2000), and the book written by Rist (1996).
2   For more details see Strasser and Randall, 1979: 51-68.
3   Weber was more a historian of social change than a theoretician. He considered power as the capacity to influence the will of other people. His approach is of interest to the notion of competition where cultural factors are important (e.g. the Protestant ethics).
4   Both conflicts are linked to regional or ethnic belongings that the respective ruling elites exploit in order to maintain their political power.
5   See Shaw (2003) for more information and details on the topic.
6   Neil J. Smelser applied theory to social actors and groups; Weber and Durkheim analyzed organizations and social change; Hagen focused on psychological factors (see Roberts and Hite, 2000: 1-23).

10

GLOBALIZATION AND SOCIAL MOVEMENTS: HUMAN AGENCY AND MOBILIZATIONS FOR CHANGE[1]

Summary

Civil society organizations have become major forces of change in a world that never stops changing and that is characterized by high levels of economic and social inequality. These groups operate all over the world to advance processes they defend and seek to resist co-optations by existing political interests and structures. One way to do so is to refuse to play politics as usual. Participating in movements has become so widespread that it influences social change. Social movements have begun to act as change agents and/or may resist changes in given societal institutions. Biographies are altered by participations in movements; alternative lifestyle options are adopted. Movements change public opinions by inserting parts of their diagnostic frameworks into popular discourses. They help create and alter policy because of their effects on state administrations and public institutions such as universities and churches. This chapter explains the role of global connections in social changes initiated by movements that arise from the contradictions and conflicts of specific local societies but also from the dominant socio-economic model. Moreover, the chapter evaluates the role of social movements in transformation processes planned by states and global institutions, such as the UN.

INTRODUCTION

Civil society organizations have become major forces of change in a world characterized by high levels of economic and social inequality. This chapter explains the role of global culture in movements that arise from the contradictions and conflicts of specific local societies and the dominant global socio-economic system.

DEBATING GLOBALIZATION AND LOCALIZATION: NEW SOCIAL MOVEMENTS

This chapter raises the question of the potential of contemporary social movements in Northern and Southern countries in terms of social transformations. Our discussion focuses on the elements that make the success or failure of a social movement. We will examine the connections between social movements and social, economic, and political changes since the 1990s. Given the recent emergence of new social movements throughout the world, it is urgent that researchers, policy analysts, and citizens understand better how an institution, such as the global economy, influences social behaviours and distributes wealth and power in the global system. The current global economic system is based on an infinite accumulation logic that excludes entire social groups in the North and even more in the South. This neoliberal economic logic primarily benefits the elites of transnational capitalist groups who contribute to produce vast inequality. Because of the fact that the process of proletarianization and the decrease of wages (e.g. China and its growing middle classes) reaches its limits, production costs rise all over the world so that economic growth and gains are increasingly limited. Indeed, the global economic system cannot continue to include huge population groups in search of work, diminish wages, and maintain peace among a growing population in the North and the South that is unemployed or poorly paid. An endless economic growth can no longer be guaranteed on a planet that has reached the limits of its energy reserves and which is exposed to growing levels of pollution.

A MORE DEMOCRATIC AND EQUITABLE ORDER

Today, globalization has proved incapable of ensuring the needs of large groups of people not only in the countries of the South but also in the countries of the Triad, the centre of the global economy. It seems as if new social movements that work towards a transformation of the current political and economic order and a more democratic and equitable order have the possibility to launch global changes in this historic moment. This hypothesis justifies the analysis of recent changes among the members of transnational social movement organizations in the North and the South in order to see how these movements can go beyond regional and national frontiers (see Bringel and Domingues, 2015). The current nature of globalization requires a better knowledge of opportunities to express viewpoints and to ask for changes by new social movements that challenge a globalization defended by elites, the international financial institutions, and the dominant institutes of economic research. Because the actors of social movements can learn from past and/or recent experiences and can articulate their visions of an improved world better, a different social and economic world that avoids the prospect of force, coercion, and marginalization of the majority of social actors may be possible. Since the struggles against austerity and exclusion of entire layers of populations in the North and the South continue (e.g. in Greece and the United Kingdom in summer 2015), journalistic impressions and findings of political actors are slowly replaced by ethnographic and sociological studies that explain why social movements do not accept the discourse of dominant institutions (states, the International Monetary Fund, the World Bank, or the media) and, by contrast, set their own agendas. These frameworks can be orientated against real socio-economic situations and the political landscape in an attempt to demand democracy from below. The question is to what extent movements in the South can go farther to tackle local issues, national political changes, and local economic and social policies, e.g. targeted towards improving the situation of young people.

This chapter aims to understand local processes in the North and the South, including continuities and disruptions, linked to transnational movements that correspond to very different national and regional realities. This will allow us to understand the specificity of social movements that continue to be local and global at the same time, corresponding to the impact of the current historical moment of globalization in different geographical and socio-economic settings. National and global elites (in organizations of the United Nations or political groups such as the G20) react to the challenges posed by social movements by reforming political institutions and creating openings or formal access to resources so that some movement leaders can continue their struggles within existing institutions. This can be regarded as an adaptation of socio-political structures to movements and as an ability to challenge the social order. Transformations imposed by battles will then contribute to changed structures that are concerned by the conflict. However, the co-optation of some movement leaders offers them a merely symbolic access to elite decisions.

INTERACTIONS WITH STATES

Social movements change while interacting with states: they can adopt reformist or anti-systemic strategies. Their choice is determined by the broader context of globalization and the particular historical situation, as we could see in North Africa in 2011 or in Greece in 2015. Indeed, the foundations of power and state justifications are challenged by transnational movements. Global change will then result from the competition between global actors operating within the institutions (World Bank and IMF) that define the standards and prevailing values. Since institutions are supposed to ensure the stability of political regimes, they have the monopoly to define sanctions against those who seek to change prevailing rules. Nevertheless, global institutions can also help to define the shape and the anti-systemic potential of transnational movements, while movement leaders can express their scepticism for achieving social change through institutions.

The goal of this chapter is thus to continue the theory of global social movements and to allow research to better reflect global structures and processes that affect the dynamics of conflict and mobilization. The suggested theoretical approach of social movements allows an understanding of the role of individuals and organizations within the broader context of collective and political struggles in an era of globalization.

Within the movement, a consensus may prevail that these organizations should function on a transnational rather than a local level because the international arena provides resources and potential allies that can promote the interests of social movements against the neoliberal globalization, supported by political and economic elites. However, international organizations and NGOs also meet in social movements and reformulate their policies. Political elites and international organizations send observers to these World Social Forums, although the leaders of these social movements debate whether these elites are welcome or not.

IS A COMMON ORGANIZATION OF SOCIAL MOVEMENTS POSSIBLE?

The question remains whether a common organization of these social movements is feasible in the current era of improved networking. Some years ago, research still considered that these movements were too disparate to achieve their goals (Caillé, 2003). This chapter will attempt to address this problem by analyzing a number of recent social movements in the North and the South in order to clarify their features and see how they can be heard, not only against local governments but against a neoliberal economic system and North-South inequality that determines multiple aspects of the social and economic life of social actors in the North and the South. Despite many similarities resulting from the structural features of contemporary capitalism, social movements in the South seem to keep some differences compared to specific social movements in the North. Forms of dominant socio-political struggles differ according to the country (e.g. Tunisia, Egypt, and Morocco). Historical peculiarities and given political trajectories bring forth a variety of social movements. For example, countries coming out of conflicts seem to be less responsive to social movements, especially those oriented towards material demands. In countries that are at the threshold of their 'democratic transition', dominant social movements are generally oriented towards issues of 'governance' and respect of human rights and the constitutional order.

A NEW WAVE OF TRANSNATIONAL CONTENTION

The political struggles that took place around the world since 2011 were quickly summarized as a new wave of transnational contention. One should ask a number of questions relating to the identification of such a transnational wave: Is it a wave defined by a similarity of movements that distinguishes it from previous waves of protests? Or is it defined by mutual interconnections, maybe a goal or a shared adversary? And how are these protests located in the changing landscape of international transactions and power? What are the social and political struggles that have recently dominated the countries in the South? What is their logic of functioning? What forms do they take? What is their political impact? Are we witnessing a resurgence of social movements? If so, is there a response to the crisis of the so-called 'representative democracy' and the rules of neoliberal globalization? Have these movements led to the emergence of new democratic forms of expression and participation? What challenges do they bring? What are the limits and/or global issues of social movements in the South and the North? What lessons can we draw from the comparison of struggles in different geographic areas? What alternative visions of the future are achievable or imaginable?

SOCIAL MOVEMENTS IN THE GLOBAL WORLD

The social movements of the last years have sometimes been vague about their preferred economic model, but it has become quite clear that people want to have a greater voice in the global economic decisions that influence their lives. There has been competition among different visions of the world that have shaped global economic institutions and social movements. It seems as if major social changes can currently be introduced with some success if those excluded from power challenge the existing social order. In times of crisis, elites have to accept pressures from social movements so that more fundamental societal changes may become possible.

Recent decades have seen an increase of transnational associations of all sorts, and in particular of those advocating for social change. Since the 1990s, networks among transnational organizations have become denser as a result of new technologies that have facilitated transnational communication, but also in response to UN international conferences. It seems as if the timing of this growing influence of social movements is linked to the global economic crisis of recent years so that various groups hope to challenge the dominant order and advance alternatives (Wallerstein, 2004: 37). These economic crises trigger opportunities not only for democratic movements but for xenophobic movements, too (Barber, 1995; Moghadam, 2008). The question is thus how political actors and the global economic system should define opportunities that social movements permit. New ideas and models of action introduced by these social movements may eventually help transform global political actors and the global economic system itself.

GLOBAL CRISIS AND CHANGING OPPORTUNITIES

Several types of crisis have appeared these last years: a global financial crisis and increased unpredictability in the financial sector, large-scale climate changes, rising energy and food costs, and rising 'expulsions' (Sassen, 2014) (exclusions and displacements) from the economy triggering high inequality levels and poverty in both the North and the South. The contemporary world economy in its form of neoliberal capitalism requires constant economic growth based on expanding markets. However, there are social and economic limits to the extraction of profits from the globe and its peoples, based on salaries and the limited possibility of including additional workers into the world economy. In the last 15 years, large-scale protests in many regions, terrorism, and military interventions have created threats to the global order. One of the main reasons for these crises is the failure of the economic system to continue assuring benefits to groups such as workers and middle classes that are impoverishing in the North and that may rise (China and India) or stay poor in most countries of the global South. Massive strikes have become frequent in multiple countries such as Greece, Spain, France, countries of the Middle East, Turkey, Chile, or Brazil. Some of them were directed against authoritarian political regimes; others were opposed to austerity measures or expressed specific grievances, such as tuition costs (Brazil and recently South Africa). The reasons for these protests are not only linked to globalization but to national and/or regional financial and economic situations that can be contested. Popular protests aimed at the policies of global financial institutions have been transmuted into electoral influence. Leaders of these movements are becoming more powerful in their countries and may unite with other movements in their demands for new rules of the global economy. The 'development project' (McMichael, 2012) launched after World War II did not mean benefits for all in the South, so that a wide range of peoples are now asking for changes in an era where global capitalism is still the dominant economic form. Yet it is not clear what sort of transformation of the existing system is possible. Will there be a world-system based on coercion and increasing violence or will there be a rise of a more democratic, more participative world economy? This possible world-system shapes the opportunity structure of movements working to transform the global economic and political system.

Globalized capitalism has extended its social and geographic reach via outsourcing and an increase in precarious forms of employments all over the world. Protests are now calling attention to the gap between ideological justifications (e.g. *free market* and *unlimited possibilities*) and actual practice. In a first step, elites have been trying to reform political institutions by opening up formal means of access in order to create the possibility for the political leaders of these movements to continue their struggle inside these institutions. Terry Boswell and Christopher Chase-Dunn have described this process and the possibilities for challenging the political and economic order via social movements (2000: 18). They write that 'from the elimination of slavery to the end of colonialism, a rough and tumbling spiral between socialist progress and capitalist reaction has resulted in higher living standards and greater freedom for working people' (2000: 11).

REFORM PROJECTS OR ANTI-SYSTEMIC STRATEGIES

Movements shape the interactions between states and global actors: either they adopt reform projects, or they follow anti-systemic strategies. These different strategies are influenced by the larger global context of international cooperation. Globalization and the neoliberal economic order challenge the capacities of states to provide for the well-being of their populations and to control activities on their territories so that new actors – such as social movements – emerge who contribute to the shifting discourse of interstate relations. Global institutions such as the UN are influenced by contestations among a multiplicity of global actors, including social movements. Some of them are human rights' movements, environmentalists, or pro-democracy movements. Within each category, some of these groups are rather influential, such as *Doctors without Borders*; others consist of a group of people around a common goal without funding. These struggles contribute to the structural change of identities of global actors and to processes of world-systemic changes. They include anti-systemic responses of transnational movements that try to achieve social transformations through institutions. For example, the feminist and the ecological movements have led to important changes worldwide in the last decades, materialized by UN resolutions and the Millennium goals.

THEORIZING GLOBAL CHANGE AND SOCIAL MOVEMENTS

A world-system perspective helps to understand the functioning of global change and to look for discontinuous changes in the basic structures of the global economic and political order. Transnational social movements contribute to the normative challenge of the global order. They expand political and economic opportunities. They create splits among elites and the emergence of new political forces through elections.

Some of the most important dynamics that have triggered protest movements are proletarianization processes caused by urbanization and the development of industrial manufacturing that integrate national economies into global markets. Moreover, small farmers are pushed out of agricultural production by transformations of local food markets and land ownership schemes. This process contributes to the expansion of urban slums and the growth of transnational agrarian movements (McMichael, 2012). As Smith and Wiest (2012: 26) have shown: 'As proletarianization reaches its limits, labor costs rise, limiting economic growth and profitability. Extensive depeasantization contributes to vulnerabilities in food supplies, generating social instability.'

SOCIAL MOVEMENTS IN WORLD-HISTORICAL TERMS

It seems as if today's social movements can only be understood in world-historical terms. The democratization of the countries of the South and the globalization of labour markets, the expansion of Internet communication, and the spread of globalizing ideologies have supported the global economic system but also the growth of transnational associations around common identities. These networks are capable of triggering of collective actions of popular groups that challenge states and global institutions but also empower less powerful states and social movements. The current multi-centric global system has emerged into a critical subsystem of global politics characterized by new forms of analyses and alternative thinking on the functioning of the global economic system. The most recent example are Greek politics of summer 2015 when a leftist government was trying to introduce a change in the functioning of the global economic system. The challenge of this tentative was expressed by disputes among political and economic elites in the principal Western European capitals, such as Berlin, Paris, and Madrid, the leaders of the international financial institutions (e.g. Christine Lagarde), and the media that discussed these political processes in talk-shows and print media. Moreover, people have begun to argue against recent austerity measures in the United Kingdom. The example of Greece constitutes a milestone on a way to change certain aspects of the dominant economic system. Global political and economic elites soon shared the viewpoint not to accept the challenge expressed by Greek political leaders so that the continuous functioning of the given financial system could be assured and Greek had finally to accept the financial conditions of the EU and the IMF.[2]

UN GLOBAL CONFERENCES

UN global conferences have helped social movements to expand. The participants in these movements have changed as more and more of them have come from the global South. In their respective countries, they take part in protest actions, advance cultural change through mass media, or engage with international institutions and their staff. Movements can thus further social change by taking part in discussions on global problems. Topics that have already been challenged include threats to indigenous peoples (Hall and Fenelon, 2009), child labour (Brooks, 2007), and gender discrimination (Moghadam, 2008). Global conferences help transnational groups to meet each other and to focus on shared global projects. World Bank projects have also involved activist groups giving them access to local networks and displaying the gap between social and community benefits and the global development project (SAPRIN, 2002). However, civil society groups' engagement with global institutions shows that parts of these groups are interested in the idea of defending changed economic outcomes and therefore want to challenge dominant assumptions. Nevertheless, the existing institutions continue to define the terms of working inside of them, so that movements remain more or less powerless if they don't create political parties, such as Podemos in Spain and Syriza in Greece (Smith and Wiest, 2012: 171).

ELITE STRATEGIES

Another strategy used by elites is to question the representativeness and accountability of social movements. This strategy aims at reasserting the monopoly of states and corporate interests in global politics (Wapner, 2002). It means limiting advantages for movements despite a larger access to global institutions. These processes help maintain the privileges and the power of elite groups by orientating activists towards interstate projects and by fostering competition and division among movements.

The strategy of bringing critics into institutions has changed movement dynamics. Earlier movements had only the street to express their criticisms; today's movements have multiple possibilities to advance critical discourses and perspectives within the institutions themselves. Movement-generated norms and different goals will thus influence world politics and contribute to a democratization of global politics. The participation in these movements already produces a critical understanding of the global political and economic order insofar as participants are exposed to new political and economic arguments. The potential for global change becomes obvious as movements, institutions, and critics are mutually reinforcing. Recent social movements show that hopelessness, despair, and self-blame do no longer constitute the only responses to global neoliberal capitalism. The hundreds of thousands who have globally protested have drawn attention to an increasing social inequality and have created some hope in difficult times. These movements have appeared in a time when social conflicts regarding wages and labour unions have been waning faced by atypical employment situations, more and more precarious jobs in the North, and an increase of the informal sector in the South.

COLLECTIVE ACTIONS WORLDWIDE

These last years, collective actions have taken place in China, India, Bangladesh, Vietnam, Cambodia, and Indonesia. In China, the new class of workers originating from the countryside asks for higher salaries. The strategy of delocalization of enterprises has thus been followed by collective actions of workers even if there has been a certain delay. This new group of workers in China contributes to rising wages on a global level. However, many companies, including Chinese companies, are moving production facilities to places like Cambodia and Vietnam where wages are closer to $.10-$.12 an hour compared to the $.50 to one dollar an hour wages in China. Traditional labour unions may be absent from conflicts but NGOs, self-help groups, and cooperatives have become instruments for expressing the interests of workers. Negotiations are no longer led at the workplace but in the local community. In this form, they may protect societies from economic outcomes of *free* markets. Workers alone - as history has shown - cannot realize changes. They need the political action of states. In India, social movements have created political parties that change politics by integrating notions such as inclusive growth and sustainable development. Elites are then obliged to undertake reforms in order to obtain electoral support. Insofar as masses have become aware of their rights, they also want to exercise power. However, if the country is small, the state can resist the neoliberal economy and the forces of globalization only with difficulty. If the country is important economically, it can - as recent politics favouring middle classes in China have shown - attack problems of equality and ask for an improved consumption level inside the country.

MUTUAL INTERACTIONS BETWEEN ELITES AND NEW SOCIAL MOVEMENTS AROUND REFORMS

It is this mutual interaction between reforms initialized by elites and new movements of contestation that will probably shape the future of societies in the South and the North. The state is no longer a neutral agent but a heavily disputed one that faces protestations and power shifts. Since the financial crisis of 2007–2009, there has been a decline in consumption nearly everywhere. Those defending austerity measures are currently opposed to defendants of a growth that is supported by salaries. Their ideological battles expressed in TV talk shows and the media may contribute to a readjustment of models of growth of the European economies but also of economies in the South. In fact, it is no longer possible to limit decisions on distribution, accumulation of wealth, conditions of employment, and production solely to national parliaments. The ruling principles of economic elites need to be extended by political processes that include several levels on top of the trans-nationalization of the economy. Different groups of actors are reclaiming their interests in the political system, such as in Spain or Greece. However, implementing new social rights as an alternative to liberal constitutions can only be the result of future social struggles. The social question is thus linked to processes of democratization, as will be shown in the following case studies. Social movements create something that has been named post-democracy. 'Across the world, squares and plazas have become *public spheres* where people can not only share alternatives, but where they can also develop a sense of continuity and incubate novel forms of collective projects and identities' (Tejerina et al., 2013: 382).

A PARTICIPATIVE DIALOGUE

The 2011–2012 protests gave democracy a new meaning, turning it into a participative dialogue between everyone, not only activists, around political issues. Decisions have been made at general assemblies using the principles of direct democracy. Activists are thus living their own utopian political ideas. Nevertheless, as the recent events in Greece have shown (2015), Prime Minister Tsiparos utilized a discourse that permitted him to gain electoral power and control the government that was much more leftist than his political actions at the international level (Troika). These politics have permitted him to introduce unpopular austerity measures imposed by the European Union – in particular Germany with Angela Merkel – and by the IMF with Christine Lagarde.

EUROPEAN MOVEMENTS

During the spring of 2011 countries such as Spain, Portugal, Italy, and Greece were facing extreme economic hardships linked to the crisis of the United States' financial system and the subsequent 'euro crisis'. In fact, the European debt crisis has been taking place in several euro-zone member states since the end of 2009. Several states (Greece, Portugal, Ireland, Spain, and Cyprus) could not repay their government debts without the assistance of money lenders, such as the IMF. Within a rather short timespan, a number of similar movements emerged in the region. These 'networks of outrage and hope' (Castells, 2012) tried to modify a situation that was considered problematic. Their goals, visions, and tactics distinguished them from former social movements such as the feminist movement of the 1970s and 1980s, or the students' movement of 1968. People felt marginalized by the socio-economic crises that had led to a decline in their standards of living. The lives of many were becoming more and more precarious and excluded from normal lives with a family and labour income (Standing, 2011). Upward mobility has been blocked even in Germany (Fratzscher, 2016) and there has been an increasing disparity between the rich and the poor (Milanovic, 2011a). People felt that governments and politicians were closed to popular concerns. A sense of injustice had arisen so that these mobilized masses reacted with indignation and anger.

The difference to former movements seems to be the new global dimension (see Tejerina et al., 2013: 380). Social contestations have been articulated in regional terms but the global diffusion of neoliberal capitalism and its social impacts were one of the essential causes. In Europe, the erosion of welfare states and the political management of the socio-economic crisis were the main mobilization factors. Among the movements were the *Indignados* movement in Spain, the '*Indignez-vous*' protests in France, the anger of Greeks in Syntagma Square, and demonstrations of young students in Britain and Belgium. Increasing levels of poverty, the precariousness of jobs, the deindustrialization processes that moved manufacturing to the Far East, and the neoliberal adjustment policies that had privileged debt payment over social benefits had adverse consequences for many groups while, at the same time, they had created wealth concentrated in a small elite. The demand was thus for 'real' democracy, not only 'democratization' as in North Africa. Everything that appeared to be wrong such as a lack of representation, political clientelism, and corruption were the targets of these movements. Often young educated and under-/unemployed citizens articulated widespread grievances. In this way, they attracted the participation of large masses with no previous political participation and knowledge. The goal was to establish a new economic and political contract that should give the priority to people's welfare.

In March 2011, university students mobilized in Spain against the unemployment rate, precariousness, and budget cuts in education. They were joined by Youth without a Future (*Juventud Sin Futuro*) who organized a mass event against the economic crisis and the two-party system. Moreover, the organization Real Democracy Now! (*¡Democracia Real Ya!*) asked people to take to the streets. This call triggered the '*indignado*' mobilizations. 'DRY incited "*the unemployed, the poorly paid, the subcontractors, the precarious, the young people...*" to take to the Spanish streets on 15 May' (Perugorría and Tejerina, 2013: 428). In 50 Spanish cities, demonstrations were organized. Supporting demonstrations were held in Dublin, Amsterdam, Bologna, Paris, London, and Lisbon. In the following evenings, an '*Occupy the Square*' ('*Toma la plaza*') movement began. Camps were built in several Spanish cities until mid-July and thematic working groups and commissions on the economy, sustainability, and politics, etc. were organized

(Perugorría and Tejerina, 2013: 428). Despite these popular protests, the right wing People's Party (PP) won the elections of May and November 2011 so that the outgoing Socialist government was punished for the economic crisis. The common language was an absence of justice regarding the acts of bankers (self-enrichment) and politicians (corruption) that derived from the outcomes of the economic crisis. The real democracy that was looked for consisted of a 'friendly atmosphere' that was 'intergenerational', and 'unrepresentable' (Perugorría and Tejerina, 2013: 436). This movement was also characterized by the possibilities of the Internet and online social networks that were seen as complementary to street actions. Both were facilitated by direct participation and open discussions.

If one takes the case study of Spain and the Podemos party, one can see how a social movement was slowly changed into a political party that has been able to challenge the existing two-party system. From low election scores at the beginning, Podemos became the most important political party in the December 2015 national elections. Political and economic elites have thus begun to challenge the reputation of their leaders, declaring them as populists, demagogues, supporters of the Basque ETA, and the political regime of Venezuela. However, the increasing scores at surveys show that the Spanish population does no longer follow the current political elites (the 'casta'), characterized by a corrupt political style favouring their personal wealth. One fourth of Spaniards are actually concerned by a difficult life situation but the number of millionaires has increased by 24 per cent to 465,000 in 2014 (Pfeiffer, 2015: 4).

The political program of Podemos is characterized by a left and social-democratic policy. Some measures are planned such as an old-age pension at 65 years, basic assistance for the unemployed, an interdiction of dismissals in enterprises which make profits, an increase of the legal minimum salary, etc. Regarding incomes, a higher taxation of high wealth, increased taxation according to rising incomes, and a taxation of luxury goods are planned. The northern European social democracies are models for this planned social state in Spain. Podemos has become a political party based on the social movements of the *Indignados* and is now a part of the political system. However, in the June elections of 2016 which repeated the legislative elections of 2015, the party lost more than one million votes. In fact, one in five Podemos voters didn't vote (*Marianne*, 2016). Observers point out the absence of a coherent program and divided leaders that begin to defend social democracy while voters still look for an alternative to the ruling parties and favour an anti-systemic approach that may not have any chance in the current political system.

MOVEMENTS IN BRAZIL

In Brazil, the protesters of 2013 took part in the global wave of indignation (Pleyers and Glasius, 2013). The protests linked general requirements to local challenges in different urban centres. At the same time, these waves also had a national character: the socio-political model of the ruling Worker's Party was questioned.

In Brazil, university graduates exposed to precarious jobs and young workers of popular suburbs, unemployed, or those that occupy difficult jobs, protested. These young people challenged the transport prices that are a heavy load in their incomes, social health services because private health organizations are expensive, education as most of them study in universities. It was a precarious generation that protested, similar to the generation of 2005–2006 in the Parisian suburbs.

The political impact of these mobilizations is difficult to measure. Several corporatist demands were satisfied as the president Dilma Rousseff took some quick political measures. The reputation of some politicians decreased in opinion polls. But there was no fundamental transformation of the political scene as in North Africa. The arrival to power of the Workers' Party in 2003 had seen the co-optation of leaders of social movements and a parallel demobilization of these movements. This system was challenged by the mobilizations of 2013 and those of 2015. In most of the urban centres, protesters wanted to maintain their distance to parties, labour unions, and other organizations of civil society.

The protest came from 'alter-activists' (Pleyers, 2010) who asked for free transport on the mainly privatized public buses. This topic was gradually expanded to other public services (health, education, police, etc.) so that it could become the focal point of a latent wave of general indignation in Brazilian society. Internet, social media, multiple identities, and transversal agendas mobilized millions of citizens questioning the government even if the initial groups had different focal points (Bringel, 2013a). Social justice, dignity, and material and post-material challenges were asked for.

These new social movements are less controlled by organizations. The engagement takes place among the young who reject ideologies introduced by parties and associations, such as labour unions. The protest is spontaneous and criticizes institutions that no longer take care of the young generation. Until now, this engagement is weakly defined and the perspectives are not clear. Collective institutions are refused because they standardize the political regime and don't suggest a political participation going further than elections. In Brazil, there is a desire to resist a Workers' Party which is challenged without the existence of an opposition that could realize better politics.

The 2015/2016 protests were those of white middle class protesters and even elite members in the streets that expressed their hate of President Dilma Rousseff of the Workers' Party and led to a process of destitution by the Chamber of Deputies and the Senate. In fact, this party has transformed the social character of the Brazilian state by creating millions of mostly precarious jobs but - faced with economic difficulties - the party has no vision to achieve economic growth. The left is disorganized and exposed to corruption scandals. There are tensions because of the economic slowdown and the failure of the government to improve public services. The middle classes that had to support the program against extreme poverty no longer support the party of the president. Organized workers are exposed to a worsening economic situation. The hostile media further contribute to trigger mass mobilizations. It seems as if 'a historical cycle of the Brazilian left is now coming to the end' (Saad-Filho, 2015). The first measures of the new government were to suppress the Ministry of Culture and the Ministry of Women, Racial Equity, and Human Rights. Further measures included questioning and suppressing programs in education, health, and parts of the labour laws. All these measures have an impact on the whole Brazilian society and most of all on the most fragile groups regarding the economic and political dimension (*L'Humanité*, 29 June 2016).

NORTH AFRICA AND THE ARAB SPRING

In North Africa, mobilizations were linked to demands for political reforms in order to initiate or deepen processes of democratization in countries such as Egypt, Morocco, and Tunisia. Although this Arab Spring was described as a political mobilization concerned with the democratization of dictatorial political regimes, these movements were caused by the particular impact that neoliberalism had in these societies. High levels of income inequality, high costs of living, the exclusion of an educated but unemployed youth, a decreasing level of government services, and a growing precarious group have characterized the Middle East and North Africa (Standing, 2011). Movements in North Africa have been popular structureless mobilizations that were quickly exposed to their limits. They have been able to mobilize but have been incapable to negotiate and sign agreements at the end of the conflict. They did not have the legitimacy of elected and representative bodies but they were directed against authoritarian former rulers and led to the emergence of pro-democracy movements in Egypt, Tunisia, and Morocco. They have shown an active civil society and a new generation of militants mainly composed of young urban educated protesters. Those who have participated in these struggles for instance in Tunisia are not those that have become powerful elected representatives. In Tunisia, like in Brazil, university graduates exposed to precarious jobs, young workers of popular suburbs, the unemployed, or those that occupy jobs for which they are over-qualified protested (Allal and Geiser, 2011). In Tunisia and Egypt, the most active of these protesters were persecuted, arrested, or assassinated, but some of them dared to protest a second time against military or Islamic governments. What has been created here is a sort of dual character of democracy (Monod, 2012: 254). On the one side, the representative democracy with elected leaders, such as Max Weber defined them; on the other side, a direct democracy, without party and without any leader but represented in the streets. This second form does not seek to put an end to their political leaders but asks them to rule in a way that respects their popular will (Cohen, 2014).

In Egypt, four years after the mobilization in Tahrir Square, political reforms continue. A new constitution was adopted in January 2014. In May 2014, the former minister of defence, Abdel Fattah Al Sissi was elected president. In October and November 2015, legislative elections were held to form a new parliament that is composed of more than 80 women and deputies from different political parties and independent deputies. However, the voter turnout was at some 30 per cent.[3] The Muslim Brotherhood continues to reject the transition process of the military forces. Former president Morsi, elected in June 2012 but deposed in July 2013, and other Muslim Brotherhood members have been sentenced to death or have been imprisoned for many years or life by the military regime.

In Tunisia, a three-party coalition ruled the country in the first three years after the mobilizations of December 2010/January 2011 and the end of the de facto single party state of president Ben Ali, the secular Constitutional Democratic Rally (RDC). In January 2014, a new constitution was adopted and the first democratic parliamentary elections since the mobilization of 2011 were organized in October 2014, resulting in a win by the secularist Nidaa Tounes party with 85 seats in the 217-member assembly. Presidential elections were organized in November/ December 2014. The President is elected for five-year terms. He appoints a Prime Minister and cabinet, who play a strong role in the execution of policy.

In Morocco, a new constitution was adopted in July 2011 which clarified the role of the head of government and the parliament. King Mohammed VI is the secular political head of State. The Prime Minister is the head of the government and a multi-party system. The government exercises executive power. Legislative power is vested in both the government and the two chambers of parliament, the House of Representatives and the House of Councilors. At the regional elections of September 2015, the *Parti de la justice et du développement* (PJD) received 25 per cent of the votes and is in fact the most important party in the country. In the current government, 11 seats are occupied by PJD members, including the head of government. The party defends democracy and the constitutional monarchy of Morocco.

In Tunisia and Morocco, 'activists have more of the "civic skills" needed to consolidate democracy', according to Moghadam (2013: 403) so that democratic transitions have been more or less successful. Unemployment continues to be a problem in the region. Morocco and Tunisia have recently seen demonstrations in defence of individual rights, such as for women wearing a mini skirt. In Tunisia, there were demonstrations and protests against terrorist acts after the attacks on tourists at the National Museum in Bardo in March 2015 and the beach in Sousse in June 2015. These events show that a population lives there that is defending individual rights and that expresses its opinion in a democratic way. However, in Egypt, the army and the acting president continue to repress street protests and political opposition so that there is not much difference to the time before the movements of 2010/2011. In fact, pre-existing conditions in Egypt included very conservative rules for women. New political parties had not enough time before elections so that the population elected two religious parties in November 2011.

CONCLUDING REMARKS

We can conclude from this overview of some recent social movements that these are networks where alternative societal visions are negotiated and where actors are engaged in struggles to achieve social changes. People reunite around projects that can influence the future. They create and promote new collective identities and eventually transform society (Polletta and Jasper, 2001). There is a certain consensus that these movements may have wide consequences in the short and/or in the long term. As these movements show, if an issue has been raised, it becomes part of a societal agenda, so that the goals may be achieved in the future. These movements try to change national discussions, for instance, in Europe, from austerity to inequality and encourage large groups of young people to become politically active. These young people will continue to support progressive government policies, faced as they are by few employment possibilities. At this moment, the outcomes of these movements in Europe remain uncertain. The events in Greece in summer 2015 around the Euro may signify that some structures of societies, and in particular the economic sector, may be changed. The changes already put into place in support of more solidarity between people and less austerity can be considered as promising signs.

I have shown in this chapter that it is difficult to suggest the outcomes of the current wave and its possible consequences on social transformations. The ideas of Castells and those reunited in the special issue of *Current Sociology* (2013) create an extensive theoretical framework. There are some common global causes, but local responses are quite different. However, these new social movements are promising signs that ascertain that the neoliberal global economy has important deficits and that it is time to look for adaptive changes that will have positive influences on inequality and poverty among an increasing part of populations in very different world regions. The movements that encourage participation of diverse groups and different political orientations may challenge the dominant economic principles in the short, but also in the long term in order to create hope instead of despair.

DISCUSSION QUESTIONS

1. How do you define social movements?
2. Do you participate in social movements in your country or your region? And why?
3. Please theorize the link between social movements and global change.
4. What are the differences between movements in the global South and those in the global North?
5. Please give a short overview of recent social movements, e.g. in Spain or Turkey.

ANNOTATED FURTHER READINGS

Bringel, B. and Domingues, J.M. (eds) (2015) *Global Modernity and Social Contestation.* **London: Sage.**
This book uses concrete social processes to link theoretical discussions to empirical case studies in order to provide an understanding of global modernity and social contestation.

Castells, M. (2012) *Networks of Outrage and Hope: Social Movements in the Internet Age.* **Cambridge: Polity Press.**
Castells' book analyzes the sudden rise of mass uprisings across the world and their political power. The variety and cultural diversity of these uprisings is considered by studying movements from Iceland and Tunisia, from the Egyptian Revolution to the Arab Spring, from the *Indignados* movements in Spain to the Occupy movements in the United States.

Khosrokhavar, F. (2012) *The New Arab Revolutions that Shook the World.* **Boulder, CO and London: Paradigm.**
While the final outcome of the Arab Spring is still unclear, these events are important as historical facts. Farhad Khosrokhavar contextualizes the demands of the protesters. He looks beyond the Arab world to show how a new conception of democracy is emerging. Looking to the future, Khosrokhavar discusses how these new social movements may change the world.

Smith, J. and Wiest, D. (2012) *Social Movements in the World-System.* **New York: Russell Sage Foundation.**
Jackie Smith and Dawn Wiest build upon theories of social movements, global institutions, and the political economy of the world-system to uncover how institutions define the opportunities and constraints on recent social movements. Smith and Wiest show how these movements have shifted the context in which states and other global actors compete and interact.

Websites

http://womhist.alexanderstreet.com/about.htm
This website is intended to serve as a resource for students and scholars of US history and US women's history. Organized around the history of women in social movements in the US between 1600 and 2000, the site seeks to advance scholarly debates and understanding of US history from a women's point of view.

http://www.encyclopedia.com/topic/Social_movements.aspx
Encyclopedia article on social movements.

https://opentextbc.ca/introductiontosociology/chapter/chapter21-social-movements-and-social-change/
An overview from *Introduction to Sociology* – 1st Canadian edition, by William Little.

http://cssm.nd.edu/
Center for the study of social movements, University of Notre Dame.

https://mobilizingideas.wordpress.com/
Blog of the Center for the study of social movements of the University of Notre Dame.

http://www.latinamericansocialmovements.org/blog/
Blog on movements in South America.

http://ssir.org/articles/entry/crowdsourcing_the_future_of_a_social_movement
An article showing how an innovative campaign lifted up the voices of people across the United States to help inform movement leaders about the hopes, fears, and ideas of the LGBTQ community.

(all websites accessed 21 October 2016)

NOTES

1　A first presentation of the results of this research project was given in a plenary session of the 3rd Forum of the International Sociological Association in July 2016 in Vienna as part of my activities as co-chair of the Research Committee 09 'Social Transformations and Sociology of Development'.

2　Available at http://www.theatlantic.com/international/archive/2016/01/global-economy-2016/422475/ (accessed 24 October 2016).

3　Available at http://www.europeanforum.net/country/egypt (accessed 24 October 2016).

11

FINAL REMARKS: SOCIAL CHANGE IN A GLOBAL WORLD

A COMPLEX WORLD

The world has become increasingly networked in recent years. Global production and international trade amounted to 60 per cent of global output in 2011 (UNDP, 2013: 2). The developing world - if one wants to continue using this encompassing notion - contributed 47 per cent to the global merchandise trade. South-South trade amounted to 26 per cent in 2013 as opposed to 8 per cent in 1980. The South consequently needs the North and the North needs, to a growing extent, the South, for example, if one thinks of the financial crisis in the European Union, the role of the Chinese Yuan, and its impact on the global economy.

Meanwhile, it can be argued in global studies that there is the South of the North (e.g. Spain, Greece), and the North of the South (e.g. Singapore, South Korea), which have different socio-economic characteristics. After the Second World War, developments in the South have led to the creation of development institutions with the task to respond more flexibly to the growing global diversity. The development paths of Brazil, India, and China, as well as the success stories of countries such as Mauritius, Bangladesh, and until recently Turkey, have changed our thinking about global transformations. Chinese and Indian enterprises invest in Africa and thereby contribute to the creation of international production networks as well as the implementation of socio-economic development processes through new products and new communication infrastructures. The diversity of transformation processes that have been considered in this book reveals principles that show the role of states, their developments, and their welfare policies in a new light. Not all developing countries have participated in the recovery of the South of the last three decades. In the least developed countries of the South, change is slow, especially in those that are distant from world markets. The development of the South also means more opportunities for global public goods, forcing a reconsideration of global issues (*inter alia* climate and water issues). The new power dynamics, as well as the changed socio-political participation of growing populations through social networking create new policies (transnational movements) and call for renewed global institutions of the UN family that have to accept changing power balances.

The rise of the South must be considered being the story of a dramatic spread of individual potentials in countries that comprise large parts of the world population (*inter alia* India and China). For the first time in 150 years, the gross domestic product of India, China, and Brazil is as high as that of the long-industrialized countries of the North – such as Canada, France, Germany, Italy, the United Kingdom, and the USA. This represents a dramatic shift in the global economy that the UNDP's Human Development Report (2013: 13) rightly points out.

The most important aspect of development in the countries of the South seems to be their internal market. The middle classes have grown numerically and in terms of their average income. Between 1990 and 2010, the proportion of middle classes of the South in the global middle class has increased from 24 to 58 per cent (UNDP, 2013: 14). In the three countries of China, India, and Brazil, the number of income-poor also declined sharply. Instead of continuing to have a centre of industrial countries and a periphery of less developed countries, the world is today complex, dynamic, and more balanced. The large number of people in the South – billions of consumers and citizens – asks for a multiplication of global development efforts by governments, enterprises, and international institutions.

PERSPECTIVES

The development of the South is driven, as the UNDP Human Development Report of 2013 underlined, by three factors: a proactive developmental state, global markets, and innovations in the field of social policy (2013: 4). Proactive and responsible states develop public and private sectors and are characterized by long-term visions, and expanding e.g. social welfare in their countries, such as the health sector, education, and social insurance (unemployment schemes and old age pension schemes). Social security covers 27 per cent of the global population; which means that 73 per cent are only partially covered or not at all (UNRISD, 2016: 44). Global markets have been opened up according to national situations, so that there has been an investment in the education of these populations (e.g. South Korea) or in the communication infrastructure (e.g. China). The rapid educational expansion in the South has created the necessity for jobs for these large population groups. If not enough jobs are made available in the foreseeable future, there will be social unrest, such as in the Arab Spring of 2011. The better people are educated, the more employment opportunities must be offered to these young people who otherwise protest or migrate to other regions. The demographic structure of the North and the South can facilitate these migrations, for example, with employment opportunities in the health and care sectors in the North for migrants from the South but also for unemployed in the North[1].

After years of government funding, some smaller states have successfully focused on niche products. Countries in the South are open to technological innovations so that new adapted products are increasingly produced in this part of the world. Technology transfer from the North to the South often calls for greater local adaptations. The South has proposed innovations that can directly benefit people: e.g. mobile phones are cheaper and easier to use locally. They make it possible to provide banking services for customers and transmit weather news. Enterprises in the South often focus on young consumers who are interested in branded goods and who can thus, for the first time, buy their products. Recent goods in the South are often better adapted to the incomes and tastes of local consumers than expensive and sophisticated products from the North.

The rise of the South has also permitted countries such as Brazil, China, India, Mexico, and Thailand to buy large foreign currency reserves and to build up a protective wall against financial crises. The financial architecture of the South is thus changing. Even in the World Bank there has been a certain power shift towards emerging economies with a change in the voting power in 2010 for e.g. China, South Korea, and Turkey. The upturn in the South is driving global economic developments (China), even if it has recently slowed down, and will continue to determine global societal change in the coming decades.

As I have shown in this book, changes are not automatic, but require responsible stakeholders that tackle global concerns in national practices. The successful among them show new transformation possibilities. Further investments in development are not only morally justified, but also by the fact that a healthy, well-educated population can contribute to a dynamic world economy. Investments that support poor population groups, and give them new opportunities therefore influence global transformation processes worldwide.

The 2014 Human Development Report underlined that there was evidence that the overall rate of progress was slowing down (UNDP, 2014: 33) due to the global financial crisis of 2008. Progress in HDI in the Arab States, in Latin America, the Caribbean, and in Asia slowed in 2008–2013 (2014: 35). All three components of the HDI have been concerned: 'Growth in gross national income (GNI) per capita has declined, particularly in the Arab States and in Europe and Central Asia. Growth rates of life expectancy at birth have recently declined in most regions – especially in Asia – though they increased in Sub-Saharan Africa. And since 2008 the growth of expected years of schooling has also declined. All four human development groups have experienced a slowdown in HDI growth' (2014: 35).

Today, we recognize further new tendencies of transformations in our societies: on a worldwide scale, post-material attitudes are increasing; Sen's capabilities (1999) have become a central notion; middle-classes are experiencing decreasing status and impoverishment; and youth without job perspectives is becoming a worldwide phenomenon. But there are other tendencies that let us hope: economies are changing with jobs that permit to share services with each other or to give a second life to goods; housing and consumption are done in new cooperative groups via networks created on the Internet. Enterprises are asked to display social, ethical, and environmental concerns while growth is criticized. Social networks of consumers and critical citizens are created that have a chance to influence economic decisions in global enterprises. Hacktivists' activities introducing themselves in networks of enterprises or banks are increasing since 2008. Moreover, the relation between enterprises and consumers has been modified: global enterprises increasingly include renewable energies, create social integration projects, and finance innovative mass media projects.

The crisis that many people live has triggered new social and economic solutions whose importance is rising. The power of a new generation of social entrepreneurs is increasing. Linked to this is the readiness of these new generations to demonstrate solidarity in mobilizations on the Internet. The tendency RAK 'Random Acts of Kindness' also illustrates this new economic attitude to show proximity to and personal interest in the consumer. Interflora in Great Britain has presented flowers to the person that was found on Twitter to live a difficult moment. Another tendency is the branded government of enterprises intervening in the social or ecological field in addition to political actors. Poor consumers have become targets of global firms in the South with products that are conceived for them (food, health, technology, etc.). Solidarity is also shown by new collecting points of food, books, or clothing where people can find what they need for free. Another new economic aspect is the form of circulatory economy where manufactured products are recycled at the end of their usefulness in order to live several lives. All these activities are known as participating in the growing social and solidarity economy (SSE) that should play an increasing role in the coming years because it gives an answer to the current absence of growth and the difficulties of the dominant neoliberal economy.

In conclusion, I would point out that new ways of living, working, thinking, and making are emerging. New technologies permit them spreading all over the world. A new collective and cooperative intelligence has been created that asks for new links between social actors, economy, nature, policy, and society. Young entrepreneurs and scholars have created new economic paradigms and challenged models that have been the legacy of the industrial era. A top-down society is probably evolving into a society that works in networks. The growing importance of civil society asks for more participation (e.g. *Nuit debout* in France in spring 2016). Today, we are in a situation of in-between: where the old is still existent and where the new finds it difficult to appear.

Globalization, increasing poverty, and inequality influence our societies. New movements, trends, and phenomena are appearing in civil society and local groups. These people invent new local and economic relations, including ecological preoccupations. Their ideas are intensely discussed in UN organizations that push for societal change in the fields of economy, politics, and labour. UN and governmental reports and websites create new perspectives that are in the making and that the younger generations will spread all over the globe. For the time being, there are still discrepancies between these political and economic futures that populations all over the world have not yet assimilated. But mass media, movements, and engaged scientific discourses will contribute to spread these visions in the discourses of national groups so that they can become political options for national governments in the near future. Political decisions have been taken by most of the national governments, for instance, on sustainable economic measures. However, it is still too early to see their impacts. Long-term visions such as the Sustainable Development Goals (SDGs) for 2030 will contribute to changes in the coming 15 years; governments will have to implement political visions that they approved and signed in UN decisions. Slowly, the world as we know it, may change in the directions that these reports suggest (see the list of websites below) and hopefully, not in the direction of threat and violence but in that of 'leaving no one behind' in the common process of the substantive transformation of global societies.

DISCUSSION QUESTIONS

1. How do you envisage the future of the topics discussed in this book?

2. Are you participating in the construction of the future society, e.g. in NGOs or in political parties or movements?

3. What do you think of the social and solidarity economy? Would a focus on this economy be an interesting development of the economic system of the future?

4. What do you think about the development of the care sector in the North and the South?

5. How could changed fiscal measures contribute to transformations in inequality worldwide?

Websites including reports on global change perspectives

http://www.unrisd.org/
The website of the United Nations Research Institute for Development.

http://www.unrisd.org/80256B3C005BB128/(httpProjects)/38DF80F450689724C1257A7
   D004BD04B?OpenDocument
How UNRISD engages with the Sustainable Development Goals.

http://www.unrisd.org/80256B3C005BB128/(httpProgrammeAreas)/76B6CE6A525FA46
   E8025790C005C4A4E?OpenDocument
Social policy measures and development.

http://www.unrisd.org/80256B3C005BB128/(httpProgrammeAreas)/6DA4DF9FA8158D3
280257F1B005A8527?OpenDocument
Gender and development.

https://www.youtube.com/watch?v=Rht4d4GdYbM
Business and sustainable development – can they work for each other?

https://www.youtube.com/watch?v=hNZa94kFMA4
The digital economy and the future of work.

http://www.worldbank.org/en/news/press-release/2016/08/04/world-bank-board-approves-
new-environmental-and-social-framework
The World Bank approves the new environmental and social framework.

http://www.ilo.org/global/research/global-reports/weso/2016-transforming-jobs/lang--en/
index.htm
Transforming jobs to end poverty – World Employment and Social Outlook 2016.

http://www.gouvernement.fr/action/la-cop-21
The Paris climate agreement signed by 196 delegations on 12 December 2015.

http://en.unesco.org/themes/building-knowledge-societies
Building knowledge societies.

(all websites accessed 21 October 2016)

NOTE

1   See e.g. UNRISD, 2016: Chapter 3, Care Policies: Realizing their Transformative Potential.

BIBLIOGRAPHY

Abbas, A.J. (2004) *Islamic Perspectives on Management and Organization*. Cheltenham and Northampton, MA: Edward Elgar.

Acción Ecológica (1999) 'No more plunder. They owe us the ecological debt!' *Bulletin of Acción Ecológica* 78 (October). Acción Ecológica: Quito, Ecuador.

Adam, B. (1990) *Time and Social Theory*. Cambridge: Polity Press.

Adams, R. (2006) 'Remittances, poverty and investment in Guatemala,' in Ç. Özden and M. Schiff (eds) *International Migration, Remittances and the Brain Drain*. Washington, DC: Palgrave-Macmillan and World Bank. pp. 53–80.

Adda, J. (2006) *La mondialisation de l'économie: Genèse et problèmes* (revised Seventh edition). Paris: La Découverte.

Adebo, G.M. (2014) 'Effectiveness of e-wallet practice in grassroots agricultural services delivery in Nigeria – a case study of Kwara State growth enhancement support scheme', *Journal of Experimental Biology and Agricultural Science* 2 (August): 410–18.

Aderinwale, A. (2000) 'Afrika und der Gobalisierungsprozess,' in R. Tetzlaff (ed.) *Weltkulturen unter Globalisierungsdruck. Erfahrungen und Antworten aus den Kontinenten*. Bonn: Dietz. pp. 232–58.

Ajayi, S. I. (2003) 'Globalisation and Africa,' *Journal of African Economies* 12 (1): 120–50.

Akindele, S.T., Gidado, T.O. and Olaopo, O.R. (2002) 'Globalisation, its implications and consequences for Africa.' *Globalization* 2 (1). Available at http://globalization.icaap.org/content/v2.1/01_akindele_etal.html (accessed 29 September 2016).

Albers, D., Haeler, S. and Meyer, H. (eds) (2006) *Social Europe: A Continent's Answer to Market Fundamentalism*. London: European Research Forum at London Metropolitan University.

Allal, A. and Geisser, V. (2011) 'Tunisie: "Révolution de jasmine" ou Intifada?' *Mouvement* 66: 62–8.

Allan, S. (2013) *Citizen Witnessing: Revisioning Journalism in Times of Crisis*. Cambridge: Policy.

Alvaredo, F., Atkinson, A.B., Piketty, T. and Saez, E. (2013) 'The Top 1 percent in international and historical perspective,' *Journal of Economic Perspectives* 27 (3): 3–20.

Amin, S. (1986) *La déconnexion*. Paris: La Découverte.

Anquetil, A. (2008) *Qu'est-ce que l'éthique des affaires?* Paris: Vrin (Chemins philosophiques).

Ansart, P. (1969) *Saint-Simon*. Paris: Presses universitaires de France.

Antweiler, C. (2011) *Mensch und Weltkultur. Für einen realistischen Kosmopolitismus im Zeitalter der Globalisierung*. Bielefeld: Transcript.

Appadurai, A. (1990) 'Disjuncture and difference in the global cultural economy,' *Public Culture* 2 (2): 1–24.

Appadurai, A. (1991) 'Global ethnoscapes: Notes and queries for a transnational anthropology,' in R.G. Fox (ed.) *Recapturing Anthropology*. Santa Fe, NM: School of American Research Press. pp. 191–210.

Appadurai, A. (1993) 'Patriotism and its futures,' *Public Culture* 42 (5): 411–29.

Appadurai, A. (1995) 'Disjuncture and difference in the global cultural economy,' in M. Featherstone (ed.) *Global Culture: Nationalism, Globalization, and Modernity* (Sixth edition). London: Sage. pp. 295–310.

Appardurai, A. (1996) *Modernity at Large. Cultural Dimensions of Globalization*. Minneapolis: University of Minnesota Press.

Appadurai, A. (2013) *The Future as Cultural Fact*. London and New York: Verso.

Appleyard, R.T. (1992) 'Migration and development: A global agenda for the future,' *International Migration* 30 (2): 251–66.

Archer, M.S. (1985) 'Structuration versus Morphogenesis,' in S.N. Eisenstadt and H.J. Helle (eds) *Macro-Sociological Theory. Perspectives on Sociological Theory*. London: Sage. pp. 58–88.

Ardichvili, A. and Gasparishvili, A. (2001) 'Socio-cultural values, internal work culture and leadership styles in four post-communist countries,' *International Journal of Cross Cultural Management* 1 (2): 227–42.

Arguello, R. (2010) 'Securing the fruits of their labours: The effect of the crisis on women farm workers in Peru's Ica Valley,' *Gender & Development* 18 (2): 241–7.

Arjomand, S.A. and Tiryakian, E.A. (eds) (2004) *Rethinking Civilizational Analysis*. London: Sage.

Aron, R. (1950) 'Social structure and the ruling class,' *British Journal of Sociology* 1 (3): 126–44.

Aron, R. (1963) *Frieden und Krieg*. Frankfurt a.M: Fischer.

Arora, A. and Gambardella, A. (2004) 'The globalization of the software industry: Perspectives and opportunities for developed and developing countries,' in A.B. Jaffe, J. Lerner, and S. Stern (eds) *Innovation Policy and the Economy*, vol. 5. Cambridge, MA: MIT Press. pp. 1–32.

Ascencio, C. and Rey, D. (2010) *Etre efficace en Chine: Le management à l'épreuve de la culture chinoise*. Paris: Pearson.

Aslund, A., Guriev, S. and Kuchins A. (eds) (2010) *Russia after the Global Economic Crisis*. Washington, DC: Peterson Institute for International Economics and Center for Strategic and International Studies.

Atzeni, M. (2010) *Workplace Conflict. Mobilization and Solidarity in Argentina*. Basingstoke: Palgrave Macmillan.

Aubert, J.E. and Landrieu, J. (eds) (2004) *Vers des civilisations mondialisées? De l'éthologie à la prospective*. La Tour-d'Aigues: Éditions de l'Aube.

Awotwi, J.E. and Owusu, G. (2010) 'Ghana Community Information Centers (CiCs) E-Governance success or mirage?' *Journal of E-Governance* 33 (3): 157–67.

Axford, B. (1995) *The Global System: Economics, Politics and Culture*. Oxford: Polity Press.

Azoulay, G. (2002) *Les théories du développement. Du rattrapage des retards à l'explosion des inégalités*. Rennes: Presses universitaires de Rennes.

Bäckstrand, K. (2006) 'Multi-stakeholder partnerships for sustainable development: Rethinking legitimacy, accountability and effectiveness,' *European Environment* 16 (5): 290–306.

Balachandran, G. and Subrahmanyam, S. (2005) 'On the history of globalization and India: Concepts, measures and debates,' in J. Assayag and C.J. Fuller (eds) *Globalizing India: Perspectives from Below*. London: Anthem Press. pp. 17–46.

Balandier, G. (1951) 'La situation coloniale: Approche théorique,' *Cahiers Internationaux de Sociologie* XI: 44–79.

Balandier, G. (1968) 'Tradition et continuité' *Cahiers Internationaux de Sociologie*, 44 (1): 1–12.

Balandier, G. (1971) *Sens et puissance*. Paris: Presses Universitaires de France.

Balandier, G. (1978) 'L'anthropologie africaniste et la question du pouvoir', *Cahiers Internationaux de Sociologie*, 65 (2): 197–211.

Balandier, G. (1985) *Sociologie des Brazzavilles noires* (Second edition). Paris: Presses de Sciences Po.

Balandier, G. (1988) *Le Désordre, éloge du mouvement*. Paris: Fayard.

Baldwin, R.E. and Martin, P. (1999) *Two Waves of Globalization: Superficial Similarities, Fundamental Differences*. Cambridge, MA: National Bureau of Economic Research. Working Paper n° 6904.

Banerjee, S.B. (2003) 'Who sustains whose development? Sustainable development and the reinvention of nature,' *Organization Studies* 24 (1): 143–80.

Barber, B. (1995) *Jihad vs. McWorld*. New York: Plume.

Baro, S.S. (2005) *Quête du savoir et strategies d'insertion professionnelle. Parcours d'émigration des étudiants et cadres sénégalais en France, aux États-Unis et au Québec*. EHESS, Paris, PhD in Sociology.

Bartnik, M. (2011) 'Qui sont ces ultra-riches que l'on veut taxer?' *Le Figaro*, 19 August. Available at http://www.lefigaro.fr/impots/2011/08/19/05003-20110819ARTFIG00471-qui-sont-ces-ultra-riches-que-l-on-veut-taxer.php (accessed 24 April 2016).

Bassi, M. and Bertossi, C. (2010) *Les doubles nationaux. Enquête sur les nouveaux entrepreneurs au Maroc*. Paris: Institut Français des Relations Internationales.

Basu, P.K. (2007) 'Critical evaluation of growth strategies: India and China,' *International Journal of Social Economics* 34 (9): 664–78.

Beaujard, P. (2005) 'The Indian Ocean in Eurasian and African world-systems before the sixteenth century,' *Journal of World History* 16 (4): 411–65.

Beine, M., Docquier, F. and Rapoport, H. (2001) 'Brain drain and economic growth: Theory and evidence,' *Journal of Development Economics* 64 (1): 275–89.

Beine, M., Docquier, F. and Rapoport, H. (2003) 'Brain drain and LDCs' growth: Winners and losers,' IZA Discussion Paper, n° 819, July.

Bell, D. (1974) *The Coming of Postindustrial Society*. London: Penguin.

Bellamy, A., Williams, P. and Griffin, S. (2004) *Understanding Peacekeeping*. Cambridge: Polity.

Ben Hammouda, H. and Sadni Jallab, M. (2010) 'La crise va-t-elle emporter le Sud?' Hors série 2010: *Revue Tiers Monde*, 77–96.

Ben-Rafael, E. and Sternberg, Y. (eds) (2005) *Comparing Modernities. Pluralism versus Homogeneity*. Leiden and Boston: Brill.

Bennett, J. (1996) 'Applied and action anthropology: Ideological and conceptual aspects,' *Current Anthropology* Supplement 37 (1): 23–53.

Bennett, L.W. and Segerberg, A. (2012) 'The logic of connective action,' *Information, Communication and Society* 15 (5): 739–68.

Benski, T., Langman, L., Perugorría, I. and Tejerina, B. (2013) 'From the streets and squares to social movement studies: What have we learned?' *Current Sociology* 61 (4): 541–61.

Benton, T. (ed.) (1996) *The Greening of Marxism*. New York: Guilford.

Berardi, F., Jacquemet, M. and Vitali, G. (2003) *Telestreet. Macchina immaginativa non omologata*. Milan: Baldini Castoldi Dalai.

Berger, I. (2016) *Women in Twentieth-century Africa*. Cambridge: Cambridge University Press.

Berger, J. (2006) 'Die Einheit der Moderne,' in T. Schwinn (ed.) *Die Vielfalt und Einheit der Moderne. Kultur- und strukturvergleichende Analysen*. Wiesbaden: VS Verlag für Sozialwissenschaften. pp. 201–26.

Berger, P.L. and Huntington S.P. (eds) (2002) *Many Globalizations. Cultural Diversity in the Contemporary World*. Oxford: Oxford University Press.

Bergson, H. (1989) *L'évolution créatrice*. Paris: Presses universitaires de France.

Berkes, F. and Folke, C. (1998) *Linking Social and Ecological Systems. Management Practices and Social Mechanisms for Building Resilience*. Cambridge: Cambridge University Press.

Bertelsmann Stiftung (2015) *Technologischer Wandel und Beschäftigungspolarisierung in Deutschland*. Policy Brief: Zukunft Soziale Marktwirtschaft.

Bertram, H. (ed.) (1995) *Ostdeutschland im Wandel: Lebensverhältnisse – politische Einstellungen*. Opladen: Leske and Budrich.

Besharov, D.J. and Lopez, M.H. (eds) (2016) *Adjusting to a World in Motion: Trends in Global Migration and Migration Policy*. Oxford: Oxford University Press.

Beyer, J. (2005) 'Pfadabhängigkeit ist nicht gleich Pfadabhängigkeit! Wider den impliziten Konservatismus eines gängigen Konzepts,' *Zeitschrift für Soziologie* 34 (1): 5–21.

Beyer, P. (1994) *Religion and Globalization*. London: Sage.

Bhagwati, J. (2004) *In Defense of Globalization*. Oxford: Oxford University Press.

Bhagwati, J. and Hamada, K. (1974) 'The brain drain, international integration of markets for professionals and unemployment,' *Journal of Development Economics* 1 (1): 19–42.

Bhorat, H., van der Westhuizen, C. and Jacobs, T. (2009) 'Income and non-Income Inequality in Post-apartheid South Africa: What are the Drivers and Possible Policy Interventions?' DPRU Working Paper 09/138. University of Cape Town. Available at http://www.researchgate.net/publication/228269383_Income_and_Non-Income_Inequality_in_Post-Apartheid_South_Africa_What_are_the_Drivers_and_Possible_Policy_Interventions (accessed 7 October 2016).

BIT [Bureau International du Travail] (2013) *Rapport mondial sur les salaires 2012/13: Salaires et croissance équitable*. BIT: Genève.

Blaney, D. and Inayatullah, N. (1998) 'International political economy as a culture of competition,' in D. Jacquin-Berdal, A. Oros, and M. Verweij (eds) *Culture in World Politics*. New York: St. Martin's Press. pp. 61–88.

Boccagni, P. (2012) 'Rethinking transnational studies: Transnational ties and the transnationalism of everyday life,' *Social Theory* 15 (1): 117–32.

Bon, H. K. (1992) *Socio-cultural Factors in the Industrialization of Korea*. San Francisco: ICS Press.

Bonacker, T. and Reckwitz, A. (eds) (2007) *Kulturen der Moderne. Soziologische Perspektiven der Gegenwart*. Frankfurt a.M. and New York: Campus.

Bond, P. (2014a) 'Tokenistic social policy in South Africa,' *Transformation* 86: 48–77.

Bond, P. (2014b) *Elite Transition: From Apartheid to Neoliberalism in South Africa*. London: Pluto Press.

Boswell, T. and Chase-Dunn, C. (2000) *The Spiral of Capitalism and Socialism*. Boulder, CO: Lynne Rieder.

Boudon, R. (1984) *La place du désordre*. Paris: Presses universitaires de France.

Bouffartigue, P. and Béroud, S. (2009) *Quand le travail se précarise, quelles résistances collectives?* Paris: La dispute/SNEDIT.

Boyer, R. (1999) 'The variety and dynamics of capitalism,' in J. Groenewegen and J. Vromen (eds) *Institutions and the Evolution of Capitalism: Implications of Evolutionary Economics*. Northampton: Edward Elgar. pp. 122–140.

Boyer, R. (2005) 'How and why capitalisms differ,' MPIfG Discussion Paper 05/4. Max-Planck-Institut für Gesellschaftsforschung Köln.

Brand, K.-W. (2010) 'Social practices and sustainable consumption: Benefits and limitations of a new theoretical approach' in M. Gross and H. Heinrichs (eds) *Environmental Sociology: European Perspectives and Interdisciplinary Challenges*. Dordrecht: Springer. pp. 217–35.

Brand, K.-W. (2014) *Umweltsoziologie: Entwicklungslinien, Basiskonzepte und Erklärungsmodelle*. Weinheim and Basel: Beltz Juventa.

Brand, K.-W., Eder, K. and Poferl, A. (eds) (1997) *Ökologische Kommunikation in Deutschland*. Opladen: Westdeutscher Verlag.

Brand, U. (2012) 'Green economy – the next oxymoron. No lessons learned from failures of implementing sustainable development,' *GAIA* 21 (1): 28–32.

Branine, M. (2011) *Managing Across Cultures: Concepts, Policies and Practices*. London: Sage.

Braudel, F. (1998) *Grammaire des civilisations*. Paris: Bussière Camedan.

Bright, C. and Geyer, M. (1987) 'For a unified history of the world in the twentieth century,' *Radical History Review* 39: 69–91.

Bringel, B. (2013a) 'Le Brésil et la géopolitique de l'indignation,' *La vie des idées* 25 (July).

Bringel, B. (2013b) 'Miopias, sentidos e tendências do levante brasileiro de 2013', *Insight Inteligência* 62: 42–51.

Bringel, B. and Pleyers, G. (2015) 'Les mobilisations de 2013 au Brésil: vers une reconfiguration de la contestation,' *Brésil(s): sciences humaines et sociales* 7: 7–18.

Bringel, B. and Domingues, J.M. (eds) (2015) *Global Modernity and Social Contestation*. London: Sage.

Brinley, T. (1954) *Migration and Economic Growth*. London: Cambridge University Press.

Brock, D. and Junge, M. (1995) 'Die Theorie gesellschaftlicher Modernisierung und das Problem gesellschaftlicher Integration,' *Zeitschrift für Soziologie* 24 (3): 165–82.

Brooks, E. (2007) *Unraveling the Garment Industry. Transnational Organizing and Women's Work*. Minneapolis: University of Minnesota Press.

Brumann, C. (1998) 'The anthropological study of globalization. Towards an agenda for the second phase,' *Anthropos* 93 (4–6): 495–506.

Brunel, S. (2005) *L'Afrique dans la mondialisation*. Paris: La Documentation française. Dossier 8048.

Bruun, O. and Kalland, A. (eds) (1995) *Asian Perception of Nature*. Richmond: Curzon Press.

Buchholt, H., Heidt, E.U. and Stauth, G. (eds) (1996) *Modernität zwischen Differenzierung und Globalisierung. Kulturelle, wirtschaftliche und politische Transformationsprozesse in der sich globalisierenden Moderne*. Hamburg: Lit.

Budhwar, P.S. (2001) 'Doing business in India,' *Thunderbird International Business Review* 43 (4): 549–68.

Budhwar, P.S., Woldu, H.G. and Ogbonna, E. (2008) 'A comparative analysis of cultural value orientations of Indians and migrant Indians in the USA,' *International Journal of Cross Cultural Management* 8 (1): 79–105.

Budlender, J., Woolard, I. and Leibbrandt, M. (2015) 'How current measures underestimate the level of poverty in South Africa,' *The Conversation*, 3 September. Available at https://theconversation.com/how-current-measures-underestimate-the-level-of-poverty-in-south-africa-46704 (accessed 7 October 2016).

Buehl, W.L. (1990) *Sozialer Wandel im Ungleichgewicht: Zyklen, Fluktuationen, Katastrophen*. Stuttgart: Enke.

Buell, F. (1994) *National Culture and the New Global System*. Baltimore, MD and London: Johns Hopkins University Press.

Caillé, A. (2003) 'Présentation,' *Revue de Mauss* 21: 5–20.

Camilleri, J.A. (2000) *States, Markets and Civil Society in Asia Pacific. The Political Economy of the Asia-Pacific Region*. Vol. 1. Cheltenham: Edward Elgar.

Canau, M. (2011) 'La disgrâce du chef. Mobilisations populaires arabes et crise du leadership,' *Movements* 66: 22–9.

Capron, M. and Quairel-Lanoizelée, F. (2004) *Mythes et réalités de l'entreprise responsable. Acteurs, enjeux, stratégies*. Paris: La Découverte.

Cardoso, F.H. and Faletto, E. (1979) *Dependency and Development in Latin America*. Berkeley: University of California Press.

Carlton-Ford, S. and Boop. D. (2010) 'Civil war and life chances: A multinational study,' *International Sociology* 25 (1): 75–97.

Carrel, P. (2011) 'Stark resignation limits Draghi's room on bond buys.' Available at http://www.easybourse.com/bourse/international/news/934379/stark-resignation-limits-draghis-room-on-bond-buys.html (accessed 26 April 2016).

Castells, M. (2000) *The Information Age*. 3 vols. Oxford: Blackwell.

Castells, M. (2009) *Communication Power*. Oxford: Oxford University Press.

Castells, M. (2012) *Networks of Outrage and Hope: Social Movements in the Internet Age*. Cambridge: Polity Press.

Castles, S. and Kosack, G. (1973) *Immigrant Workers and Class Structure in Western Europe*. Oxford: Oxford University Press.

Castles, S. and Miller, M.J. (1998) *The Age of Migration: International Population Movements in the Modern World* (Second edition). London: Macmillan.

Causa, O. and Cohen, D. (2006) *The Ladder of Competitiveness: How to Climb it*. Paris: OECD.

Centre Tricontinental (2000) *Cultures et mondialisation. Résistances et alternatives*. Paris and Montreal: L'Harmattan.

Cernea, M.M. (1998) 'La sociologie des déplacements forcés: un modèle théorique,' *Autrepart* 5: 11–28.

Cesana, A. (1988) *Geschichte als Entwicklung? Zur Kritik des geschichtsphilosophischen Entwicklungsdenkens*. Berlin: W. de Gruyter.

Chabanet, D. (ed.) (2011) *Les mobilisations sociales à l'heure du précariat*. Rennes: Presses de l'EHESP.

Chambers, E. (1987) 'Applied anthropology in the post-Vietnam era: Anticipations and irony,' *Annual Review of Anthropology* 16: 309–37.

Chang, H.-J. (2007) *The East Asian Development Experience. The Miracle, the Crisis and the Future*. London: Zed Books.

Chaponnière, J.-R. (2010) 'L'Asie émergente face à la crise mondiale,' in Hors série 2010: *Revue Tiers Monde*, 127–56.

Chatterton, P., Featherstone, D. and Routledge, P. (2012) 'Articulating climate justice in Copenhagen: Antagonism, the commons, and solidarity,' *Antipode*. Available at http://cccep.ac.uk/wp-content/uploads/2015/10/articulating-climate-justice.pdf (accessed 21 December 2016).

Chen, W. and Wellman, B. (2004) 'The global digital divide - Within and between countries,' *IT & Society* 1 (7): 18–25.

Chew, S.C. (2001) *World-Ecological Degradation: Accumulation, Urbanization, and Deforestation 3000 BC–AD 2000*. Lanham, MD: AltaMira Press, Rowman and Littlefield.

Chieng, A., d'Iribarne, P. and Lewis, R.D. (2006) 'Cultures d'entreprises,' *Revue des deux mondes* 2 (Feb.): 93–155.

Chintan, Environmental Research and Action Group (2009) *Cooling Agents: An Examination of the Role of the Informal Recycling Sector in Mitigating Climate Change*. New Delhi: Chintan.

Chow, E.N.-L. (ed.) (2003) 'Gender, globalization and social change in the 21st century,' Special Issue of *International Sociology* 18 (3): 441–640.

Christoff, P. (2000) 'Ecological modernisation, ecological modernities,' in S.C. Young (ed.) *The Emergence of Ecological Modernisation. Integrating the Environment and the Economy?* London and New York: Routledge. pp. 209–31.

Chua-Franz, C. (2002) *Indonesiens Chinesen. Konstruktion und Instrumentalisierung einer ethnischen Minderheit*. Hamburg: Mitteilungen des Instituts für Asienkunde, n° 361.

Cingolani, P. (2014) *Révolutions précaires. Essai sur l'avenir de l'émancipation*. Paris: La Découverte.

Cohen, J. (2010) 'How the global economic crisis reaches marginalised workers: The case of street traders in Johannesburg, South Africa,' *Gender & Development* 18 (2): 277–89.

Cohen, Y. (2014) 'Crowds without a master: A Transnational approach between past and present,' *FocaalBlog*, 10 November. Available at http://www.focaalblog.com/2014/11/10/yves-cohen-crowds-without-a-master-a-transnational-approach-between-past-and-present (accessed 21 October 2016).

Cole, L. and Foster, S. (2001) *From the Ground Up: Environmental Racism and the Rise of the Environmental Justice Movement*. New York: New York University Press.

Coleman, N. (2013) 'The national development plan: The devil is in the economic detail,' *Daily Maverick*. Available at http://www.dailymaverick.co.za/opinionista/2013-04-03-national-development-plan-the-devil-is-in-the-economic-detail/#.Vn904FIpV4M (accessed 24 October 2016).

Collins, R. (1975) *Conflict Sociology: Toward an Explanatory Science*. New York: Academic Press.

Comisión Económica para América Latina y el Caribe [CEPAL] (2009) *Balance preliminar de las economías de América Latina y el Caribe*. Santiago de Chile: Publicación de las Naciones Unidas.

Commission for Africa (2005) *Our Common Interest: An Argument*. London and New York: Penguin Books.

Conaghan, C. M. and Malloy, J.M. (1994) *Unsettling Statecraft: Democracy and Neo-liberalism in the Central Andes*. Pittsburgh: University of Pittsburgh Press.

Condé, J., Diagne, P.S., Ouaidou, N. G., Boye, K. and Kader, A. (1986) *Les Migrations internationales Sud–Nord: Une étude de cas des migrants maliens, mauritaniens et sénégalais de la vallée du fleuve Sénégal en France*. Paris: Development Centre of the OECD.

Cook, S. (2006) 'Commodity cultures, Mesoamerica and Mexico's changing indigenous economy,' *Critique of Anthropology* 26(2): 181–208.

Cordey, P.-A. (2005) 'Business and state relations in Latin America: The role of transnational corporations in Peru'. PhD Thesis, University of Fribourg, Switzerland. Available at https://doc.rero.ch/record/4974/files/1_CordeyPA.pdf (accessed 29 September 2016).

Córdova Alcaraz, R. (2012) *Rutas y dinámicas migratorias entre los países de América Latina y el Caribe (ALC), y entre ALC y la Unión Europea* [Migration Routes and Dynamics between the Countries of Latin America and the Caribbean (LAC), and between LAC and the European Union]. Belgium: IOM.

Cornia, G.A. and World Institute for Development Economics Research (2004) *Inequality, Growth, and Poverty in an Era of Liberalization and Globalization*. Oxford and New York: Oxford University Press.

Coser, L.A. (1967a) *Continuities in the Study of Social Conflict*. London and New York: The Free Press, Collier-MacMillan.

Coser, L.A. (1967b) 'Social conflict and the theory of social change,' in L.A. Coser, *Continuities in the Study of Social Conflict*. London and New York: The Free Press, Collier-MacMillan. pp. 17–35.

Crouch, C. (2008) *Postdemokratie*. Frankfurt a.M.: Suhrkamp.

Crouch, C. (2011) *The Strange Non-Death of Neo-liberalism*. Wiley: Cambridge.

Crow, G. and Heath, S. (ed.) (2002) *Social Conceptions of Time: Structure and Process in Work and Everyday Life*. Basingstoke: Palgrave Macmillan.

Cutler, S.J. (2007) 'Aging and technology,' in G. Ritzer (ed.) *Blackwell Encyclopedia of Sociology*. Malden, MA: Blackwell Publishing.

d'Iribarne, P. (2003) *Le Tiers Monde qui réussit*. Paris: Odile Jacob.

d'Iribarne, P. (2004) 'Mondialisation et maintien de la diversité des cultures au sein des enterprises,' in J.E. Aubert and J. Landrieu (eds) *Vers des civilisations mondialisées? De l'éthologie à la prospective*. La Tour-d'Aigues: Éditions de l'Aube. pp. 171–180.

d'Iribarne, P. (2007) *Successful Companies in the Developing World: Managing in Synergy with Cultures*. Paris: Agence Française de Développement.

d'Iribarne, P., Henry, A., Segal, J.-P. and Chevrier, S. (1998) *Cultures et mondialisation: gérer par-delà les frontières*. Paris: Seuil.

Dabla-Norris, E., Kochhar, K., Suphaphiphat, N., Ricka, F. and Tsounta, E. (2015) *Causes and Consequences of Income Inequality: A Global Perspective*. International Monetary Fund: Strategy, Policy, and Review Department. Available at https://www.imf.org/external/pubs/ft/sdn/2015/sdn1513.pdf (accessed 2 October 2016).

Dahmani, M. (1983) *L'Occidentalisation des pays du Tiers Monde. Mythes et réalités*. Algiers: Economia.

Dahrendorf, R. (1964) 'Toward a theory of social conflict,' in A. Etzioni and E. Etzioni (eds) *Social Change*. New York and London: Basic Books. pp. 98–111.

Dahrendorf, R. (1967) *Class and Class Conflict in Industrial Society*. Stanford, CA: Stanford University Press.

Dahrendorf, R. (1969) 'Zu einer Theorie des sozialen Konflikts,' in W. Zapf (ed.), *Theorien des sozialen Wandels*. Köln: Kiepenheuer & Witsch. pp. 108–23.

Dallago, B., Guri, G. and McGowan, J. (2016) *A Global Perspective on the European Economic Crisis*. New York: Routledge.

Daly, H.E. (1996) *Beyond Growth. The Economics of Sustainable Development*. Boston: Beacon Press.

Damon, J. and Igué, J.O. (eds) (2003) *L'Afrique de l'Ouest dans la compétition mondiale. Quels atouts possibles?* Paris: Karthala, Club du Sahel et de l'Afrique de l'Ouest - OECD.

Dasgupta, S. (ed.) *Understanding the Global Environment*. New Delhi: Pearson Education India.

Daum, C. (1998) *Les associations de Maliens en France. Migration, développement et citoyenneté*. Paris: Karthala.

Davies, J.B., Sandström, S., Shorrocks, A. and Wolff, E.N. (2008) *The World Distribution of Household Wealth*. Discussion Paper n° 2008/03 (Helsinki, UNU-WIDER). Available at http://www.wider.unu.edu/publications/working-papers/discussion-papers/2008/en_GB/dp2008-03/ (accessed 24 October 2016).

Davis, G.F. (2009) *Managed by the Market: How Finance Reshaped America*. Oxford: Oxford University Press.

Davis, S.H. (1999) 'Bringing culture into the development paradigm: The view from the World Bank,' *Development Anthropology* 16 (1–2): 25–31.

de Gaulejac, V. (2011) *Travail, les raisons de la colère*. Paris: Seuil.

Deibert, R., Palfrey, J., Rohozinski, R. and Zittrain, J. (eds) (2008) *Access Denied: The Practice and Policy of Global Internet Filtering*. Cambridge, MA: MIT Press.

Deibert, R., Palfrey, J., Rohozinski, R. and Zittrain, J. (eds) (2010) *Access Controlled: The Shaping of Power, Rights, and Rule in Cyberspace*. Cambridge, MA: MIT Press.

Della Porta, D. and Tarrow, S. (2005) 'Transnational protest and social activism: An introduction,' in D. Della Porta and S. Tarrow (eds) *Transnational Protest and Global Activism*. Lanham, MD: Rowman & Littlefield. pp. 1–17.

Devall, B. and Sessions, G. (1985) *Deep Ecology: Living as if Nature Mattered*. Layton, UT: Gibbs Smith.

Di Giulio, A. (2004) *Die Idee der Nachhaltigkeit im Verständnis der Vereinten Nationen. Anspruch, Bedeutung und Schwierigkeiten*. Münster: Lit.

Diachronia (1984) 'Zum Verhältnis von Ethnologie, Geschichte und Geschichtswissenschaft,' *Ethnologica Helvetica* 8.

Diamond, I. and Orenstein, G.F. (eds) (1990) *Reweaving the World: The Emergence of Ecofeminism*. San Francisco: Sierra Club Books.

Diamond, J. (1998) *Guns, Germs and Steel: A Short History of Everybody for the Last 13,000 Years*. Vintage: London.

Dimier, V. (1999) *Le discours idéologique de la méthode coloniale chez les Français et les Britanniques de l'entre-deux-guerres à la décolonisation (1920–1960)*. Bordeaux: Université Montesquieu, Centre d'Étude d'Afrique Noire.

Docquier, F. and Marfouk, A. (2006) 'International migration by educational attainment (1990–2000),' in Ç. Özden and M. Schiff (eds) *International Migration, Remittances and the Brain Drain*. Washington, DC: Palgrave-Macmillan and World Bank. pp. 151–65.

Docquier, F. and Rapoport, H. (2004) 'Skilled migration: The perspective of developing countries,' *World Bank Policy Research Working Paper* n° 3382.

Docquier, F. and Sekkat, K. (2006) *The Brain Drain: What Do We Know?* Agence Française de Développement, Working Paper 31.

Docquier, F., Lohest, O. and Marfouk, A. (2005) 'Union européenne et migrations internationales: l'UE15 contribue-t-elle à l'exode des travailleurs qualifiés?' *Revue Économique* 56 (6): 1301–30.

Dossani, R. (2008) *India Arriving: How This Economic Powerhouse is Redefining Global Business*. New York: AMACOM, American Management Association.

Dreher, A. (2006) 'Does globalization affect growth? Evidence from a new Index of Globalization,' *Applied Economics* 38 (10): 1091–110.

Dreher, A., Gaston, N. and Martens, P. (2008) *Measuring Globalization – Gauging Its Consequences*. New York: Springer.

Dryzek, J.S. (1997) *The Politics of the Earth. Environmental Discourses*. Oxford: Oxford University Press.

Duby, G. (1973) *Le Dimanche de Bouvines*. Paris: Gallimard.

Dumont, J.C. and Lemaître, G. (2005) 'Counting immigrants and expatriates in OECD countries: A new perspective,' Mimeo, OECD.

Dunning, J.H. and Mucchielli, J.-L. (eds) (2002) *Multinational Firms: The Global-Local Dilemma*. London and New York: Routledge.

Edelman, M. and Haugerud, A. (eds) (2006) *The Anthropology of Development and Globalization: From Classical Political Economy to Contemporary Neoliberalism*. Oxford: Blackwell.

Eisenstadt, S.N. (2000a) *Die Vielfalt der Moderne*. Weilerswist: Velbrück.

Eisenstadt, S.N. (2000b) 'Multiple modernities,' *Daedalus* 129: 1–30.

Eisenstadt, S.N. (2006) 'Multiple Modernen im Zeitalter der Globalisierung,' in T. Schwinn (ed.) *Die Vielfalt und Einheit der Moderne. Kultur- und strukturvergleichende Analysen*. Wiesbaden: VS Verlag für Sozialwissenschaften. pp. 37–62.

Ekholm-Friedman, K. and Friedman, J. (1995) 'Global complexity and the simplicity of everyday life,' in D. Miller (ed.) *Worlds Apart: Modernity through the Prism of the Local*. London and New York: Routledge. pp. 134–89.

El-Hinnawi, E. (1985) *Environmental Refugees*. Nairobi: United Nations Environment Programme.

Elson, D. (2002) 'The international financial architecture – a view from the kitchen,' *Femina Politica – Zeitschrift für feministische Politik-Wissenschaft* 11 (1): 26–37.

Elson, D. (2010) 'Gender and the global economic crisis in developing countries: A framework for analysis,' *Gender & Development* 18 (2): 201–12.

Emirbayer, Mustapha (ed.) (2003) *Emile Durkheim: Sociologist of Modernity*. Malden, MA: Wiley, Blackwell.

Engelhard, P. (1998) *L'Afrique miroir du monde? Plaidoyer pour une nouvelle économie*. Paris: Karthala.

Escobar, A. (1995a) 'Encountering development: The making and unmaking of the Third World 1945–1992,' *Social Text* 31/32: 20–56.

Escobar, A. (1995b) *Encountering Development: The Making and Unmaking of the Third World*. Princeton: Princeton University Press.

Escobar, A. (1997) 'Anthropology and development,' *International Social Science Journal* 49 (154): 497–515.

Esser, K. (2000) 'Gehemmte Modernisierung in Lateinamerika,' in R. Tetzlaff (ed.), *Weltkulturen unter Globalisierungsdruck. Erfahrungen und Antworten aus den Kontinenten*. Bonn: Dietz. pp. 260–95.

European Commission (2009) *Monthly Monitor EU Employment Situation and Social Outlook May*. Available at http://www.zukunfteuropa.at/DocView.axd?CobId=34789 (accessed 24 October 2016).

European Union (2013) *European Report on Development 2013 – Post-2015: Global Action for an Inclusive and Sustainable Future*. Brussels: EU.

Evans, P. (1995) *Embedded Autonomy: States and Industrial Transformation*. Princeton, NJ: Princeton University Press.

Evans, V. (2003) *The Structure of Time. Language, Meaning, and Temporal Cognition*. Amsterdam, Philadelphia, PA : J. Benjamins.

Evers Rosander, E. (2005) 'Cosmopolites et locales: femmes sénégalaises en voyage,' *Afrique et Histoire: Revue internationale* 4: 103–22.

Fadairo, O.S., Olutegbe, N.S. and Tijan, A.M. (2015) 'Attitude of crop farmers towards e-wallet platform of the growth enhancement support scheme for input delivery in Oke-Ogun area of Oyo state,' *Journal of Agricultural Informatics* 6 (2): 62–71.

Faist, T. (2014) 'The public role of social scientists in constituting the migration-development nexus,' *New Diversities* 16 (2): 112–23.

Falch, M. and Anyimadu, A. (2003) 'Tele-centres as a way of achieving universal access – The case of Ghana,' *Telecommunications Policy* 27 (1–2): 21–39.

Falquet, J., Hirata, H., Kergoat, D., Labari, B., Lefeuvre, N. and Sow, F. (2010) *Le sexe de la mondialisation. Genre, classe, race et nouvelle division du travail.* Paris: Presses de la Fondation de Sciences po.

Fassmann, H. (2003) 'Transnationale Mobilität: Konzeption und Fallbeispiel,' *SMS-Rundschau* 43 (4): 429–49.

Featherstone, M. (1995) 'Global culture: An introduction', in M. Featherstone (ed.) *Global Culture: Nationalism, Globalization and Modernity* (Sixth edition). London: Sage. pp. 1–14.

Ferguson, J. (1990) *The Anti-Politics Machine: 'Development,' Depoliticization, and Bureaucratic Power in Lesotho.* Cambridge: Cambridge University Press.

Fernández-Macías, E. and Vacas-Soriano, C. (2015) *Recent Developments in the Distribution of Wages in Europe.* Luxembourg: Publications Office of the European Union.

Firebaugh, G. and Goesling, B. (2007) 'Globalization and global inequalities: Recent trends,' in G. Ritzer (ed.) *The Blackwell Companion to Globalization.* Oxford: Blackwell Publishing.

Fischer, P.A., Martin, R. and Straubhaar, T. (1997) 'Interdependencies between development and migration,' in T. Hammar, G. Brochmann, K. Tamas, and T. Faist (eds) *International Migration – Immobility and Developement: Multidisciplinary Perspectives.* Oxford and New York: Berg. pp. 91–132.

Fleming, P. and Sewell, G. (2002) 'Looking for the good soldier, Svejk: Alternative modalities of resistance in the contemporary workplace,' *Sociology* 36 (4): 857–73.

Flesher Fominaya, C. and Cox, L. (eds) (2013) *Understanding European Movements: New Social Movements, Global Justice Struggles, Anti-Austerity Protest.* London and New York: Routledge.

Foran, J., Lane, D. and Zivkovic, A. (eds) (2008) *Revolution in the Making of the Modern World: Social Identities, Globalization, and Modernity.* London and New York: Routledge.

Forslund, D. (2012) 'Wages, profits and labour productivity in South Africa,' *Amandla!*, 24 January.

Foucault, M. (1975) *Discipline and Punish: The Birth of the Prison.* New York: Random House.

Fougère, M. and Solitander, N. (2009) 'Against corporate responsibility: Critical reflections on thinking, practice, content and consequences,' *Corporate Social Responsibility and Environmental Management* 16: 217–27.

Fougier, E. (2004) *Altermondialisme. Le nouveau mouvement d'émancipation?* Paris: Lignes de repères.

Fourcade, M. and Khurana, R. (2013) 'From social control to financial economics: The linked ecologies of economics and business in twentieth-century America,' *Theory and Society* 42 (2): 121–59.

Francis, Holy Father (2015) *Encyclical Letter Laudato Si' on Care for Our Common Home.* Available at http://w2.vatican.va/content/francesco/en/encyclicals/documents/papa-francesco_20150524_enciclica-laudato-si.html (accessed 24 October 2016).

Frank, A.G. (1967) *Capitalism and Underdevelopment in Latin America.* Harmondsworth: Penguin Books.

Frankfurter Allgemeine Zeitung (2008) 'Finanzkrise könnte 20 Millionen Jobs kosten,' October 21.

Fratzscher, M. (2016) *Verteilungskampf: Warum Deutschland immer ungleicher wird.* Munich: Carl Hanser Verlag.

Freeman, G.P. and Mirilovic, N. (2016) *Handbook in Migration and Social Policy.* Cheltenham and Northampton, MA: Edward Elgar Publishing.

Friedman, J. (1994) *Cultural Identity and Global Process.* London: Sage.

Friedman, J. (1995) 'Being in the world: Globalisation and localisation,' in M. Featherstone (ed.) *Global Culture: Nationalism, Globalization and Modernity* (Sixth edition). London: Sage. pp. 311–28.

Friedman, J. and Randeria, S. (eds) (2004) *Worlds on the Move: Globalization, Migration and Cultural Security.* New York: Palgrave Macmillan.

Fuentes Nieva, R. and Galasso, N. (2014) *Working for the Few: Political Capture and Economic Inequality.* Oxford: Oxfam.

Fukuda, J.K. (1989) 'China's management tradition and reform,' *Management Decision* 27 (3): 45–9.

Gaillard, A.M. and Gaillard, J. (1999) *Les enjeux des migrations scientifiques internationales: De la quête du savoir à la circulation des compétences.* Paris: L'Harmattan.

Galbraith, J.K. (2008) *Inequality and Economic and Political Change.* UTIP Working Paper 51.

Galtung, J. (1984) 'On the dialectics between crisis and crisis perception,' in E.A. Tiryakian (ed.) *The Global Crisis, Sociological Analyses and Responses.* Leiden: Brill. pp. 4–32.

Gane, N. (2004) 'Back to the future of social theory: An interview with Nicholas Gane,' *Sociological Research Online.* Available at http://www.socresonline.org.uk/9/4/beer.html (accessed 24 October 2016).

Gardner, G.T. and Stern, P.C. (1996) *Environmental Problems and Human Behavior.* Boston: Allyn and Bacon.

Garrett, G. (2003) 'Global markets and national politics,' in D. Held and A. McGrew (eds) *The Global Transformations Reader* (Second edition). Cambridge: Polity. pp. 384–402.

Garvey, J. (2008) *The Ethics of Climate Change.* London: Continuum.

Gauchon, P. (ed.) (2006) *Inde, Chine à l'assaut du monde: rapport Antheios.* Paris: Presses universitaires de France.

Gaudillière, J.-P. and Flipo, F. (2009) 'Inégalités écologiques, croissance verte et utopies technocratiques,' *Mouvements* 60: 78–91.

Geertz, C. (1986) *Savoir local, savoir global.* Paris: PUF. (1st American edition 1983, *Local Knowledge: Further Essays in Interpretative Anthropology*).

Geschiere, P. (1997) *The Modernity of Witchcraft: Politics and the Occult in Postcolonial Africa.* Charlottesville, VA: University Press of Virginia.

Gibson, N.C. (2004) 'Africa and globalization: Marginalization and resistance,' *Journal of Asian and African Studies* 39 (1–2): 1–28.

Giddens, A. (1984) *The Constitution of Society: Outline of the Theory of Structuration.* Cambridge: Polity.

Giddens, A. (1990) *The Consequences of Modernity.* Stanford, CA: Stanford University Press.

Giddens, A. (2009) *The Politics of Climate Change.* London: Polity Press.

Glick Schiller, N., Basch, L.G. and Szanton-Blanc, C. (1995) 'From immigrant to transmigrant: Theorizing transnational migration,' *Anthropological Quarterly* 68 (1): 48–63.

Global Financial Integrity (2015) *Illicit Financial Flows from Developing Countries.* Washington, DC. Available at http://www.gfintegrity.org/report/illicit-financial-flows-from-developing-countries-2004-2013/ (accessed 24 October 2016).

Globalization (1999) *International Social Science Journal* 51, 160 (4): 135–261.

Godelier, M. (1995) 'L'anthropologie sociale est-elle indissolublement liée à l'Occident, sa terre natale?' *International Social Science Journal* 47, 143 (1): 165–83.

Godong Bend, S.A. (2011) *Implanter le capitalisme en Afrique: Bonne gouvernance et meilleures pratiques de gestion face aux cultures locales.* Paris: Karthala.

Goldberg, N. (2005) *Measuring the Impact of Microfinance: Taking Stock of What We Know.* Grameen Foundation USA. Publication Series. Available at http://www.grameenfoundation.org/sites/default/files/resources/Measuring-Impact-of-Microfinance_Nathanael_Goldberg.pdf (accessed 24 October 2016).

Goldstein, A., Pinaud, N., Reisen, H. and Chen, X. (2006) *The Rise of China and India: What's in it for Africa?* Paris: OECD.

Goldstone, J. A. (1998) 'Initial conditions, general laws, path dependence, and explanation in historical sociology' *American Journal of Sociology* 104 (3): 829–45.

Golini, A., Gerano, G. and Heins, F. (1991) 'South–North migration with special reference to Europe,' *International Migration* 29 (2): 253–79.

Gomes, R.C. and de Oliveira Miranda Gomes, L. (2009) 'Depicting the arena in which Brazilian local government authorities make decisions: What is the role of stakeholders?' *International Journal of Public Sector Management* 22 (2): 76–90.

Gosh, B. (1992) 'Migration-development linkages: Some specific issues and practical policy measures,' *International Migration* 30 (3–4): 423–56.

Gould, W.T.S. and Findlay, A.M. (1994) *Population Migration and the Changing World Order.* London: John Wiley.

Gouldson, A. and Murphy, J. (1997) 'Ecological modernization: Restructuring industrial economics,' in M. Jacobs (ed.) *Greening the Millennium? The New Politics of the Environment,* Oxford: Blackwell. pp. 74–86.

Gourvish, T. R. and Wilson, R. G. (1994) *The British Brewing Industry 1830–1980.* Cambridge: Cambridge University Press.

Gow, D. (2002) 'Anthropology and development: Evil twin or moral narrative?' *Human Organization* 61 (4): 299–313.

Graeber, D. (2002) 'The anthropology of globalization (with notes on Neomedievalism, and the end of the Chinese model of the state),' *American Anthropologist* 104 (4): 1222–7.

Graeber, D. (2010) 'Les fondements moraux des relations économiques,' *Revue du MAUSS* 2 (36): 51–70.

Grégoire, E. (2002) 'La difficile insertion de l'Afrique de l'Ouest dans la mondialisation,' *Les Temps Modernes* 57 (620–621): 392–409.

Greig, A., Hulme, D. and Turner, M. (2007) *Challenging Global Inequality: Development Theory and Practice in the 21st Century.* Basingstoke: Palgrave MacMillan.

Gross, M. (2007) 'Non-knowledge and related concepts. The unknown in process: Dynamic connections of ignorance,' *Current Sociology* 55 (5): 742–59.

Gruzinski, S. (2004) *Les quatre parties du monde: Histoire d'une mondialisation.* Paris: Éditions de la Martinière.

Guilmoto, C.Z. and Sandron, F. (2003) *Migration et développement.* Paris: La Documentation Française.

Gumplowicz, L. (1885 [1926]) *Grundriss der Soziologie.* Innsbruck: Universitätsbuchhandlung Wagner.

Gupta, N. (2015) 'Rethinking the relationship between gender and technology: A study of the Indian example,' *Work, Employment and Society* 29 (4): 661–72.

Haggard, S.M. (1998) 'Business, politics and policy in East and Southeast Asia,' in H.S. Rowen (ed.) *Behind East Asian Growth. The Political and Social Foundations of Prosperity.* London and New York: Routledge. pp. 78–104.

Halimi, S. (2011) 'Ne rougissez pas de vouloir la lune: il nous la faut,' *Le Monde diplomatique,* July. Available at http://www.monde-diplomatique.fr/2011/07/HALIMI/20760 (accessed 24 October 2016).

Hall, E.T. (1984) *La danse de la vie. Temps culturel, temps vécu.* Paris: Seuil.

Hall, P. A. and Soskice, D. (eds) (2001) *Varieties of Capitalism. The Institutional Foundations of Comparative Advantage.* Oxford: Oxford University Press.

Hall, T.D. and Fenelon, J.F. (2009) *Indigenous Peoples and Globalization.* Boulder, CO: Paradigm.

Hamelink, C. (1999) *ICTs and Social Development: The Global Policy Context.* UNRISD Discussion Paper n° 116.

Hammar, T., Brochmann, G., Tamas, K. and Faist, T. (eds) (1997) *International Migration, Immobility and Development: Multidisciplinary Perspectives.* Oxford and New York: Berg.

Hampden-Turner, C. and Trompenaars, F. (1993) *The Seven Cultures of Capitalism: Value Systems for Creating Wealth in the United States, Britain, Japan, Germany, France, Sweden and the Netherlands.* New York: Doubleday.

Hannerz, U. (1983) 'Tools of identity and imagination,' in A. Jacobson-Widding (ed.) *Identity: Personal and Socio-Cultural.* Uppsala: Academia Upsaliensis/Atlantic Highlands, NJ: Humanities Press. pp. 347–60.

Hannerz, U. (1987) 'The world in Creolization,' *Africa* 57 (4): 546–59.

Hannerz, U. (1989a) 'Culture between center and periphery: Toward a macroanthropology,' *Ethnos* 54 (3–4): 200–16.

Hannerz, U. (1989b) 'Notes on the global ecumene,' *Public Culture* 1 (2): 66–75.

Hannerz, U. (1991) 'The global ecumene as a network of networks,' in Adam Kuper (ed.) *Conceptualizing Societies.* London and New York: Routledge. pp. 34–56.

Hannerz, U. (1992) *Cultural Complexity: Studies in the Social Organization of Meaning.* New York: Columbia University Press.

Hannerz, U. (1993) 'Mediations in the global ecumene,' in G. Pâlsson (ed.) *Beyond Boundaries.* Oxford: Berg. pp. 41–57.

Hannerz, U. (1995a) 'Cosmopolitans and locals in world culture,' in M. Featherstone (ed.) *Global Culture: Nationalism, Globalization and Modernity* (Sixth edition). London: Sage. pp. 237–251.

Hannerz, U. (1995b) '"Kultur" in einer vernetzten Welt. Zur Revision eines ethnologischen Begriffes,' in W. Kaschuba (ed.) *Kulturen – Identitäten – Diskurse. Perspektiven Europäischer Ethnologie.* Berlin: Akademie Verlag. pp. 64–84.

Hannerz, U. (1996) *Transnational Connections: Cultures, People, Places.* London and New York: Routledge.

Hansen, N., Postmes, T., Tovote, A.K. and Bos, A. (2014) 'How modernization instigates social change: Laptop usage as a driver of cultural value change and gender equality in a developing country,' *Journal of Cross-Cultural Psychology* 45 (8): 1229–48.

Harmsen, A. (1999) *Globalisierung and lokale Kultur. Eine ethnologische Betrachtung.* Hamburg: Lit.

Hartmann, M. (2016) *Die globale Wirtschaftselite. Eine Legende.* Frankfurt a.M.: Campus Verlag.

Hauff, V. (1987) *Unsere gemeinsame Zukunft. Der Brundtland-Bericht der Weltkommission für Umwelt und Entwicklung.* Greven: Eggenkamp.

Hausmann, R., Tyson, L.D., Bekhouche, Y. and Zahidi, S. (2009) *The Global Gender Gap Report*. Geneva: World Economic Forum.

Haynes, A., Power, M.J., Devereux, E., Dillane, A. and Power, M.J. (2016) *Public and Political Discourses on Migration: International Perspectives*. London and New York: Rowman & Littlefield International.

Heeks, R. (2011) 'ICT and economic growth: Evidence from Kenya, ICTs for development: Talking about information and communication technologies and socio-economic development.' Available at http://ict4dblog.wordpress.com/2011/06/26/ict-and-economic-growth-evidence-from-kenya (accessed 23 October 2016).

Helbling, J. (1984) 'Evolutionismus, Strukturfunktionalismus und die Analyse von Geschichte in der Ethnologie,' in P. Kamber, R. Moser, E. von Buettner, H. Lotz (eds) *Diachronica: Zum Verhältnis von Ethnologie, Geschichte und Geschichtswissenschaft*. Bern: Schweizerische Ethnologische Gesellschaft. pp. 83–102.

Held, D. and Kaya, A. (2007) 'Introduction,' in D. Held and A. Kaya, *Global Inequality: Patterns and Explanations*. Cambridge: Polity Press. pp. 1–25.

Hendrix, C.S. and Salehyan, I. (2012) 'Climate change, rainfall, and social conflict in Africa,' *Journal of Peace Research* 49 (1): 35–50.

Henry, A. (2004) 'Entreprises mondialisées en Afrique: Comportements et formes institutionnelles,' in J.-E. Aubert and J. Landrieu (eds) *Vers des civilisations mondialisées? De l'éthologie à la prospective*. La Tour-d'Aigues: Éditions de l'Aube. pp. 195–203

Hettne, B. (1995) *Development Theory and the Three Worlds* (Second edition). Harlow: Longman.

Hickson, D.J. and Pugh, D.S. (2001) *Management Worldwide: Distinctive Styles among Globalization* (Second edition). Harmondsworth: Penguin.

Hintz, A. and Milan, S. (2009a) 'Movimenti sociali e governance della communicazione globale: La sfida della partecipazione nei processi decisionali transnazionali,' *Partecipazione e conflitto* 2: 111–34.

Hintz, A. and Milan, S. (2009b) 'At the margins of Internet governance: Grassroots tech groups and communication planning,' *International Journal of Media and Culture Policy* 5 (122): 23–38.

Hirschman, A.O. (1970) *Exit, Voice and Loyalty. Response to Decline in Firms, Organizations, and States*. Cambridge, MA: Harvard University Press.

Hoffmann-Nowotny, H.-J. (1970) *Migration – ein Beitrag zu einer soziologischen Erklärung*. Stuttgart: Enke.

Hoffmann-Nowotny, H.-J. (1973) *Soziologie des Fremdarbeiterproblems: eine theoretische und empirische Analyse am Beispiel der Schweiz*. Stuttgart: Enke.

Hoffmann-Nowotny, H.-J. (1988) 'Paradigmen und Paradigmenwechsel in der sozialwissenschaftlichen Wanderungsforschung – Versuch einer neuen Migrationstheorie', in G. Jaritz and A. Müller (eds) *Migration in der Feudalgesellschaft*. Frankfurt a.M. and New York: Campus. pp. 21–42.

Hoffmann-Nowotny, H.-J. (1989) 'Weltmigration – Eine soziologische Analyse,' in W. Kälin and R. Moser (eds) *Migration aus der Dritten Welt – Ursachen und Wirkungen*. Bern and Stuttgart: P. Haupt. pp. 29–40.

Hofstede, G. (1980) *Culture's Consequences: International Differences in Work Related Values*. London: Sage.

Hofstede, G. (1991) *Culture and Organizations: Software of the Mind*. London: McGraw-Hill.

Hofstede, G. (1998) 'Think locally, act globally: Cultural constraints in personnel management,' *Management International Review*, Special Issue, 98 (2): 7–26.

Hopper, P. (2012) *Understanding Development. Issues and Debates*. Cambridge, UK and Malden, MA: Polity.

Horowitz, M. (1994) 'Development anthropology in the mid-1990s,' *Development Anthropology Network* 12 (1–2): 1–14.

House, R. J., Hanges, P.J., Javidan, M., Dorfman, P.W. and Gupta, V. (2004) *Culture, Leadership and Organization: The GLOBE Study of 62 Societies*. London: Sage.

Hradil, S. (1996) 'Die Transformation der Transformationsforschung,' *Berliner Journal für Soziologie* 6 (3): 299–303.

Huang, X. (1998) 'What is "Chinese" about Chinese civilization? Culture, institutions and globalization?' in D. Jacquin-Berdal, A. Oros, and M. Verweij (eds) *Culture in World Politics*. New York: St. Martin's Press. pp. 218–240.

Huber, J. (1991) *Unternehmen Umwelt. Weichenstellungen für eine ökologische Marktwirtschaft*. Frankfurt a.M.: Fischer.

Huber, J. (2011) *Allgemeine Umweltsoziologie*. Wiesbaden: VS Verlag für Sozialwissenschaften.

Hugon, P. (2006) *L'économie de l'Afrique* (Fifth edition). Paris: La Découverte.

Hugon, P. (2010) 'La crise mondiale et l'attractivité des pays émergents et en développement,' in Hors série 2010: *Revue Tiers Monde*, 49–75.

Hugon, P. (2016) *Afriques: entre puissance et vulnérabilité*. Malakoff: Armand Collin.

Hugon, P. and Salama, P. (2010) 'Introduction: Les Suds dans la crise,' in Hors série 2010: *Revue Tiers Monde*, 5–21.

Hugon, P. and Salama, P. (eds) (2010) *Les Suds dans la crise*. Hors série 2010: *Revue Tiers Monde*.

Imbusch, P. and Rucht, D. (2007a) 'Wirtschaftseliten und ihre gesellschaftliche Verantwortung,' *Aus Politik und Zeitgeschichte* 4–5: 3–10.

Imbusch, P. and Rucht, D. (eds) (2007b) *'Ohne Druck bewegt sich nichts' – Fallstudien zur gesellschaftlichen Verantwortung von Eliten*. Wiesbaden: VS Verlag für Sozialwissenschaften.

Inglehart, R., Basàñez, M.E. and Menéndez Moreno, A. (1998) *Human Values and Beliefs: A Cross-cultural Sourcebook: Political, Religious, Sexual, and Economic Norms in 43 Societies; Findings from the 1990–1993 World Values Survey*. Ann Arbor: University of Michigan Press.

Inglis, D. and Bone, J. (eds) (2006) *Social Stratification: Critical Concepts in Sociology*. London and New York: Routledge.

Ingold, T. (1986) *Evolution and Social Life*. Cambridge: Cambridge University Press.

International Labour Office [ILO] (2006) *Decent Work in the Americas: An Agenda for the Hemisphere, 2006–15,* Report of the Director General, 16th American Regional Meeting, Brasilia, May. Geneva: ILO.

International Labour Office [ILO] (2007) *Equality at Work: Tackling the Challenges*. Genf: ILO. Available at http://www.ilo.org/wcmsp5/groups/public/---dgreports/---dcomm/---webdev/documents/publication/wcms_082607.pdf (accessed 12 October 2016).

International Labour Office [ILO] (2008) *World of Work Report 2008: Income Inequalities in the Age of Financial Globalization*. Genf: ILO. Available at http://www.ilo.org/wcmsp5/groups/public/@dgreports/@dcomm/@publ/documents/publication/wcms_100354.pdf (accessed 5 October 2016).

International Labour Office [ILO] (2009) *Global Wage Report 2008/09. Minimum Wages and Collective Bargaining: Towards Policy Coherence*. Available at http://www.ilo.org/global/publications/WCMS_100786/lang--en/index.htm (accessed 24 October 2016).

International Labour Office [ILO] (2011) *Global Employment Trends 2011. The Challenge of a Jobs Recovery*. Genf: ILO. Available at http://www.ilo.org/global/publications/books/WCMS_150440/lang--en/index.htm. (accessed 24 October 2016).

International Monetary Fund [IMF] (2013) 'South Africa: 2013 Article IV Consultation,' Washington, DC. Available at http://www.imf.org/external/pubs/cat/longres.aspx?sk=40971.0 (accessed 3 October 2016).

International Monetary Fund (2015) *Causes and Consequences of Income Inequality: A Global Perspective*. Staff Discussion Note.

International Organization for Migration [IOM] (2005) *World Migration Report – Costs and Benefits of International Migration*. Geneva: International Organization for Migration.

International Organization for Migration [IOM] (2013) *Migration and the United Nations post-2015 Development Agenda*. Geneva: International Organization for Migration. Available at http://publications.iom.int/system/files/pdf/migration_and_the_un_post2015_agenda.pdf (accessed 10 October 2016).

International Organization for Migration [IOM] and the United Nations Department of Economic and Social Affairs [UN DESA] (2012) *Migration and Human Mobility*. Thematic think piece prepared for the United Nations System Task Team on the post-2015 United Nations Development Agenda. Available at www.un.org/en/development/desa/policy/untaskteam_undf/them_tp.shtml (accessed 10 October 2016).

ISSC-UNESCO (2013) *World Social Science Report: Changing Global Environments*. Paris: UNESCO. Available at http://www.worldsocialscience.org/activities/world-social-science-report/the-2013-report/changing-global-environments/ (accessed 13 October 2016).

Jackson, P. (1989) *Maps of Meaning. An Introduction to Cultural Geography*. London and New York: Routledge.

Jackson, G. and Deeg, R. (2006) 'How many varieties of capitalism? Comparing the Comparative Institutional Analyses of Capitalist Diversity,' MPIfG Discussion Paper 06/2. Köln: Max-Planck-Institut für Gesellschaftswissenschaften.

Jacquin-Berdal, D., Oros, A. and Verweij, M. (eds) (1998a) *Culture in World Politics*. New York: St. Martin's Press.

Jacquin-Berdal, D., Oros, A. and Verweij, M. (1998b) 'Culture in world politics: An introduction,' in D. Jacquin-Berdal, A. Oros, and M. Verweij (eds) *Culture in World Politics*. New York: St. Martin's Press. pp. 1–10.

Jänicke, M. (2008) *Megatrend Umweltinnovation. Zur ökologischen Modernisierung von Wirtschaft und Staat*. München: oekom.

Jansen, M. and Lee, E. (2007) *Trade and Employment: Challenges for Policy Research*. Geneva: International Labour Office and World Trade Organisation.

Javidan, M. and Dastmalchian, A. (2009) 'Managerial implications of the GLOBE project: A study of 62 societies,' *Asia Pacific Journal of Human Resources* 47 (1): 41–58.

Joffrin, L. (2011) 'Crise: l'autre stratégie pour en sortir,' *Le Nouvel Observateur*, 17 August. Available at http://tempsreel.nouvelobs.com/actualite/laurent-joffrin/20110817.OBS8670/crise-l-autre-strategie-pour-en-sortir.html (accessed 24 October 2016).

Johnson, H. (2007) 'Women, information technology and (Asia),' in G.Ritzer (ed.) *The Blackwell Encyclopedia of Sociology*. Malden, MA: Blackwell Publishing.

Jomo, K. S. and Baudot, J. (eds) (2007) *Flat World, Big Gaps. Economic Liberalization, Globalization, Poverty and Inequality*. London and New York: Zed Books, Orient Longman, TWN.

Jones, R.J. (1998) 'Remittances and inequality: A question of migration stage and geographic scale,' *Economic Geography* 74 (1): 8–25.

Jones, S. (1999) *Doing Internet Research*. Newbury Park, CA: Sage.

Joshi, I. (ed.) (1997) *Asian Women in the Information Age: New Communication Technology, Democracy, and Women*. Singapore: Asian Media Information and Communication Center.

Junne, G. and Verkoren, W. (eds) (2005) *Postconflict Development: Meeting New Challenges*. London: Lynne Rienner.

Juris, J.S. (2012) 'Reflections on #Occupy everywhere: Social media, public space, and emerging logics of aggregation,' *American Ethnologist* 39 (2): 259–79.

Kahanec, M. and Zimmermann, K.F. (eds) (2016) *Labor Migration, EU Enlargement, and the Great Recession*. Berlin and Heidelberg: Springer.

Kamoche, K.N., Debrah, Y.A., Horwitz, F.M. and Muuka, G.N. (eds) (2004) *Managing Human Resources in Africa*. London and New York: Routledge.

Kanter, R.M. (1995) *World Class: Thinking Locally in the Global Economy*. New York: Simon & Schuster.

Kaplinsky, R. (2005) *Globalization, Poverty and Inequality: Between a Rock and a Hard Place*. Cambridge: Polity.

Kappel, R. (2000) 'Afrikas Entwicklungspotenziale im Globalisierungssprozess,' in R. Tetzlaff (ed.) *Weltkulturen unter Globalisierungsdruck. Erfahrungen und Antworten aus den Kontinenten*. Bonn: Dietz. pp. 202–31.

Kasrils, R. (2013) *Armed and Dangerous*. Johannesburg: Jacana Media.

Kearney, M. (1995) 'The local and the global: The anthropology of globalization and transnationalism,' *Annual Review of Anthropology* 24: 547–65.

Keniston, K. (2004) 'Introduction: The four digital divides,' in K. Keniston and D. Kumar (eds) *IT Experience in India: Bridging the Digital Divide*. New Delhi: Sage. pp. 11–36.

Keping, Y. (2000) 'Chinesische Sichtweisen auf Globalisierung: von "sino—westlichem" zum "Globalisierungs"– Diskurs,' in R. Tetzlaff (ed.) *Weltkulturen unter Globalisierungsdruck. Erfahrungen und Antworten aus den Kontinenten*. Bonn: Dietz. pp. 151–73.

Khosrokhavar, F. (2012) *The New Arab Revolutions that Shook the World*. Boulder, CO and London: Paradigm Publishers.

Kiggundu, M.N. (1989) *Managing Organizations in Developing Countries: An Operational and Strategic Approach*. West Hartford, CT: Kumarian Press.

Kohl, R. and Organization for Economic Co-operation and Development, Development Center (2003) *Globalisation, Poverty and Inequality*. Paris: Development Center of the Organization for Economic Co-operation and Development.

Kohli, M. (1985) 'Gesellschaftszeit und Lebenszeit. Der Lebenslauf im Strukturwandel der Moderne,' in J. Berger (ed.) Die Moderne – Kontinuitäten und Zäsuren. *Soziale Welt* Special Issue 4: 183–208.

Kollmorgen, R. (1999) 'Transformationstheorien. Postsozialistische Karriere und metatheoretische Kritik'. PhD thesis, Friedrich-Schiller Universität, Jena.

Korzeniewicz, R.P. and Moran, T.P. (2007) 'World inequality in the twenty-first century: Patterns and tendencies,' in G. Ritzer (ed.) *The Blackwell Companion to Globalization*. Oxford: Blackwell.

Krier, D. (2009) 'Finance capital, neo-liberalism and critical institutionalism,' *Critical Sociology* 35 (3): 395–416.

Krugman, P. (2011) 'Rule by rentiers,' *The New York Times*, 9 June. Available at http://www.nytimes.com/2011/06/10/opinion/10krugman.html (accessed 12 October 2016).

Kuran, T. (2004) 'Why is the Middle East economically underdeveloped? Historical mechanisms of institutional stagnation,' *Journal of Economic Perspectives* 18 (3): 71–90.

Laczko, F. and Brian, T. (2013) 'North-south migration: A different look at the migration and development debate,' *Migration Policy Practice* 3 (3): 14–19.

Lakner, C. and Milanovic, B. (2015) 'Global income distribution: From the fall of the Berlin Wall to the Great Recession,' *The World Bank Economic Review* 1–30. Available at https://www.gc.cuny.edu/CUNY_GC/media/LISCenter/brankoData/wber_final.pdf (accessed 2 October 2016).

Lammers, C.J. and Hickson, D.J. (1979) *Organizations Alike and Unlike: International and Inter-institutional Studies in the Sociology of Organizations*. London: Routledge & Kegan Paul.

Latouche, S. (1998) *L'Autre Afrique. Entre don et marché*. Paris: Albin Michel.

Latouche, S. (2009) *Farewell to Growth*. Cambridge: Polity Press.

Laurent, A. (1983) 'The cultural diversity of Western conceptions of management,' *International Studies of Management and Organization* 13 (1–2): 75–96.

Laville, J.L. (dir.) (2011) *Economie solidaire*. CNRS Éditions, coll. 'Les Essentiels d'Hermès'.

Lebaron, F. (2009) 'Le rapport Stiglitz: vers une revolution statistique,' *Savoir/Agir*. Available at https://www.savoir-agir.org/IMG/pdf/SA10AlterLebaron.pdf (accessed 12 October 2016).

Lebaron, F. (2010a) 'Les conséquences sociales de la crise mondiale: Quelques réflexions à partir de données récentes,' *Savoir/Agir* 2 (12): 91–101.

Lebaron, F. (2010b) *La crise de la croyance économique*. Bellecombe-en-Bauges: Éditions du Croquant.

Lechner, F. and Boli, J. (2005) *World Culture*. Oxford: Blackwell.

Lejeune, Z. (2015) 'La justice et les inégalités environmentales: concept, méthodes et traduction politique aux États-Unis et en Europe', *Revue française des affaires sociales*, 1: 51–78.

Lenz, I. (2010) 'Gender, inequality, and globalization' in U. Schuerkens (ed.) *Globalization and Transformations of Social Inequality*. New York and London: Routledge. pp. 93–111.

Lewis, R.D. (2004) *When Cultures Collide: Leading, Team-working and Managing Across the Globe*. London: Nicholas Brealey.

Light, I.H. and Gold, S.J. (2000) *Ethnic Economies*. San Diego: Academic Press.

Lin, Y.-M. (2001) *Between Politics and Markets: Firms, Competition, and Institutional Change in Post-Mao China*. Cambridge: Cambridge University Press.

Lindsay, B. (ed.) (1985) *African Migration and National Development*. University Park, PA and London: Pennsylvania State University Press.

Ling, R. (2012) *Taken for Grantedness: The Embedding of Mobile Communication into Society*. Cambridge, MA: MIT Press.

Ling, R. and Schroeder, R. (2014) 'Durkheim and Weber on the social implications of new information and communication technologies,' *New Media & Society* 16 (5): 789–805.

Lituchy, T.R., Punnett, B.J. and Puplampu, B.B. (eds) (2013) *Management in Africa: Macro and Micro Perspectives*. New York and London: Routledge.

Lockwood, D. (1964) 'Social integration and system integration,' in G. K. Zollschan and W. Hirsch (eds) *Explorations in Social Change*. Boston, MA: Houghton Mifflin. pp. 244–57.

Lodge, G. and Wilson, C. (2006) *A Corporate Solution to Global Poverty: How Multinationals Can Help the Poor and Invigorate Their Own Legitimacy*. Princeton: Princeton University Press.

Long, N. (1996) 'Globalization and localization: New challenges to rural research,' in H.L. Moore (ed.) *The Future of Anthropological Knowledge*. London and New York: Routledge. pp. 37–59.

Long, N. (2001) *Development Sociology: Actor Perspectives*. London and New York: Routledge.

Lowell, L.B. (2002) *Some Developmental Effects of the International Migration of Highly Skilled Persons*. International Migration Papers n° 46. Geneva: International Labour Office.

Luhmann, N. (1984) 'The self-description of society: Crisis fashion and sociological theory,' in E.A. Tiryakian (ed.) *The Global Crisis, Sociological Analyses and Responses*. Leiden: Brill. pp. 59–72.

Luhmann, N. (1997) *Die Gesellschaft der Gesellschaft*. Frankfurt a.M.: Suhrkamp.

Lynn, R. and Vanhanen, T. (2002) *IQ and the Wealth of Nations*. Westport, CT: Praeger.

Lynn, R. and Vanhanen, T. (2008) 'Intelligence and the wealth and poverty of nations.' Available at http://www.rlynn.co.uk/index.php?page=intelligence-and-the-wealth (accessed 19 October 2016).

Lyon, D. (1988) *The Information Society: Issues and Illusions*. Cambridge: Polity Press.

Lyon, D. (1999) *Postmodernity*. Oxford: Oxford University Press.

Lyon, D. (2003) *Surveillance after September 11*. Cambridge: Polity Press.

Lyon, D. (2007) 'Information technology,' in G. Ritzer (ed.) *Blackwell Encyclopedia of Sociology*. Oxford: Blackwell Publishing.

Macias, F., Vacas, E. and Soriano, C. (2015) *Recent Developments in the Distribution of Wages in Europe*. European Monitoring Centre on Change. Available at http://www.eurofound.europa.eu/publications/report/2015/working-conditions-labour-market/recent-developments-in-the-distribution-of-wages-in-europe (accessed 17 December 2016).

Macleod, A.E. (1991) *Accommodating Protest: Working Women, the New Veiling, and Change in Cairo*. New York: Columbia University Press.

Mahler, V.A. and Jesuit, D.K. (2006) 'Fiscal redistribution in the developed countries: New insights from the Luxembourg Income Study,' *Socio-Economic Review* 4 (3): 483–511.

Mahler, V.A. and Jesuit, D.K. (2008) *Redistribution Dataset, Version 2, February*. Available at http://www.lisdatacenter.org/wp-content/uploads/2011/02/fiscal-redistribution-details.pdf (accessed 26 April 2016).

Mahoney, J. (2000) 'Path dependence in historical sociology,' *Theory and Society* 29 (4): 507–48.

Maia, J. (2012) 'Economic overview,' Industrial Development Corporation, *Access Newsletter*, April. Available at http://www.idc.co.za/access/economicoverview-april-2012 (accessed 7 October 2016).

Majumdar, S.K. (2012) *India's Late, Late Industrial Revolution: Democratizing Entrepreneurship*. Cambridge: Cambridge University Press.

Manstetten, R. and Faber, M. (1999) 'Umweltökonomie. Nachhaltigkeitsökonomie und ökologische Ökonomie. Drei Perspektiven auf Mensch und Natur,' *Jahrbuch für Ökologie* 1: 53–97.

Manzo, A. (2016) 'La Microfinance dans une économie locale dominée par l'informel: Le cas du Niger'. PhD thesis in socio-economy of development. Paris: EHESS.

Marchand, M.H. and Runyan, A.S. (eds) (2011) *Gender and Global Restructuring: Sightings, Sites, and Resistances*. London and New York: Routledge.

Margairaz, D. and Philippe, M. (2006) 'Présentation du numéro spécial: Le marché dans son histoire,' *Revue de Synthèse*, 5 (2): 241–52.

Marianne (2016) 'La revanche des peuples,' 1 July: 1004.

Marmorá, L. (2002) *Les Politiques de migrations internationales*. Paris: L'Harmattan.

Martinez-Alier, J. (2002) 'Ecological debt and property rights on carbon sinks and reservoirs,' *Capitalism Nature Socialism* 13 (1): 115–19.

Martínez-Alier, j. (2014) *L'écologisme des pauvres. Une* étude *des conflits environnementaux dans le monde*. Les Petits matins/Inst. Veblen.

Marx, K. (1975) *Das Kapital zum Selbststudium* (Erhart Löhnberg, ed.). Frankfurt a.M.: Fischer.

Massey, D.S. (1988) 'Economic development and international migration in comparative perspective,' *Population and Development Review* 14 (3): 383–413.

Massey, D.S., Arango, J., Hugo, G., Kouaouci, A., Pellegrino, A. and Taylor, J.E. (1998) *Worlds in Motion: Understanding International Migration at the End of the Millennium*. Oxford: Clarendon Press.

Massey, G. (2012) *Ways of Social Change: Making Sense of Modern Times*. London: Sage.

Mattelart, A. (1983) *Transnationals and the Third World: The Struggle for Culture*. South Hadley, MA: Bergin and Garvey.

Mattelart, A., Delcourt, X. and Mattelart, M. (1984) *International Image Markets: In Search of an Alternative Perspective*. New York: Comedia Publishing Group.

Mauss, M. (2012) *Essai sur le don. Forme et raison de l'échange dans les sociétés archaïques*. Paris: Presses Universitaires de France.

Mayer, K.U. (1990) 'Lebensverläufe und sozialer Wandel – Anmerkungen zu einem Forschungsprogramm,' in *Lebensverläufe und sozialer Wandel*, Special Issue 31 *Kölner Zeitschrift für Soziologie und Sozialpsychologie*: 7–21.

Mazumdar, D. (2008) *Globalization, Labor Markets and Inequality in India*. London and New York: Routledge.

McAdam, J. (2015) 'Relocation and resettlement from colonisation to climate change: The perennial solution to "danger zones",' *London Review of International Law* 3 (1): 93–130.

McCormick, B. and Wahba, J. (2001) 'Overseas work experience, savings and entrepreneurship amongst return migrants to LDCs,' *Scottish Journal of Political Economy* 48 (2): 164–78.

McGrew, A. and Poku, N.K. (eds) (2007) *Globalization, Development and Human Security*. Cambridge: Polity.

McLeman, R.T.F. and Schade, J. (eds) (2016) *Environmental Migration and Social Inequality*. Advances in Global Change Research: 61. New York: Springer.

McMichael, P. (2012) *Development and Social Change. A Global Perspective* (Fifth edition). London: Sage.

Mead, M. (2003) *Sex and Temperament in Three Primitive Societies* (1st Perennial ed.). New York: Perennial.

Meadows, D. (1972) *The Limits to Growth: A Report for the Club of Rome's Project on the Predicament of Mankind*. London: A Potomac Associates Book. Earth Island Ltd.

Meadows, D.H., Meadows, D.L. and Randers, J. (2004) *The Limits to Growth: The 30-Year Update*. White River Junction, VT: Chelsea Green.

Menzel, U. (1992) *Das Ende der Dritten Welt und das Scheitern der großen Theorie*. Frankfurt a.M.: Suhrkamp.

Merchant, C. (1992) *Radical Ecology*. London and New York: Routledge.

Meyer, J.W. (2005) *Weltkultur. Wie die westlichen Prinzipien die Welt durchdringen*. Frankfurt a.M.: Suhrkamp.

Mezouar, A. and Sémériva, J.-P. (2004) 'Entreprises et modernité dans les sociétés arabo-islamiques,' in J.-Eric Aubert and Josée Landrieu (eds) *Vers des civilisations mondialisées? De l'éthologie à la prospective*. La Tour-d'Aigues: Éditions de l'Aube. pp. 204–14.

Mies, M. and Shiva, V. (1995) *Ökofeminismus. Beiträge zur Theorie und Praxis*. Zürich: Rotpunktverlag.

Milan, S. (2013) *Social Movements and their Technologies: Wiring Social Change*. Basingstoke: Palgrave Macmillan.

Milanovic, B. (2005) *Worlds Apart: Measuring International and Global Inequality*. Princeton, NJ and Woodstock, UK: Princeton University Press.

Milanovic, B. (2011a) *The Haves and the Have-Nots. A Brief and Idiosyncratic History of Global Inequality*. Nova Iorque: Basic Books.

Milanovic, B. (2011b) *Global Income Inequality: The Past two Centuries and Implications for 21st Century*. Presentation delivered at the University of Barcelona. Available at https://web. archive.org/web/20140209042330/http://www.ub.edu/histeco/pdf/milanovic.pdf (accessed 10 October 2016).

Milanovic, B. (2011c) *Global Inequality: From Class to Location, from Proletarians to Migrants*. World Bank, Policy Research Working Paper 5820.

Milanovic, B. (2016) 'Did Post-Marxist theories destroy Communist regimes?' *Globalinequality*. Available at http://glineq.blogspot.fr/ (accessed 17 December 2016).

Miller, D. (1990) 'Fashion and ontology in Trinidad,' *Culture and History* 7: 49–77.

Miller, D. (1992) 'The young and the restless: A case of the local and the global in mass consumption,' in R. Silverstone and E. Hirsch (eds) *Consuming Technologies*. London and New York: Routledge. pp. 163–182.

Miller, D. (1994) *Modernity, an Ethnographic Approach: Dualism and Mass Consumption in Trinidad*. Oxford: Berg.

Miller, D. (ed.) (1995a) *Worlds Apart: Modernity through the Prism of the Local*. London and New York: Routledge.

Miller, D. (1995b) 'Introduction: Anthropology, modernity and consumption,' in D. Miller (ed.) *Worlds Apart: Modernity through the Prism of the Local*. London and New York: Routledge. pp. 1–22.

Miller, D. (1997) *Capitalism: An Ethnographic Approach*. Oxford: Berg.

Miller, D. (2006) 'A theory of virtualism: Consumption as negation,' in M. Edelman and A. Haugerud (eds) *The Anthropology of Development and Globalization. From Classical Political Economy to Contemporary Neoliberalism*. Oxford: Blackwell. pp. 224–31.

Miller, J. (2005) 'Perspectives and policies on ICT in Africa,' in J. Berleur and C. Avgerou (eds) *Perspective and Policies on ICT in Society*. New York: Springer. pp. 15–26.

Miller, M. (2005) *Welten des Kapitalismus. Institutionelle Alternativen in der globalisierten Ökonomie*. Frankfurt a.M. and New York: Campus.

Milton, K. (1996) *Environmentalism and Cultural Theory. Exploring the Role of Anthropology in Environmental Discourse*. London and New York: Routledge.

Mlinar, Z. (1992a) 'Introduction,' in Z. Mlinar (ed.) *Globalisation and Territorial Identities*. Farnham: Ashgate. pp. 1–14.

Mlinar, Z. (1992b) 'Individualisation and globalisation: The transformation of territorial social organisation,' in Z. Mlinar (ed.) *Globalisation and Territorial Identities*. Farnham: Ashgate. pp. 15–34.

Mlinar, Z. (1992c) 'Epilogue,' in Z. Mlinar (ed.) *Globalisation and Territorial Identities*. Farnham: Ashgate. pp. 165–169.

Moghadam, V. (2008) *Globalization and Social Movements: Islamism, Feminism and the Global Justice Movement*. Lanham, MD: John Hopkins University Press.

Moghadam, V. (2013) 'What is democracy? Promises and perils of the Arab Spring,' *Current Sociology* 61 (4): 393–408.

Mohapatra, S., Scott, R. and Huang, J. (2006) 'Climbing the development ladder: Economic development and the evolution of occupations in rural China,' *Journal of Development Studies* 42 (6): 1023–55.

Mol, A.P.J. (1995) *The Refinement of Production. Ecological Modernization Theory and the Chemical Industry*. Utrecht: Van Arkel.

Mol, A.P.J. (1996) 'Ecological modernisation and institutional reflexivity: Environmental reform in the late modern age,' *Environmental Politics* 5: 302–23.

Mol, A.P.J. (1997) 'Ecological modernization: Industrial transformations and environmental reform,' in M. Redclift and G. Woodgate (eds) *The International Handbook of Environment Sociology*. Cheltenham: Edward Elgar. pp. 138–49.

Mol, A.P.J. (2010) 'Ecological modernization as a theory of environmental reform,' in M. Redclift and G. Woodgate (eds) *The International Handbook of Environment Sociology* (Second edition). Cheltenham: Edward Elgar. pp. 63–76.

Mol, A.P.J. and Spaargaren, G. (eds) (2000) *Ecological Modernization around the World: Perspectives and Critical Debates*. London: Frank Cass.

Mol, A.P.J. and Spaargaren, G. (2006) 'Towards a theory of environmental flows: A new agenda for twenty-first century environmental sociology,' in G. Spaargaren, A.P.J. Mol and F.H. Buttel (eds) *Governing Environmental Flows: Global Challenges for Social Theory*. Cambridge, MA: MIT Press. pp. 39–83.

Mol, A.P.J., Sonnenfeld, D.A. and Spaargaren, G. (2009) *The Ecological Modernisation Reader. Environmental Reform in Theory and Practice*. London and New York: Routledge.

Momayezi, N. (2006) 'Globalization: Impact on development,' in T.M. Leonard (ed.) *Encyclopedia of the Developing World*, vol. 2. London and New York: Routledge. pp. 707–712.

Monod, J.-C. (2012) *Qu'est-ce qu'un chef en démocratie? Politiques du charisme*. Paris: Seuil.

Montaño, S. and Milosavljevic, V. (2010) 'La crisis económica y financiera. Su impacto sobre la pobreza, el trabajo y el tiempo de las mujeres,' *Serie Mujer y Desarrollo* N° 98, February. Santiago de Chile: Comisión Económica para América Latina y el Caribe (CEPAL).

Moon, J. (2007) 'The contribution of corporate social responsibility to sustainable development,' *Sustainable Development* 15: 296–306.

Moore, B. (1978) *Injustice. The Social Bases of Obedience and Revolt*. New York: M. E. Sharpe.

Moore, W.E. (ed.) (1972) *Technology and Social Change*. Chicago: Quadrangle Books.

Moran, R.T., Harris, P.R. and Moran, S.V. (2007) *Managing Cultural Differences: Global Leadership Strategies for the 21st Century* (Eighth edition). London and New York: Routledge.

Morin, E. (1973) 'Vers une théorie de la crise,' *Éducation et Gestion* 34: 13–19.

Morin, E. (1976) 'Pour une crisologie,' *Communications* 25: 149–63.

Morris, A.D. and Staggenborg, S. (2004) 'Leadership in social movements,' in D.A. Snow, S.A. Soule and H. Kriesi (eds) *The Blackwell Companion to Social Movements*. Oxford: Blackwell. pp. 171–96.

Morrissey, J. (2009) *Environmental Change and Forced Migration: A State of the Art Review*. Oxford: Refugee Studies Centre, University of Oxford.

Mosco, V. (1998) *The Political Economy of Communication*. London: Sage.

Mosco, V. (2004) *The Digital Sublime*. Cambridge, MA: MIT Press.

Mozaffari, M. (ed.) (2002) *Globalization and Civilizations*. London and New York: Routledge.

Mrozowicki, A. and van Hootegem, G. (2008) 'Unionism and workers' strategies in capitalist transformation: The Polish case reconsidered,' *European Journal of Industrial Relations* 14 (2): 197–216.

Muchie, M. and Li, Xing (2006) *Globalization, Inequality, and the Commodification of Life and Well-being*. London: Adonis and Abbey.

Mulholland, K. (2004) 'Workplace resistance in an Irish call centre: Slammin', scammin' smokin' an' leavin',' *Work, Employment and Society* 18 (4): 709–24.

Müller, H.-P. (ed.) (1996) *Weltsystem und kulturelles Erbe. Gliederung und Dynamik der Entwicklungsländer aus ethnologischer und soziologischer Sicht*. Berlin: D. Reimer Verlag.

Müller, H.-P., Kock, C. and von Ditfurth, A. (1991) *Kulturelles Erbe und Entwicklung: Indikatoren zur Bewertung des sozio-kulturellen Entwicklungsstandes*. München: Weltforum Verlag.

Müller, K. (1998) 'Kontingenzen der Transformation,' *Berliner Journal für Soziologie* 6 (4): 449–66.

Münch, R. (1997) *Globale Dynamik, lokale Lebenswelten*. Frankfurt a.M: Suhrkamp.

Naím, M. and Tulchin, J.S. (eds) (1999) *Competition Policy, Deregulation and Modernization in Latin America*. Boulder, CO: Lynne Rienner.

Nederveen Pieterse, J. (1993) *Globalization as Hybridization*. Working Paper 152. The Hague: Institute of Social Studies.

Nederveen Pieterse, J. (1996) 'The development of development theory: Towards critical globalism,' *Review of International Political Economy* 3 (4): 541–64.

Nederveen Pieterse, J. (1998) 'My paradigm or yours? Alternative development, post-development, reflexive development,' *Development and Change* 29 (4): 343–73.

Nederveen Pieterse, J. (2004a) *Globalization & Culture. Global Mélange*. New York: Rowman & Littlefield.

Nederveen Pieterse, J. (2004b) *Globalization or Empire?* London and New York: Routledge.

Neubert, D. and Daniel, A. (2012) 'Introduction: Translating globalization, world society and modernity in everyday life – thereotical reflections and empirical perspectives,' *Sociologus* 62 (1): 1–23.

Neubert, D., Kößler, R. and von Oppen, A. (eds) (1999) *Gemeinschaften in einer entgrenzten Welt*. Berlin: Arabisches Buch.

Neverla, I. (2007) 'The climatic turn. How and why journalism has discovered climate Change.' Unpublished paper presented at the Conference 'Communicating Climate Change' at University of Braga, Portugal, November.

Neveu, E. (2011) *Sociologie des mouvements sociaux*. Paris: La Découverte.

Newell, P. and Frynas, J.G. (2007) 'Beyond CSR? Business, poverty and social justice: An introduction,' *Third World Quarterly* 28 (4): 669–81.

Nicholas, H. (2005) *Forum 2005*. Special issue of *Development and Change* 36 (6, November).

Nichols, T. and Sugur, N. (2004) *Global Management, Local Labour: Turkish Workers and Modern Industry*. Houndmills, UK and New York: Palgrave Macmillan.

Nissanke, M. and Thorbecke, E. (eds) (2007) *The Impact of Globalization on the World's Poor: Transmission Mechanisms*. Basingstoke and New York: Palgrave Macmillan in Association with UNU World Institute for Development Economics Research.

Nissanke, M. and World Institute for Development Economics Research (2005) *Channels and Policy Debate in the Globalization-Inequality-Poverty Nexus*. Helsinki: UNU World Institute for Development Economics Research.

Nolan, P. (2001) *China and the Global Business Revolution.* London: Palgrave, New York: St. Martin's Press.

Nora, P. (1974) 'Le retour de l'évènement,' in J. Le Goff and P. Nora (eds) *Faire de l'Histoire.* Paris: Gallimard. pp. 210–28.

Norris, P. (2001) *Digital Divide: Civic Engagement, Information Poverty and the Internet Worldwide.* Cambridge: Cambridge University Press.

O'Leary, G. (ed.) *Adjusting to Capitalism: Chinese Workers and the State.* Armonk, NY and London: M.E. Sharpe.

O'Rourke, K.H. (2002) 'Europe and the causes of globalization: 1700–2000,' in H. Kierzkowski (ed.) *Europe and Globalization.* New York: Palgrave, Macmillan. pp. 64–86.

Ohemeng, F.L.K. and Ofosu-Adarkwa, K. (2014) 'Overcoming the digital divide in developing countries: An examination of Ghana's strategies to promote universal access to information communication technologies (ICTs),' *Journal of Developing Societies* 30 (3): 297–322.

Organisation for Economic Co-operation and Development [OECD] (2001) *Understanding the Digital Divide.* Paris: OECD.

Organisation for Economic Co-operation and Development [OECD] (2002) *Trends in International Migration.* Paris: OECD Editions.

Organisation for Economic Co-operation and Development [OECD] (2006) *Promoting Pro-Poor Growth. Private Sector Development.* Paris: OECD.

Organisation for Economic Co-operation and Development [OECD] (2008) *Growing Unequal? Income Distribution and Poverty in OECD Countries.* Available at http://www.oecd.org/dataoecd/45/42/41527936.pdf (accessed 24 October 2016).

Organisation for Economic Co-operation and Development [OECD] (2015) *In It Together: Why Less Inequality Benefits All.* Paris: OECD Publishing. Available at http://www.oecd-ilibrary.org/employment/in-it-together-why-less-inequality-benefits-all_9789264235120-en (accessed 24 October 2016).

Osterhammel, J. and Petersson, N.P. (2004) *Geschichte der Globalisierung. Dimensionen – Prozesse – Epochen.* Münich: C.H. Beck.

OXFAM (2014) *Even it up. Time to End Extreme Inquality.* Oxford: Oxfam. Available at https://www.oxfam.org/sites/www.oxfam.org/files/file_attachments/cr-even-it-up-extreme-inequality-291014-en.pdf (accessed 17 December 2016).

Paech, N. (2012) *Befreiung vom Überfluss. Auf dem Weg in die Postwachstumsökonomie.* Münich: oekom.

Parkes, R. (2016) *People on the Move: The New Global (Dis)order.* Paris: EU Institute for Security Studies. Available at http://www.iss.europa.eu/uploads/media/CP_138_online.pdf (accessed 24 October 2016).

Parks, B.C. and Roberts, J.T. (2010) 'Climate change, social theory and justice,' *Theory, Culture and Society* 27 (2–3): 134–66.

Parnell, J.A. (2008) 'Strategy execution in emerging economies: Assessing strategic diffusion in Mexico and Peru,' *Management Decision* 46 (9): 1277–98.

Parrochia, D. (2008) *La forme des crises: Logique et épistémologie.* Seyssel: Champ Vallon.

Paulmier, T. (2004) 'Métaphysique chinoise et mentalité économique,' in J.-E. Aubert and J. Landrieu (eds) *Vers des civilisations mondialisées? De l'éthologie à la prospective.* La Tour-d' Aigues: Éditions de l'Aube. pp. 181–194.

Peiperl, M. and Estrin, S. (1998) 'Managerial markets in transition in Central and Eastern Europe: A field study and implications,' *The International Journal of Human Resource Management* 9 (1): 58–78.

PEKEA (2003) 'Prolegomena to the building of a political and ethical knowledge regarding economic activities (PEKEA)', *Économies et Societés* Hors Série XXXVII (6). Paris: Les Presses de l'ISMEA.

Perrons, D. (2004) *Globalization and Social Change. People and Places in a Divided World.* London and New York: Routledge.

Perroux, F. (1961) *L'économie au XXe siècle.* Paris: Presses universitaires de France.

Perugorría, I. and Tejerina, B. (2013) 'Politics of the encounter: Cognition, emotions, and networks in the Spanish 15M,' *Current Sociology* 61 (4): 424–42.

Peters, B. (1993) *Die Integration moderner Gesellschaften.* Frankfurt a.M.: Suhrkamp.

Pew Research Center (2015) 'Climate change seen as top global threat.' Available at http://www.pewglobal.org/2015/07/14/climate-change-seen-as-top-global-threat/ (accessed 21 December 2016).

Pew, R.W. and van Hemel, S.B. (eds) (2004) *Technology for Adaptive Aging.* Washington, DC: National Academies Press.

Pfeffer, J. (1994) *Competitive Advantage Through People: Unleashing the Power of the Work Force.* Boston, MA: Harvard Business School Press.

Pfeiffer, C. (2015) 'Podemos: Eine neue Partei bedroht Spaniens "bipartidismo,"' *Forschungsjournal Soziale Bewegungen-PLUS* 1: 1–15.

Pietrobelli, C. and Sverrisson, A. (eds) (2004) *Linking Local and Global Economies: The Ties That Bind.* London and New York: Routledge.

Piguet, E. (2013) 'From "primitive migration" to "climate refugees": The curious fate of the natural environment in migration studies,' *Annals of the Association of American Geographers* 103 (1): 148–62.

Piketty, T. (2009) 'Qui seront les gagnants de la crise?' *Libération*, 12 December.

Piketty, T. (2014) *Capital in the Twenty-First Century.* Cambridge, MA: The Harvard University Press.

Pleyers, G. (2010) *Alter-globalization: Becoming Actors in the Global Age.* Cambridge: Polity Press.

Pleyers, G. and Glasius, M. (2013) 'La resonance des mouvements des places: connexions, emotions, valeurs', *Socio* [Online], 2. Available at https://socio.revues.org/393 (accessed 19 December 2016).

Polletta, F. and Jasper, J.M. (2001) 'Collective identity and social movements,' *Annual Review of Sociology* 27: 283–305.

Pons, P. (1988) *D'Edo à Tokyo: mémoires et modernités.* Paris: Gallimard.

Portes, A. (1997) 'Immigration theory for a new century: Some problems and opportunities,' *International Migration Review* 31 (4): 799–825.

Poster, M. (2001) *What's the Matter with the Internet.* Minneapolis: University of Minnesota Press.

Poujol, C. (2004) 'Les nouveaux États d'Asie centrale face au processus de mondialisation,' in J.-E. Aubert and J. Landrieu (eds) *Vers des civilisations mondialisées? De l'éthologie à la prospective.* La Tour-d'Aigues: Éditions de l'Aube. pp. 143–158.

PricewaterhouseCoopers (2014) *Global Economic Crime Survey 2014: A Threat to Business Globally,* Johannesburg. Available at http://www.micci.com/downloads/digests/eberita/2014/15/pwc.pdf (accessed 17 December 2016).

PricewaterhouseCoopers (2016). *Global Economic Crime Survey 2016: Adjusting the Lens on Economic Crime,* Johannesburg. Available at http://www.pwc.com/gx/en/services/advisory/consulting/forensics/economic-crime-survey.html (accessed 17 December 2016).

Pries, L. (ed.) (1999) *Migration and Transnational Social Spaces.* Aldershot: Ashgate.

Punnett, B.J. (2012) *Management: A Developing Country Perspective.* London and New York: Routledge.

Rajan, R.S. (2003) *Economic Globalization and Asia. Essays on Finance, Trade, and Taxation.* Singapore: Institute of Policy Studies, World Scientific Publishing.

Rajasingham-Senanayake, D. (2004) 'Between reality and representation: Women's agency in war and post-conflict Sri Lanka,' *Cultural Dynamics* 16 (2/3): 141–68.

Rajesh, R. (2002) *Bridging the Digital Divide: Gyandoot – The Model for Community Networks.* New Delhi: Tata McGraw-Hill.

Ramonet, I. (2004) '50 années qui ont changé notre monde,' Paris, *Le Monde diplomatique.* March.

Randeria, S. (1999) 'Geteilte Geschichte und verwobene Moderne,' in J. Rüsen, H. Leitgeb and N. Jegelka (eds) *Zukunftsentwürfe. Ideen für eine Kultur der Veränderung.* Frankfurt a.M. and New York: Campus. pp. 87–96.

Randeria, S. (2000) 'Jenseits von Soziologie und soziokultureller Anthropologie. Zur Ortsbestimmung der nicht-westlichen Welt in einer zukünftigen Sozialtheorie,' in U. Beck and A. Kieserling (eds) *Ortsbestimmungen der Soziologie. Wie die kommende Generation Gesellschaftswissenschaften betreiben wird.* Baden-Baden: Nomos. pp. 41–50.

Ratha, D. (2012) 'Remittances: Funds for the folks back home,' *Finance & Development,* March 28, International Monetary Fund. Available at http://www.imf.org/external/pubs/ft/fandd/basics/remitt.htm (accessed 24 October 2016).

Ratha, D. and Shaw, W. (2007) *South-South Migration and Remittances.* Washington, DC: World Bank.

Ratha, D., Mohapatra, S. and Silwal, A. (2011) *Migration and Remittances Factbook 2011.* Washington, DC: Development Prospects Group, World Bank.

Ratzenhofer, G. (1907) *Soziologie: Positive Lehre von den menschlichen Wechselbeziehungen.* Leipzig: F. A. Brockhaus.

Rauch, J.E. and Casella, A. (2003) 'Overcoming informational barriers to international resource allocation: Prices and ties,' *Economic Journal* 113 (484): 21–42.

Redman, T. and Keithley, D. (1998) 'Downsizing goes east? Employment restructuring in post-socialist Poland,' *The International Journal of Human Resource Management* 9 (2): 274–95.

Rex, J. (1981) *Social Conflict – A Theoretical and Conceptual Analysis.* London: Longman.

Riley, M.W., Kahn, R.L. and Foner, A. (eds) (1994) *Age and Structural Lag: Society's Failure to Provide Meaningful Opportunities in Work, Family, and Leisure.* New York: Wiley-Interscience.

Rist, G. (1996) *Le développement, histoire d'une croyance occidentale.* Paris: Presses de la Fondation Nationale de Sciences Po.

Rivière, C. (1978) *L'analyse dynamique en sociologie.* Paris: Presses Universitaires de France.

Roberts, J.T. and Hite, A.B. (2000) *From Modernization to Globalization. Perspectives on Development and Social Change.* Malden, Oxford, Melbourne: Wiley-Blackwell.

Robertson, R. (1987) 'Globalization theory and civilizational analysis,' *Comparative Civilizations Review* 17 (1): 20–30.

Robertson, R. (1992) *Globalization. Social Theory and Global Culture.* London: Sage.

Robertson, R. and Lechner, F. (1985) 'Modernization, globalization and the problem of culture in world-system theory,' *Theory, Culture & Society* 2 (3): 103–17.

Robins, K. (1995) 'Cyberspace and the world we live in,' *Body & Society* 1 (3–4): 135–55.

Rocca, J.-L. (2006) *La condition chinoise: La mise au travail capitaliste à l'âge des réformes (1978–2004)*. Paris: Karthala.

Rodríguez, M.D. and Ríos, F.R. (2009) 'Paternalism at a crossroads: Labour relations in Chile in transition,' *Employee Relations* 31 (3): 322–33.

Rodrik, D. (1999) *The New Global Economy and Developing Countries: Making Openness Work*. Washington, DC: Overseas Development Council.

Roniger, L. (2011) 'Connected histories, power and meaning: Transnational forces in the construction of collective identities,' *Journal of Classical Sociology* 11 (3): 251–68.

Rostow, W.W. (1960) *The Stages of Economic Growth. A Non-Communist Manifesto*. Cambridge: Cambridge University Press.

Roudometof, V. (2005) 'Transnationalism, cosmopolitanism and glocalization,' *Current Sociology* 53 (1): 113–35.

Rugumamu, S.M. (2005) *Globalization Demystified. Africa's Possible Development Futures*. Dar Es Salaam: Dar Es Salaam University Press.

Ruppenthal, S. and Lück, D. (2009) 'Jeder fünfte Erwerbstätige ist aus beruflichen Gründen mobil,' *Informationsdienst Soziale Indikatoren* 42: 1–5.

Russell Sage Foundation, Bardhan, P.K., Bowles, S. and Wallerstein, M. (2006) *Globalization and Egalitarian Redistribution*. New York and Princeton, NJ: Russell Sage Foundation and Princeton University Press.

Russell, S.S. (1992) 'Migrant remittances and development,' *International Migration* 30 (3–4): 267–87.

Saad-Filho, A. (2015) 'The debacle of the workers' party in Brazil.' Available at https://www.opendemocracy.net/alfredo-saadfilho/debacle-of-workers%E2%80%99-party-in-brazil (accessed 21 October 2016).

Sabeg, Y. and Méhaignerie, L. (2004) *Les oubliés de l'égalité des chances. Participation, pluralité, assimilation ou repli*. Paris: Institut Montaigne.

Sachs, W. (2002) *Nach uns die Zukunft. Der globale Konflikt um Gerechtigkeit und Ökologie*. Frankfurt a.M.: Brandes and Apsel.

Sale, K. (1985) *Dwellers in the Land: The Bioregional Vision*. San Francisco: Sierra Club Books.

Sands, P. (2005) *Lawless World: America and the Making and Breaking of Global Rules*. London: Allen Lane.

Sanjuan, T. (2004) 'Refonder la mondialisation chinoise,' in J.-E. Aubert and J. Landrieu (eds) *Vers des civilisations mondialisées? De l'éthologie à la prospective*. La Tour-d'Aigues: Éditions de l'Aube. pp. 122–30.

Sapir, J. (2006a) 'La concurrence, un mythe,' *Le monde diplomatique*, June. Available at https://www.monde-diplomatique.fr/2006/07/SAPIR/13645 (accessed 24 April 2016).

Sapir, J. (2006b) *La fin de l'eurolibéralisme*. Paris: Seuil.

SAPRIN (2002) *The Policy Riots of Economic Crisis and Poverty*. Washington, DC: The Structural Adjustment Participatory Review International Networks.

Sarr, P.A. (2007) *Migrations et développement. Transferts d'argent des migrants du Sénégal et du Mali: Motivations et impacts sur le développement économique et social*. Mémoire de Master 2, Étude comparative du développement, EHESS.

Sartre, J.-P. (1971) 'Préface,' in Paul Nizan *Aden Arabie*. Paris: Maspero.

Sassen, S. (2014) *Expulsions: Brutality and Complexity in the Global Economy*. Cambridge, MA: Harvard University Press.

Saul, J.S. and Bond, P. (2014) *South Africa – Present as History*. London: James Currey Press.

Schäfer, A. (2009) 'Krisentheorien der Demokratie: Unregierbarkeit, Spätkapitalismus und Postdemokratie,' *der moderne staat* 2 (1): 159–83.

Schäfer, W. (2004) 'Global civilization and local cultures,' in S. A. Arjomand and E.A. Tiryakian (eds) *Rethinking Civilizational Analysis*. London: Sage. pp. 71–86.

Schein, L. (2006) 'Market mentalities, iron satellite dishes, and contested cultural developmentalism,' in M. Edelman and A. Haugerud (eds) *The Anthropology of Development and Globalization. From Classical Political Economy to Contemporary Neoliberalism*. Oxford: Blackwell. pp. 216–23.

Scherer, A.G. and Palazzo, G. (2011) 'The new political role of business in a globalized world – A review of a new perspective on CSR and its implications for the firm, governance, and democracy,' *Journal of Management Studies* 48 (4): 899–931.

Schifferes, S. (2007) 'Globalisation shakes the world,' *BBC News Online*, 21 January. Available at http://news.bbc.co.uk/2/hi/business/6279679.stm (accessed 23 September 2016).

Schmidt, V.H. (2004) 'Erfolgsbedingungen des konfuzianischen Wohlfahrtskapitalismus. Kultursoziologische und modernisierungstheoretische Überlegungen,' in P. Stykow and J. Beyer (eds) *Gesellschaft mit beschränkter Hoffnung. Reformfähigkeit und die Möglichkeit rationaler Politik*. Wiesbaden: VS Verlag für Sozialwissenschaften. pp. 175–196.

Schmidt, V.H. (2006) 'Multiple modernities or varieties of modernity?' *Current Sociology* 54 (1): 77–97.

Schmidt, V.H. (2007) 'One world, one modernity,' in V.H. Schmidt (ed.) *Modernity at the Beginning of the 21st Century*. New Castle: Cambridge Scholars Publishing. pp. 205–28.

Schmitter Heisler, B. (2000) 'The sociology of immigration, from the American experience to the global arena,' in C.B. Brettell and J.F. Hollifield (eds) *Migration Theory: Talking across Disciplines*. London and New York: Routledge. pp. 77–96.

Schmitz, H. (ed.) (2004) *Local Enterprises in the Global Economy: Issues of Governance and Upgrading*. Cheltenham and Northampton, MA: Edward Elgar.

Scholte, J. A. (2005) *Globalization: A Critical Introduction* (Second edition). London: Palgrave Macmillan.

Schroeder, R. (2007) *Rethinking Science, Technology, and Social Change*. Stanford, CA: Stanford University Press.

Schubert, G. (2000) 'Die Asienkrise als Grenzmarkierung der Globalisierung? Bewertungen aus der Region,' in R. Tetzlaff (ed.) *Weltkulturen unter Globalisierungsdruck. Erfahrungen und Antworten aus den Kontinenten*. Bonn: Dietz. pp. 120–50.

Schuerkens, U. (1981) *Regionale Disparitäten – individuelle Statuskonfiguration und Migration: Am Beispiel zweier afrikanischer Staaten: Kongo und Sudan*. Frankfurt a.M. and Bern: P. D. Lang.

Schuerkens, U. (1990) 'Veränderung der sozialen Ungleichheit in einem Entwicklungsland von der vorkolonialen Zeit bis zur heutigen Zeit: Ein theoretisches Konzept und seine empirische Überprüfung,' *Zeitschrift für Ethnologie* 115: 199–208.

Schuerkens, U. (1993) *L'évolution sociale: Problématique théorique et portée empirique*. Thèse (nouveau régime) en anthropologie sociale et ethnologie à l'EHESS: Paris.

Schuerkens, U. (1995a) 'The notion of development in Great Britain in the XXth century and some aspects of its application in Togoland under British Mandate and trusteeship,' *Sociologus* 45 (2): 122–39.

Schuerkens, U. (1995b) 'Gesellschaften im Umbruch und *Longue Durée*: Am Beispiel der Begriffe Struktur und Zeit,' in H. Sahner, L. Clausen and S. Schwendtner (eds)

Gesellschaften im Umbruch. 27. Kongress der Deutschen Gesellschaft für Soziologe, Halle an der Saale (Germany), 3–7 April 1995. pp. 103–7.

Schuerkens, U. (2000) 'Migrants africains à Paris: L'intégration sociale en tant que problématique interculturelle,' *International Review of Sociology* 10 (3): 365–84.

Schuerkens, U. (2001a) *Changement social sous régime colonial: Du Togo allemand aux Togo et Ghana indépendants*. Paris: L'Harmattan.

Schuerkens, U. (2001b) *Transformationsprozesse in der Elfenbeinküste und in Ghana: Eine historisch-vergleichende Analyse des Verhältnisses von Lebensgeschichten und strukturellen Wandlungsprozessen*. Münster: Lit.

Schuerkens, U. (ed.) (2003) 'Social transformations between global forces and local life-worlds', *Current Sociology* 51 (1–2; 3/4) [Special Issue].

Schuerkens, U. (ed.) (2004) *Global Forces and Local Life-Worlds*. London: Sage.

Schuerkens, U. (ed.) (2005) 'Transnational migrations and social transformations,' *Current Sociology* 53 (2, 4): 527–742. [Monograph Issue].

Schuerkens, U. (ed.) (2008) *Globalization and Transformations of Local Socio-Economic Practices*. London and New York: Routledge.

Schuerkens, U. (2009) 'Conflict, competition, co-operation in the sociology of development and social transformations,' in A. Denis and D. Kalekin-Fishman (eds) *New Handbook in Contemporary International Sociology: Conflict, Competition, Cooperation*. London: Sage. pp. 109–23.

Schuerkens, U. (ed.) (2010) *Globalization and Transformations of Social Inequality*. London and New York: Routledge.

Schuerkens, U. (ed.) (2012) *Socioeconomic Outcomes of the Global Financial Crisis: Theoretical Discussion and Empirical Case Studies*. London and New York: Routledge.

Schuerkens, U. (ed.) (2014a) *Global Management, Local Resistances*. London and New York: Routledge.

Schuerkens, U. (2014b) *Soziale Transformationen und Entwicklung(en) in einer globalisierten Welt: Eine Einführung*. Beltz-Juventa: Weinheim.

Schuerkens, U. and Khondker, H.H. (2014) 'Social transformations, development, and globalization,' *Sociopedia article*, International Sociological Association.

Schuerkens, U. and Kuagbénou, V.K. (2001) 'African women and migration in France,' in *The Perspectives of African Women in the Globalizing Economy, African Development Perspectives Yearbook*, vol. 8. Münster: Lit. pp. 765–782.

Schuler, R.S., Jackson, S.E. and Luo, Y. (2004) *Managing Human Resources in Cross Border Alliances*. London and New York: Routledge.

Schulz, M. (ed.) (1997) *Entwicklung: Theorie – Empirie – Strategie*. Festschrift für Volker Lühr. Münster: Lit.

Schwinn, T. (2005) 'Weltgesellschaft, multiple Moderne und die Herausforderungen für die soziologische Theorie. Plädoyer für eine mittlere Abstraktionshöhe,' in B. Heintz, R. Münch and H. Tyrell (eds) *Weltgesellschaft. Theoretische Zugänge und empirische Problemlagen*. Stuttgart: Lucius & Lucius. pp. 205–22.

Schwinn, T. (ed.) (2006) *Die Vielfalt und Einheit der Moderne. Kultur- und strukturvergleichende Analysen*. Wiesbaden: VS Verlag für Sozialwissenschaften.

Scrase, T.J., Todd, J.M.H. and Baum, S. (2003) *Globalization, Culture and Inequality in Asia*. Melbourne and Abingdon, UK: Trans Pacific Press.

Seguino, S. (2010) 'The global economic crisis, its gender and ethnic implications, and policy responses,' *Gender & Development* 18 (2): 179–99.

Selmer, J. (2001) 'Adjustment of Western European vs. North American expatriate managers in China,' *Personnel Review* 30 (1): 6–21.

Sen, A. (1999) *Development as Freedom*. Oxford: Oxford University Press.

Sen, A. (2011) 'Hohe moral des Opferns,' *Der Freitag*, 25 June. Available at http://www.freitag.de/politik/1125-Hohe-Moral-des-Opferns (accessed 12 October 2016).

Sen, R. (2013) 'Organizing the unorganized workers: The Indian scene,' *Indian Journal of Intercultural Relations* 415–27.

Sen, R. and Lee, C.-H. (2015) 'Travailleurs et mouvements sociaux dans le monde en développement: Il faut revoir le champ des relations professionnelles,' *Revue Internationale du Travail* 154 (1): 43–52.

Shaw, M. (2003) 'Guerre et globalité. Le rôle et le caractère de la guerre à l'intérieur de la transition globale,' in P. Hassner and R. Marchal (eds) *Guerres et sociétés. État et violence après la Guerre froide*. Paris: Karthala. pp. 49–75.

Sinha, J.B.P. (1995) *The Cultural Context of Leadership and Power*. New Delhi: Sage.

Sklair, L. (2001) *The Transnational Capitalist Class*. Oxford and Malden, MA: Blackwell.

Smart, A. and Smart, J. (eds) (2005) *Petty Capitalists and Globalization: Flexibility, Entrepreneurship, and Economic Development*. Albany, NY: SUNY Press.

Smith, J. and Wiest, D. (2012) *Social Movements in the World-System*. New York: Russell Sage Foundation.

Smith, M.P. and Guarnizo, L.E. (eds) (1998) *Transnationalism from Below*. New Brunswick, NJ: Transaction Publishers.

Smith, T.B. (2004) *France in Crisis: Welfare, Inequality, and Globalization since 1980*. Cambridge: Cambridge University Press.

Sociologie et Sociétés (1990) Special Issue: 'Théorie sociologique de la transition,' 32 (1).

Somers, M.R. and Block, F. (2005) 'From poverty to perversity: Ideas, markets, and institutions over 200 years of welfare debate,' *American Sociological Review* 70 (2): 260–87.

Sommers, M. (2015) *The Outcast Majority: War, Development, and Youth in Africa*. Athens: The University of Georgia Press.

Sood, A. (2012) 'A future for informal services? The cycle rickshaw sector as case study,' *Economic and Political Weekly* 47 (42): 95–102.

Sorj, B. (2014) 'La politique brésilienne dans une nouvelle ère?,' *Socio* 3: 367–74.

Spaargaren, G., Mol, A.P.J. and Buttel, F.H. (2000) *Environment and Global Modernity*. London: Sage.

Spaargaren, G., Mol, A.P.J. and Buttel, F.H. (2006) *Governing Environmental Flows. Global Challenges to Social Theory*. Cambridge MA: MIT Press.

Srinivas, K.M. (1995) 'Globalization of business and the Third World: Challenges of expanding the mindsets,' *Journal of Management Development* 14 (3): 26–49.

Standing, G. (2011) *The Precariat: The New Dangerous Class*. London and New York: Bloomsbury Academic.

Stella, G.A. and Rizzo, S. (2007) *La casta. Così i politici italiani sono diventati intoccabili*. Milan: Rizzoli.

Stiglitz, J.E. (2002) *Globalization and its Discontents*. London: Penguin.

Stiglitz, J.E. (2006) *Making Globalization Work*. New York: W. W. Norton & Co.

Stockhammer, E. and Onaran, Ö. (2009) 'National and sectoral influences on wage determination in Central and Eastern Europe,' *European Journal of Industrial Relations* 15 (3): 317–38.

Strakes, J.E. (2006) 'War and development,' in Thomas M. Leonard (ed.) *Encyclopedia of the Developing World*, Vol. 3. New York and London: Routledge. pp. 1676–80.

Strasser, H. and Randall, S.C. (eds) (1979) *Einführung in die Theorien des sozialen Wandels*. Darmstadt and Neuwied: Luchterhand.

Strassoldo, R. (1992) 'Globalism and localism: Theoretical reflections and some evidence,' in Z. Mlinar (ed.) *Globalisation and Territorial Identities*. Farnham: Ashgate. pp. 35–59.

Stratfor (2013) *Migration and Remittances in the Eurozone Periphery*. 14 May.

Streeck, W. (2013) *Gekaufte Zeit: Die vertagte Krise des demokratischen Kapitalismus*. Berlin: Suhrkamp.

Subrahmanyam, S. (1997) 'Connected histories: Notes towards a reconfiguration of early modern Eurasia,' *Modern Asian Studies* 31 (3): 735–62.

Subrahmanyam, S. (2005) *Explorations in Connected History: From the Tagus to the Ganges*. Oxford: Oxford University Press.

Suliman, A.M.T. (2006) 'Human resource management in the United Arab Emirates,' in P.S. Budhwar and K. Mellahi (eds) *Managing Human Resources in the Middle East*. Abington: Routledge. pp. 59–78.

Sutcliffe, B. (2005) *100 imágenes de un mundo desigual*. Icaria/Intermon, Barcelona (previous edition in English: *100 Ways of Seeing an Unequal World*. Zed Books: London, 2001).

Sztompka, P. (1991) *Society in Action: The Theory of Social Becoming*. Chicago: University of Chicago Press.

Sztompka, P. (1993) *Sociology of Social Change*. Oxford: Basil Blackwell.

Tejerina, B., Perugorría, I., Benski, T. and Langman, L. (2013) 'From indignation to occupation: A new wave of global mobilization,' *Current Sociology* Monograph 2, 61 (4): 377–92.

Tetzlaff, R. (ed.) (2000) *Weltkulturen unter Globalisierungsdruck. Erfahrungen und Antworten aus den Kontinenten*. Bonn: Dietz.

Teune, H. and Mlinar, Z. (1978) *The Development Logic of Social Systems*. London: Sage.

Thom, R. (1979) *Théorie des catastrophes et biologie: plaidoyer pour une biologie théorique*. København: E. Munksgaard.

Thomas, B. (1954) *Migration and Economic Growth*. London: Cambridge University Press.

Tilly, C. (2005) 'Historical perspectives on inequality,' in M. Romero and E. Margolis (eds) *The Blackwell Companion to Social Inequalities*. Oxford: Blackwell.

Tombs, S. (2015) *Social Protection after the Crisis: Regulation without Enforcement*. Bristol: Policy Press.

Tomlinson, J. (1991) *Cultural Imperialism: A Critical Introduction*. London: Pinter.

Tong, J. and Mitra, A. (2009) 'Chinese cultural influences on knowledge management practice,' *Journal of Knowledge Management* 13 (2): 49–62.

Tonkiss, F. (2006) *Contemporary Economic Sociology: Globalization, Production, Inequality*. London and New York: Routledge.

Touraine, A. (2000) 'Les conflits sociaux,' *Encyclopaedia Universalis*. Paris: Encylopaedia Universalis.

Trompenaars, F. (1993) *Riding the Waves of Culture: Understanding Cultural Diversity in Business*. London: The Economist Books.

Trompenaars, F. and Hampden-Turner, C. (2004) *Managing People Across Cultures*. Oxford: Capstone.

Tsing, A. (2000) 'The global situation,' *Cultural Anthropology* 15 (3): 327–60.

Tsui, A.S., Nifadkar, S.S. and Ou, A.Y. (2007) 'Cross-national, cross-cultural organizational behaviour research: Advances, gaps, and recommendations,' *Journal of Management* 33 (3): 426–78.

Tulchin, J.S. and Bland, G. (eds) (2005) *Getting Globalization Right: The Dilemmas of Inequality.* Boulder, CO and London: Lynne Rienner.

Tyrell, H. (2005) 'Singular oder Plural – Einleitende Bemerkungen zu Globalisierung und Weltgesellschaft,' in B. Heintz, R. Münch and H. Tyrell (eds) *Weltgesellschaft. Theoretische Zugänge und empirische Problemlagen.* Stuttgart: Lucius. pp. 1–50.

[UN DESA] United Nations Department for Economic and Social Affairs (2002) *International Migration Report 2002.* New York: United Nations.

[UN DESA] United Nations Department for Economic and Social Affairs (2004) *World Economic and Social Survey 2004: International Migration.* New York: United Nations.

[UN DESA] (United Nations Department of Economic and Social Affairs) (2011a) *World Population Prospects: The 2010 Revision.* New York: UN DESA Population Division.

[UN DESA] (United Nations Department for Economic and Social Affairs) (2011b) *International Migration Report 2009: A Global Assessment.* New York: United Nations. Available at http://www.un.org/esa/population/publications/migration/WorldMigrationReport2009.pdf (accessed 15 October 2016).

[UN DESA] United Nations Department of Economic and Social Affairs (2011c) *The Great Green Technological Transformation. World Economic and Social Survey.* New York: UN DESA.

[UN DESA] United Nations Department for Economic and Social Affairs (2012a) *Migrants by Origin and Destination: The Role of South–South Migration.* Population Facts n° 2012/3, United Nations. Available at http://www.un.org/esa/population/publications/popfacts/popfacts_2012-3_South-South_migration.pdf (accessed 10 October 2016).

[UN DESA] United Nations Department for Economic and Social Affairs (2012b) *The United Nations Development Strategy Beyond 2015.* New York: Committee for Development Policy, United Nations.

[UN DESA] United Nations Department for Economic and Social Affairs (2014) *International Migration 2013: Migrants by Origin and Destination.* Population Facts n° 2013/3, United Nations. Available at http://esa.un.org/unmigration/documents/PF_South-South_migration_2013.pdf (accessed 24 October 2016).

[UN DESA] United Nations Department for Economic and Social Affairs (2016a) *International Migration Wall Chart 2015.* Population Division. New York: UN. Available at http://www.un.org/en/development/desa/population/migration/publications/wallchart/docs/MigrationWallChart2015.pdf (accessed 24 October 2016).

[UN DESA] United Nations Department for Economic and Social Affairs (2016b) *World Economic Situations and Prospects for 2016.* Development Policy and Analysis Division. Available at http://www.un.org/en/development/desa/policy/wesp/ (accessed 21 December 2016).

[UNCTAD] United Nations Conference on Trade and Development (2006) *The Digital Divide Report: ICT Diffusion Index.* New York: United Nations.

[UNCTAD] United Nations Conference on Trade and Development (2012a) *The Least Developed Countries Report 2012: Harnessing Remittances and Diaspora Knowledge to Build Productive Capacities.* New York and Geneva: United Nations.

[UNCTAD] United Nations Conference on Trade and Development (2012b) *Remittances to Poorest Countries Could Play Greater Role in Broadening and Empowering their Economies, Report Says.* UNCTAD Press Release, 26 November. Available at http://unctad.org/en/pages/PressRelease.aspx?OriginalVersionID=108 (accessed 24 October 2016).

[UNCTAD] United Nations Conference on Trade and Development (2016) *Rethinking Development Strategies after the Financial Crisis. 2, Country Studies and International Comparisons.* New York: United Nations.

[UNDP] United Nations Development Programme (2003) *Human Development Report 2003: Millenium Development Goals: A Compact to Nations to End Human Poverty.* New York: Oxford University Press.

[UNDP] United Nations Development Programme (2013) *Human Development Report 2013: The Rise of the South: Human Progress in a Diverse World.* New York: UNDP.

[UNDP] United Nations Development Programme (2014) *Human Development Report 2014: Sustaining Human Progress: Reducing Vulnerabilities and Building Resilience.* New York: UNDP.

[UNDP] United Nations Development Programme (2015) *Human Development Report 2015: Work for Human Development.* New York: UNDP.

UNESCO (1996) *The Cultural Dimensions of Global Change: An Anthropological Approach.* Paris: UNESCO.

UNESCO (1998) *World Culture Report. Culture, Creativity and Markets.* Paris: UNESCO.

[UNRISD] United Nations Research Institute for Social Development (2016) *UNRISD 2016 Flagship Report: Policy Innovations for Transformative Change.* Geneva: UNRISD.

UNRISD Report. Available at: http://www.unrisd.org/80256B42004CCC77/(httpInfoFiles)/2D9B6E61A43A7E87C125804F003285F5/$file/Flagship2016_FullReport.pdf (accessed 3 March 2017).

Urry, J. (2011) *Climate Change and Society.* Cambridge: Polity Press.

Utting, P. (2002) 'Regulating business via multi-stakeholder initiatives: A preliminary assessment' in UNRISD, *Voluntary Approaches to Corporate Responsibility.* Geneva: NGLS. pp. 61–126.

van Binsbergen, W. and Geschiere, P. (eds) (2005) *Commodification: Things, Agency, and Identities (The Social Life of Things Revisited).* Berlin and Münster: Lit.

van der Berg, S. (2009) 'Fiscal incidence of social spending in South Africa: 2006,' Working Papers 10/2009. Department of Economics, Stellenbosch University. Available at http://www.ekon.sun.ac.za/wpapers/2009/wp102009 (accessed 7 October 2016).

van Dijk, M. P. (2006) 'Different effects of globalisation for workers and the poor in China and India, comparing countries, cities and ICT clusters,' *Tijdschrift voor Economische en Sociale Geografie* 97 (5): 503–14.

Verver, M. and Dahles, H. (2013) 'The anthropology of Chinese capitalism in Southeast Asia,' *Journal of Business Anthropology* 2 (1): 93–114.

Vidal, J.-P. (1998) 'The effect of emigration on human capital formation,' *Journal of Population Economics* 11 (4): 589–600.

Vinz, D. (2005) 'Nachhaltigkeit und Gender: Umweltpolitik aus der Perspektive der Geschlechterforschung,' *Gender-Politik-Online,* January. Available at http://www.fu-berlin.de/sites/gpo/int_bez/globalisierung/Nachhaltigkeit_und_Gender/vinz.pdf (accessed 12 October 2016).

Visser, E.-P. and van Dijk, M.P. (2006) 'Economic globalisation and workers: Introduction,' *Tijdschrift voor Economische en Sociale Geografie* 97 (5): 463–69.

Vlassenroot, K. (2003) 'Économie de guerre et entrepreneurs militaires: la rationalité économique dans le conflit au Sud-Kivu (République démocratique du Congo),' in P. Hassner and R. Marchal (eds), *Guerres et sociétés. État et violence après la Guerre froide*. Paris: Karthala. pp. 339–68.

Vlassopoulos, C.-A. (2013) 'Defining environmental migration in the climate change era: Problem, consequence or solution?' in T. Faist and J. Schade (eds) *Disentangling Migration and Climate Change: Methodologies, Political Discourses and Human Rights*. Dordrecht, Heidelberg, New York, and London: Springer. pp. 145–63.

Volti, R. (2001) *Society and Technological Change* (Fourth edition). New York: Basic Books.

Wade, R.H. (2007) 'Should we worry about income inequality?' in D. Held and A. Kaya (eds) *Global Inequality*. Cambridge: Polity Press. pp. 104–31.

Wagner, P. (2000) *Theorizing Modernity*. London: Sage.

Wajcman, J. (1991) *Feminism Confronts Technology*. Cambridge: Polity Press.

Wallerstein, I. (1979) *The Capitalist World-Economy*. Cambridge: Cambridge University Press.

Wallerstein, I. (2004) *World-Systems Analysis: An Introduction*. Durham, NC: Duke University Press.

Wallerstein, I. (2011) 'The world consequences of U.S. decline.' Available at http://www.binghamton.edu/fbc/commentaries/ (accessed 24 October 2016).

Wapner, P. (2002) 'Horizontal politics: Transnational environmental activism and global cultural change', *Global Environmental Politics* 2 (2): 37–62.

Warner, M. (ed.) (2003) *Culture and Management in Asia*. London: Routledge Curzon.

Warner, M. and Rowley, C. (eds) (2011) *Chinese Management in the 'Harmonious Society': Managers, Markets and the Globalized Economy*. London and New York: Routledge.

Warnier, J.-P. (1999) *La mondialisation de la culture*. Paris: Éditions de la Découverte.

Waters, M. (1995) *Globalization*. London and New York: Routledge.

Weber, M. (1959 [1919]) *Le Savant et le politique*. Paris: Plon.

Weber, M. (1984) *Die protestantische Ethik I. Eine Aufsatzsammlung*. Gütersloh: Mohn.

Weber, M. (1991) *Die Wirtschaftsethik der Weltreligionen. Konfuzianismus und Taoismus (Schriften 1915–1920)*. Tübingen: Mohn (MWG 1/19).

Webster, E. (2015) 'Les frontières mouvantes des relations professionnelles: L'exemple sud-africain,' *Revue internationale du travail* 154: 31–41.

Webster, F. (ed.) (2004) *The Information Society Reader*. New York and London: Routledge.

Webster, F. and Robins, K. (1986) *Information Technology: A Luddite Analysis*. Norwood, NJ: Ablex.

Wehler, H.-U. (1998) *Die Herausforderung der Kulturgeschichte*. München: Beck.

Wei, Y.D. (2000) *Regional Development in China: States, Globalization, and Inequality*. London and New York: Routledge.

Weiss, T.G. (2007) *Humanitarian Intervention: Ideas in Action*. Cambridge: Polity.

Wellman, B. and Haythornthwaite, C. (2002) *The Internet in Everyday Life*. Oxford: Wiley-Blackwell.

Werner, M. and Zimmermann, B. (2002) 'Vergleich, Transfer, Verflechtung: Der Ansatz der *histoire croisée* und die Herausforderung des Transnationalen,' *Geschichte und Gesellschaft* 28: 607–36.

Werner, M. and Zimmermann, B. (2006) 'Beyond comparison: *Histoire croisée* and the challenge of reflexivity,' *History and Theory* 45 (1): 30–50.

Wieviorka, M. (2009) 'La sociologie et la crise. Quelle crise, et quelle sociologie?' *Cahiers Internationaux de Sociologie* 2 (127): 181–98.

Wihtol de Wenden, C. (2016a) *Atlas des migrations: Un équilibre mondial à inventer* (Fourth edition). Paris: Autrement.

Wihtol de Wenden, C. (2016b) 'L'Europe et la crise des réfugiés', *Études*, 3: 7–16.

Wilk, R. (1996) *Economies and Cultures*. Boulder, CO: Westview.

Williamson, J.G. and O'Rourke, K.H. (2002) 'When did globalization begin?' *European Review of Economic History* 6 (1): 23–50.

Wilson, C. and Dunn, A. (2011) 'Digital media in the Egyptian Revolution: Descriptive analysis from the Tahrir data sets,' *International Journal of Communication* 5: 1248–72.

Wobbe, T. (2000) *Weltgesellschaft*. Bielefeld: Transcript.

Wolf, M. (2004) *Why Globalization Works*. New Haven, NJ: Yale University Press.

Wong, R.B. (1997) *China Transformed: Historical Change and the Limits of European Experience*. Ithaca, NY: Cornell University Press.

World Bank (2006) *Global Economic Prospects 2006 – Economic Implications of Remittances and Migration*. Washington, DC: World Bank.

World Bank (2007) *Understanding Poverty*. Available at http://www.worldbank.org/en/news/video/2015/10/06/understanding-poverty-data (accessed 21 December 2016).

World Bank (2013a) *Migration and Development Brief 20*. Washington, DC: World Bank.

World Bank (2013b) *Migration and Development Brief 21*. Washington, DC: World Bank. Available at http://siteresources.worldbank.org/INTPROSPECTS/Resources/334934-1288990760745/MigrationandDevelopmentBrief21.pdf (accessed 24 October 2016).

World Bank (2015) *Migration and Development Brief 24*. Washington, DC: World Bank. Available at https://siteresources.worldbank.org/INTPROSPECTS/Resources/334934-1288990760745/MigrationandDevelopmentBrief24.pdf (accessed 10 October 2016).

Yahiaoui, D. and Zoubir, Y.H. (2005) 'Human resource management in Tunisia: Emerging HRM models,' in P. Budhwar and K. Mellahi (eds) *Managing Human Resources in the Middle East*. London and New York: Routledge. pp. 233–49.

Yang, D. and Martinez, C.A. (2006) 'Remittances and poverty in migrants' home areas: Evidence from the Philippines,' in Ç. Özden and M. Schiff (eds) *International Migration, Remittances and the Brain Drain*. Washington, DC: Palgrave-Macmillan and World Bank. pp. 81–121.

Yongnian, Z. and Tong, S.Y. (eds) (2010) *China and the Global Economic Crisis*. Hackensack, NJ: World Scientific Publishing.

Yoshihara, K. (2000) *Asia Per Capita. Why National Incomes Differ in East Asia*. London: Curzon Press.

Yousef, A.D. (2001) 'Islamic work ethic: A moderator between organizational commitment and job satisfaction in a cross-cultural context,' *Personnel Review* 30 (2): 152–69.

Zaccai, E. (2011) *Vingt-cinq ans de développement durable, et après?* Paris: Presses universitaires de France.

Zapf, W. (1994) *Modernisierung, Wohlfahrtsentwicklung und Transformation*. Berlin: editions sigma.

Zhang, S., Doorn, J.V. and Leeflang, P. S. H. (2012) 'Changing consumer markets and marketing in China,' *International Journal of Business and Emerging Markets* 4 (4): 328–51.

INDEX